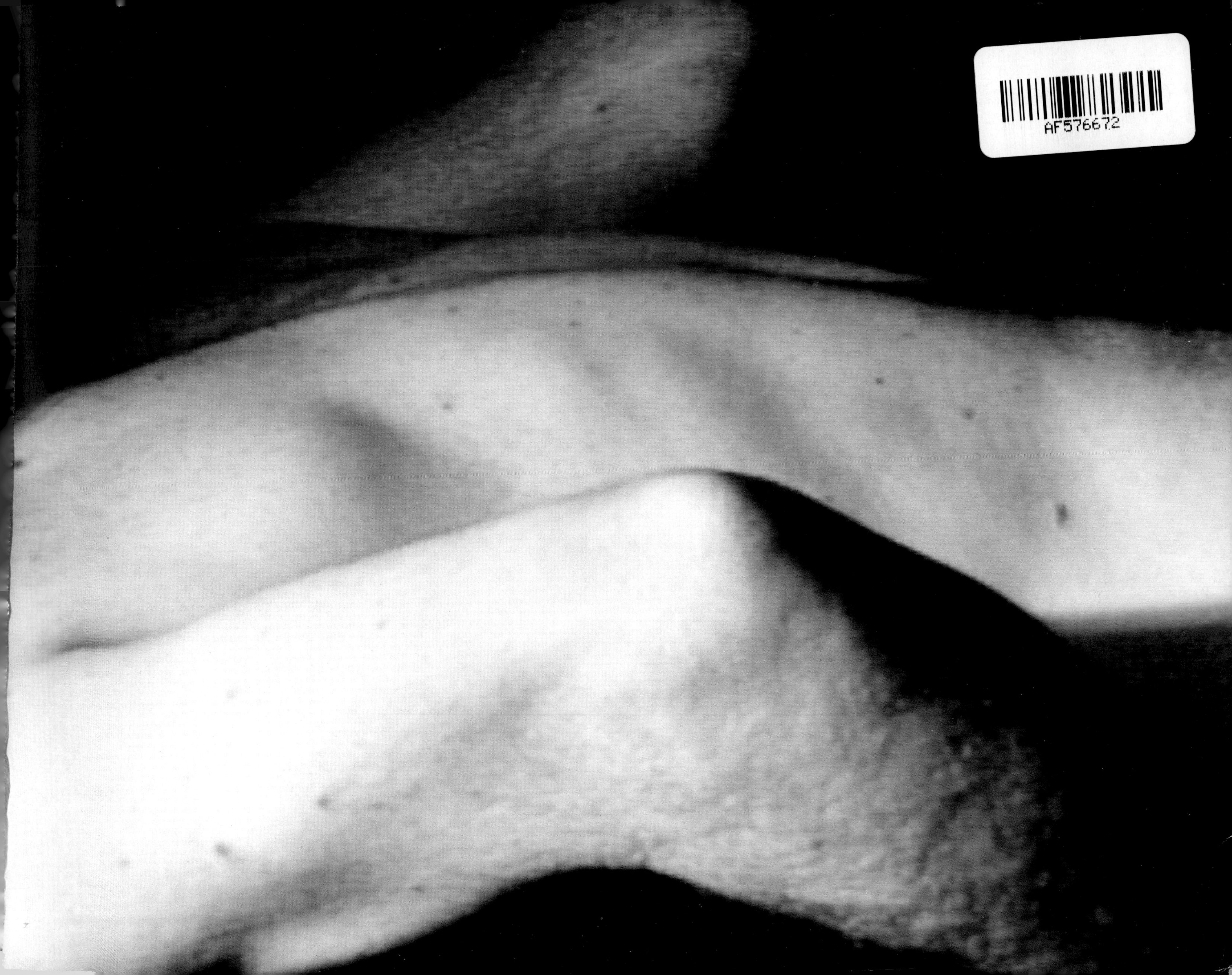

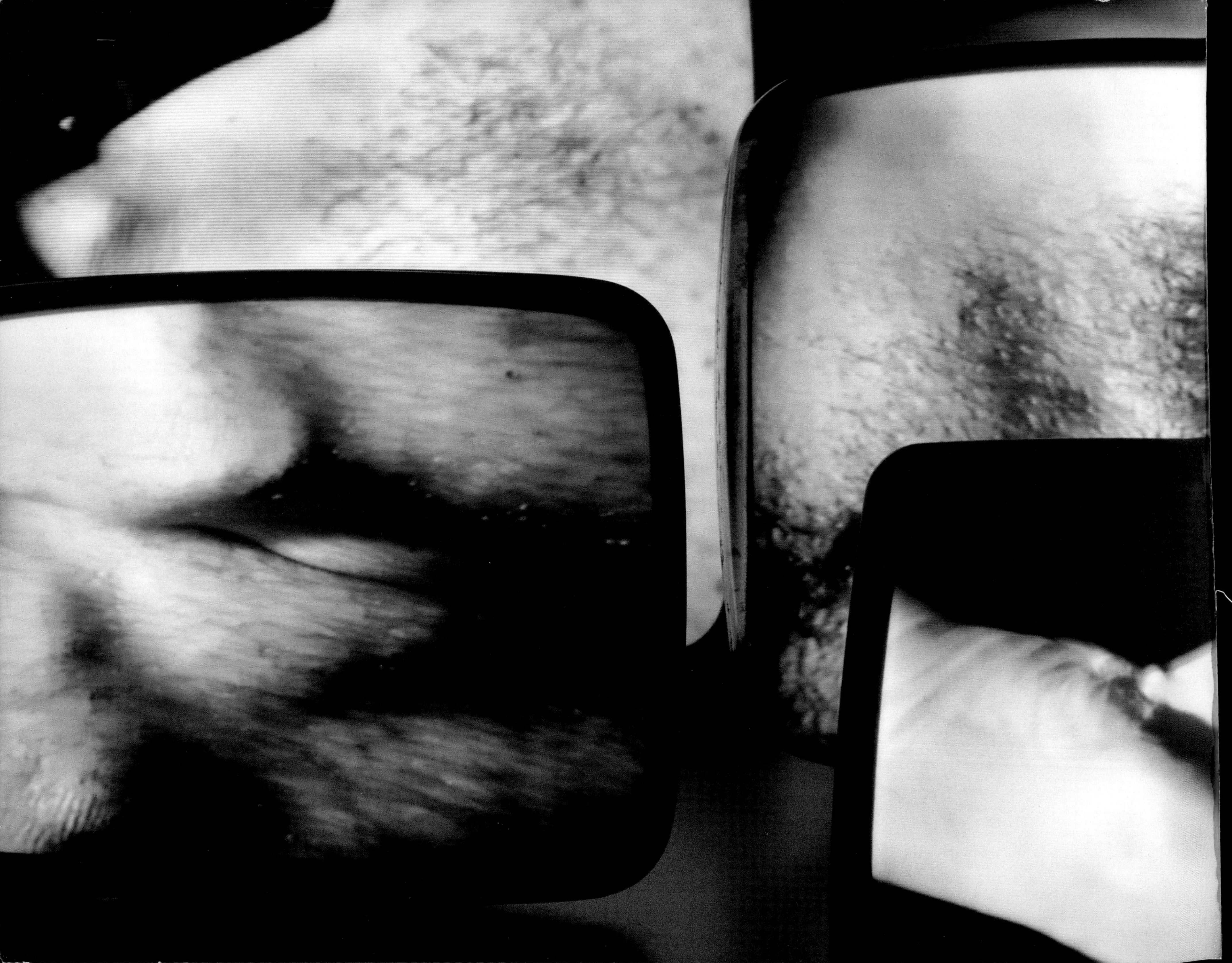

Gary Hill

Essays by Chris Bruce
Lynne Cooke
Bruce W. Ferguson
John G. Hanhardt
Robert Mittenthal

Henry Art Gallery
University of Washington
Seattle
1994

First published in the United States of America by the Henry Art Gallery Association in conjunction with the exhibition, *Gary Hill,* organized by the Henry Art Gallery. Chris Bruce, curator.

Support for this exhibition and publication has come from the National Endowment for the Arts, a federal agency, PONCHO, the Lannan Foundation, SAFECO, and the Seattle Arts Commission.

Exhibition itinerary

Hirshhorn Museum
Washington, D.C.
February 17-May 8, 1994

Henry Art Gallery
University of Washington
Seattle, Washington
June 10-August 14, 1994

Museum of Contemporary Art
Chicago, Illinois
September 22-November 27, 1994

Museum of Contemporary Art
Los Angeles, California
December 19, 1994-March 12, 1995

Guggenheim Museum Soho
New York City
April-July, 1995

Full details on each work appear on pages 98 and 99.

Library of Congress Cataloging-in-Publication Data

Hill, Gary. 1951-
Gary Hill / essays by Chris Bruce... (et al.).
p. cm.
Catalog of an exhibition held at the Hirshhorn Museum, Washington, D.C., Feb. 14-May 8, 1994, and at other museums.
Includes bibliographical references.
ISBN 0-935558-32-2
1. Hill, Gary, 1951- —Exhibitions. 2. Video art—United States—Exhibitions. 3. Installations (Art)—United States—Exhibitions. I. Bruce, Chris. II. Henry Art Gallery. III. Hirshhorn Museum and Sculpture Garden. IV. Title.
N6537.H533A4 1994
709'.2—dc20 93-2971
CIP

ISBN: 0-935558-32-2

Publication Coordinator: Tamara Moats
Editors: Sigrid Asmus and Lane Morgan
Graphic Designer: Douglas Wadden

Typography by Thomas and Kennedy, set in Univers
Printed by Nissha on Satin-Kinfuji in Kyoto, Japan

And Sat Down Beside Her is published courtesy of M.J.S., Paris. All other works are published courtesy of the Donald Young Gallery, Seattle.

The quotation from *Thomas The Obscure* by Maurice Blanchot is published courtesy of Station Hill Press, Barrytown, New York.

The *Site Re:cite* essay was originally published in *Camera Obscura,* No. 24, 1991.

Cover image: detail from *Inasmuch As It Is Always Already Taking Place,* 1990, installed at the Museum of Modern Art, New York

Acknowledgments

The work of Gary Hill has attracted increasing attention in the past few years in exhibitions in the U.S. and abroad. Hill's installations and video objects are compelling, haunting works that engage the viewer in real time. Electronic and viewer space are interwoven in these works and the experience is not so much looking at (as in television viewing) as it is engaging with (as in personal relationships). Beautiful, and sometimes disquieting, these works give us insight into art forms now emerging which create art from the raw materials of late 20th-century technology.

This is the first exhibition to provide a view of major installation works by Gary Hill in the United States. As organized by Henry Art Gallery Senior Curator Chris Bruce, the exhibition provides an opportunity for a national audience to experience key works of the last five years. We are most grateful for the assistance and cooperation of the artist in the development of the exhibition and catalogue. Organization of a traveling exhibition of this scope and technical complexity is always difficult but our work was immeasurably aided by the knowledge and efforts of Gary Hill and his assistants Dave Jones, Paul Kuranko, and Mark McLoughlin. Donald Young of the Donald Young Gallery has long been a supporter of Gary Hill and was an essential partner in the organization of this important exhibition.

We are most grateful to have the opportunity to work with our colleagues at the museums participating in the exhibition tour and particularly want to thank James Demetrian, director, Neal Benezra, chief curator, and Phyllis Rosenzweig, curator, Hirshhorn Museum and Sculpture Garden, Washington, D.C.; Kevin Consey, director, Richard Francis, chief curator, and Beryl Wright, associate curator of exhibitions, Museum of Contemporary Art, Chicago; Richard Koshalek, director, and Paul Schimmel, chief curator, The Museum of Contemporary Art, Los Angeles; and Thomas Krens, director, and Nancy Spector, associate curator, Guggenheim Museum, Soho. In addition we received much assistance in the organization of the exhibition and preparation of the catalogue from Tina Oldknow and Cara Kennedy of the Donald Young Gallery, Seattle.

As always the staff of the Henry Art Gallery rose to the challenge of an exacting and complicated exhibition. In addition to the insightful and continuous involvement of Chris Bruce, I particularly want to thank Jim Rittimann and Dan Gurney for their work on exhibition preparation and design, Anne Gendreau for her efficient organization of the tour logistics, and Claudia Bach for the dissemination of information about the exhibition. Assistant Director Joan Caine provided invaluable administrative oversight of the complex negotiations and logistics for this large exhibition and tour.

This catalogue was conceived during discussions between Gary Hill, Chris Bruce, and graphic designer Douglas Wadden. We are pleased to be able to publish thoughtful essays on Hill's work by Lynne Cooke of the Dia Art Foundation, independent curator Bruce W. Ferguson, New York, John G. Hanhardt from the Whitney Museum of American Art and Seattle writer Robert Mittenthal. We appreciate being able to include the Mittenthal essay, which originally appeared in the catalogue for the Gary Hill exhibition jointly organized by the Museum of Modern Art, Oxford, and the Tate Gallery, Liverpool, England. Coordination of the catalogue was ably handled by Tamara Moats, curator of education, with the capable collaboration of editor Sigrid Asmus and the assistance of Lane Morgan, and Jennifer Reidel, editorial assistant. Douglas Wadden's beautiful design of the catalogue was assisted by Karen Hara.

Generous support for the exhibition was provided by the Museum Program of the National Endowment for the Arts, PONCHO, Lannan Foundation, SAFECO, Seattle Arts Commission and Pioneer New Media Technologies. Additional support was contributed by the Henry Gallery Association, under the leadership of Board President Walter Parsons and Phoebe Caner, director of the Association. The University of Washington is an important contributor to the success of our exhibitions and we are most appreciative of the support given by Dean Joe Norman and Associate Dean for the Arts Arthur Grossman of the College of Arts and Sciences.

Richard Andrews
Director

Table of Contents

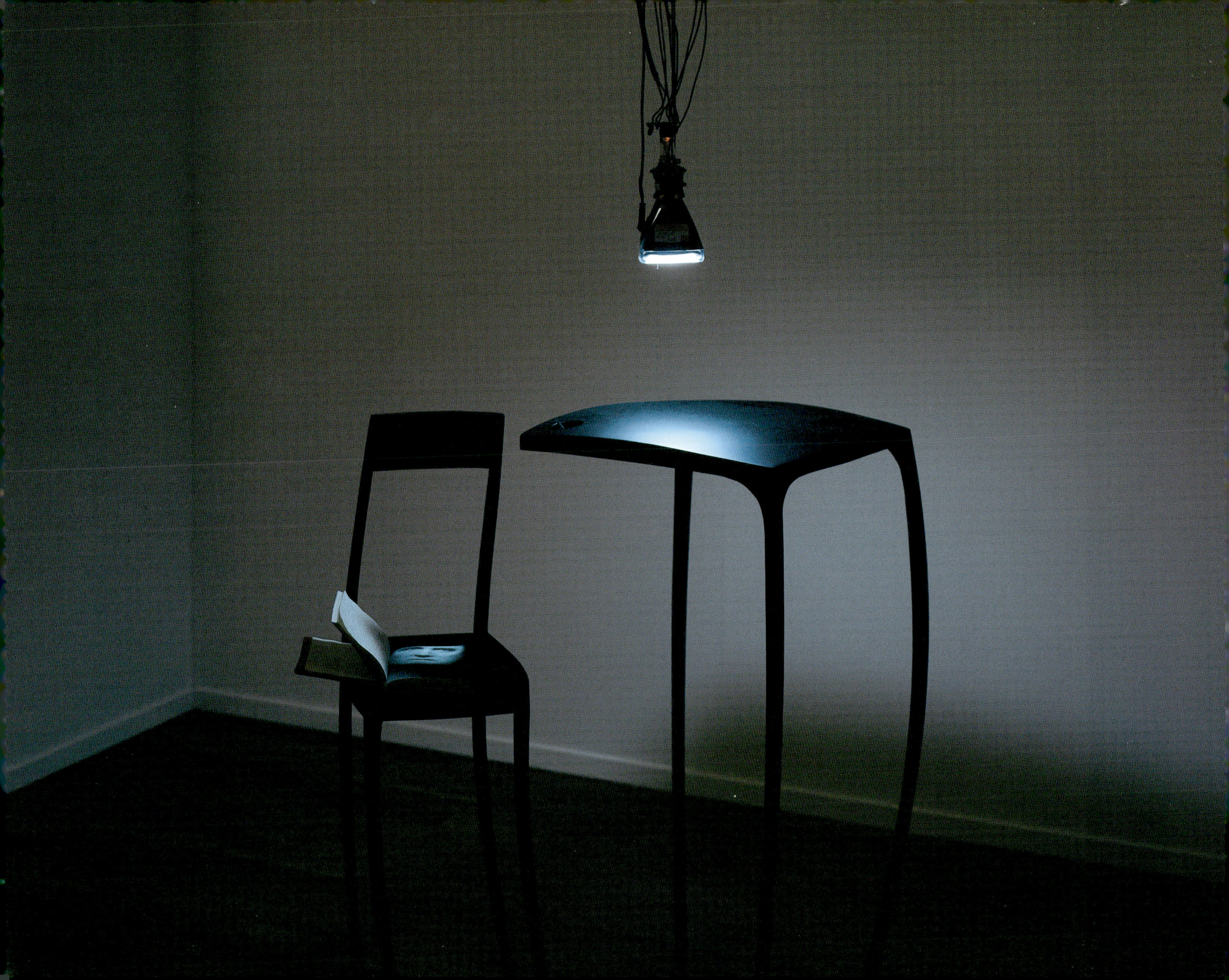

closest thing to the void, she yet found there the debris of beings with whom she maintained, in the midst of the holocaust, a sort of familial resemblance in her features. If he came straight up to her, brutally, to surprise her, she always presented him a face. She changed without ceasing to be Anne. She was Anne, having no longer the slightest resemblance to Anne. In her face and in all her features, while she was completely identical to another, she remained the same, Anne, Anne complete and undeniable. On his path, he saw her coming like a spider which was identical to the girl and, among the vanished corpses, the emptied men, walked through the deserted world with a strange peace, last descendant of a fabulous race. She walked with eight enormous legs as if on two delicate ones. Her black body, her ferocious look which made one think she was about to bite when she was about to flee, were not different from the clothed body of Anne, from the delicate air she had when one tried to see her close up. She came forward jerkily, now devouring space in a few bounds, now lying down on the path, brooding it, drawing it from herself like an invisible thread. Without even drawing in her limbs, she entered the space surrounding Thomas. She approached irresistibly. She stopped before him. Then, that day, seized by this incredible bravery and perseverance, recognizing in her something carefree which could not disappear in the midst of trials and which resounded like a memory of freedom, seeing her get up on her long legs, hold herself at the level of his face to communicate with him, secreting a whirlwind of nuances, of odors and thoughts, he turned and looked bitterly behind him, like a traveler who, having taken a wrong turn, moves away, then draws within himself and finally disappears in the thought of his journey. Yes, this woods, he recognized it.

And sat down beside her,

43

And Sat Down Beside Her, 1990 (detail)

From *Thomas the Obscure* by Maurice Blanchot, translated by Robert Lamberton (New York: Station Hill Press, 1988)

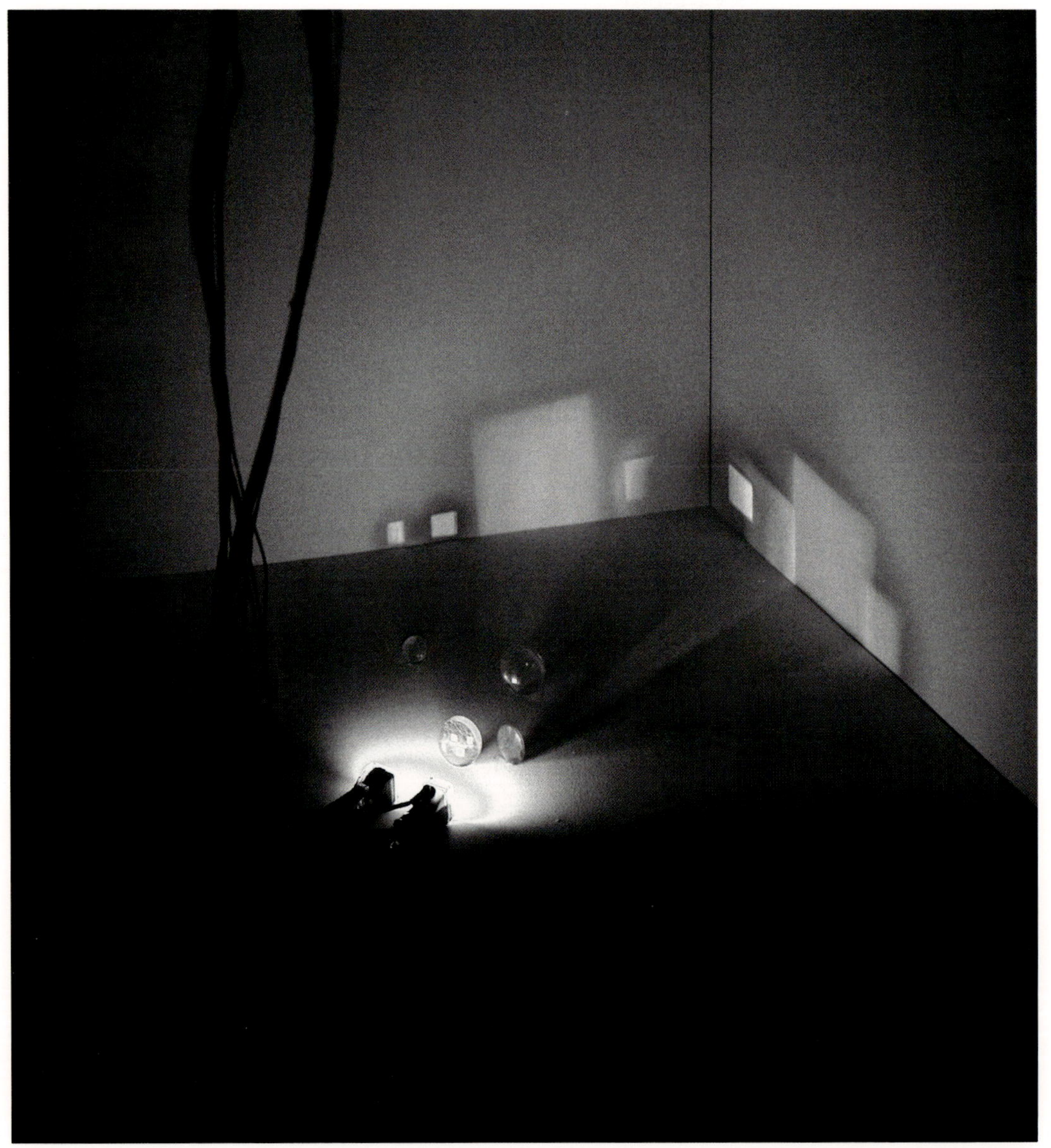

And Sat Down Beside Her, 1990 (detail)

This has always been it, a bewildering object in my path

collecting more and more of whatever collecting tends to collect

when nothing clicks when things just couple

becoming twos instead of ones. And then it stops.

Stops dead in its tracks. Backlogs.

Rolls back on one of its many convoluted surfaces and sits there perfecting stillness.

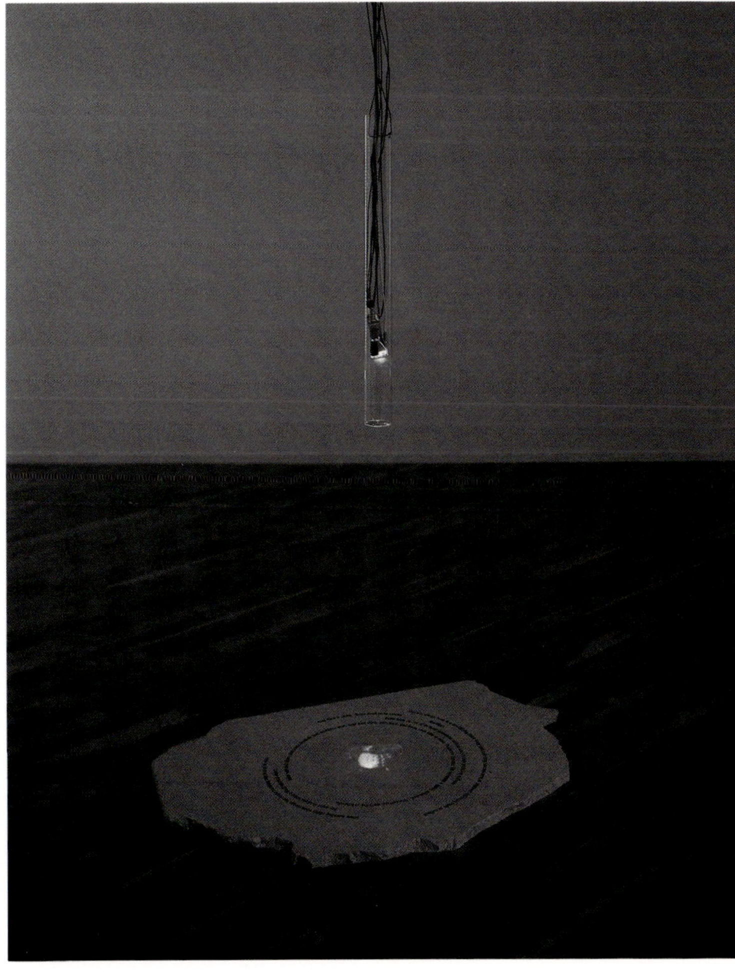

My gaze thickens before a black spherical object laden with dull, silvery characters,

symbols and numbers that, now and then,

jolts forth and back, each time to rotate its discrete distance.

The movement is quick, animated…like certain walking arachnids.

And Sat Down Beside Her, 1990 (detail)

Following pages
And Sat Down Beside Her, 1990

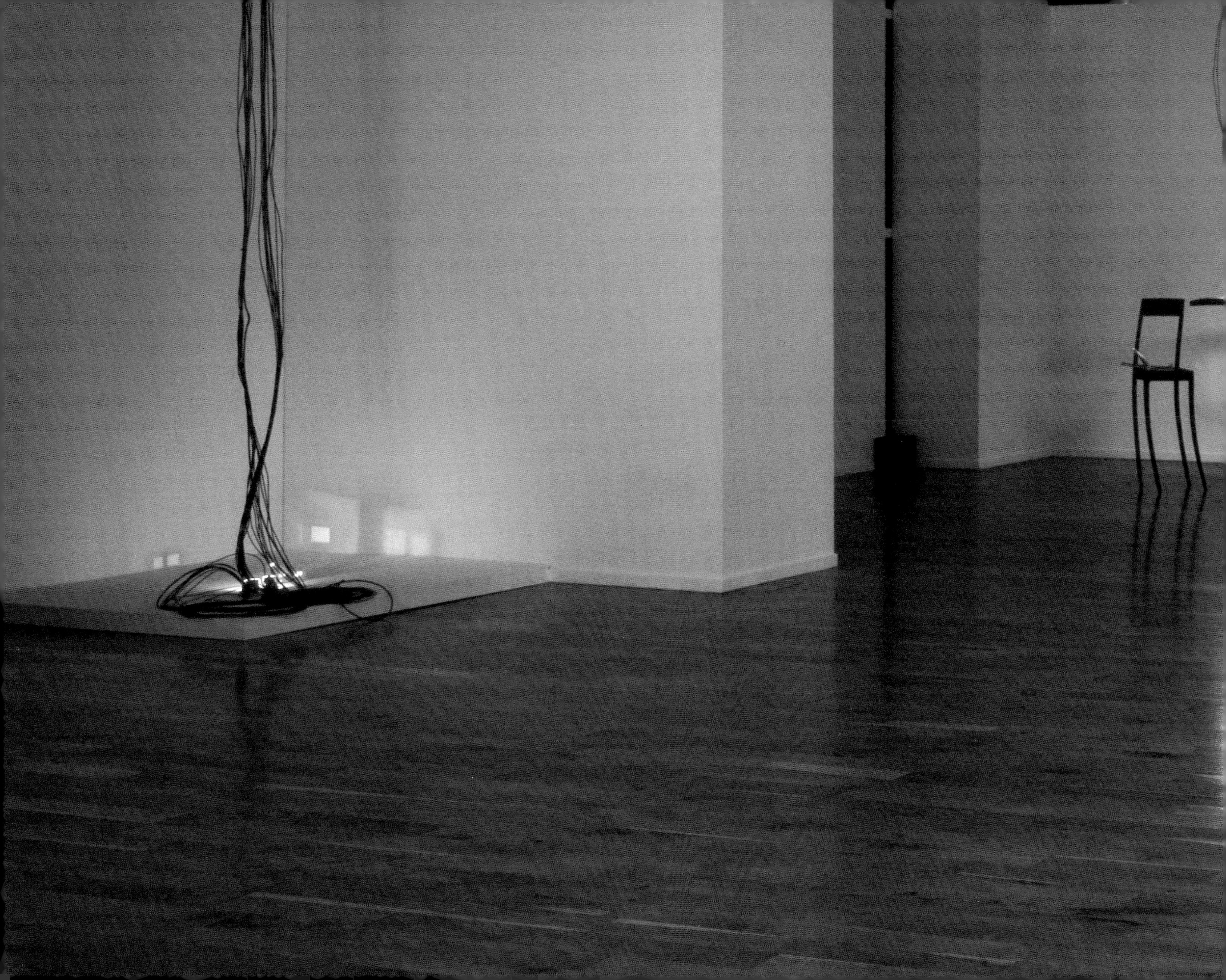

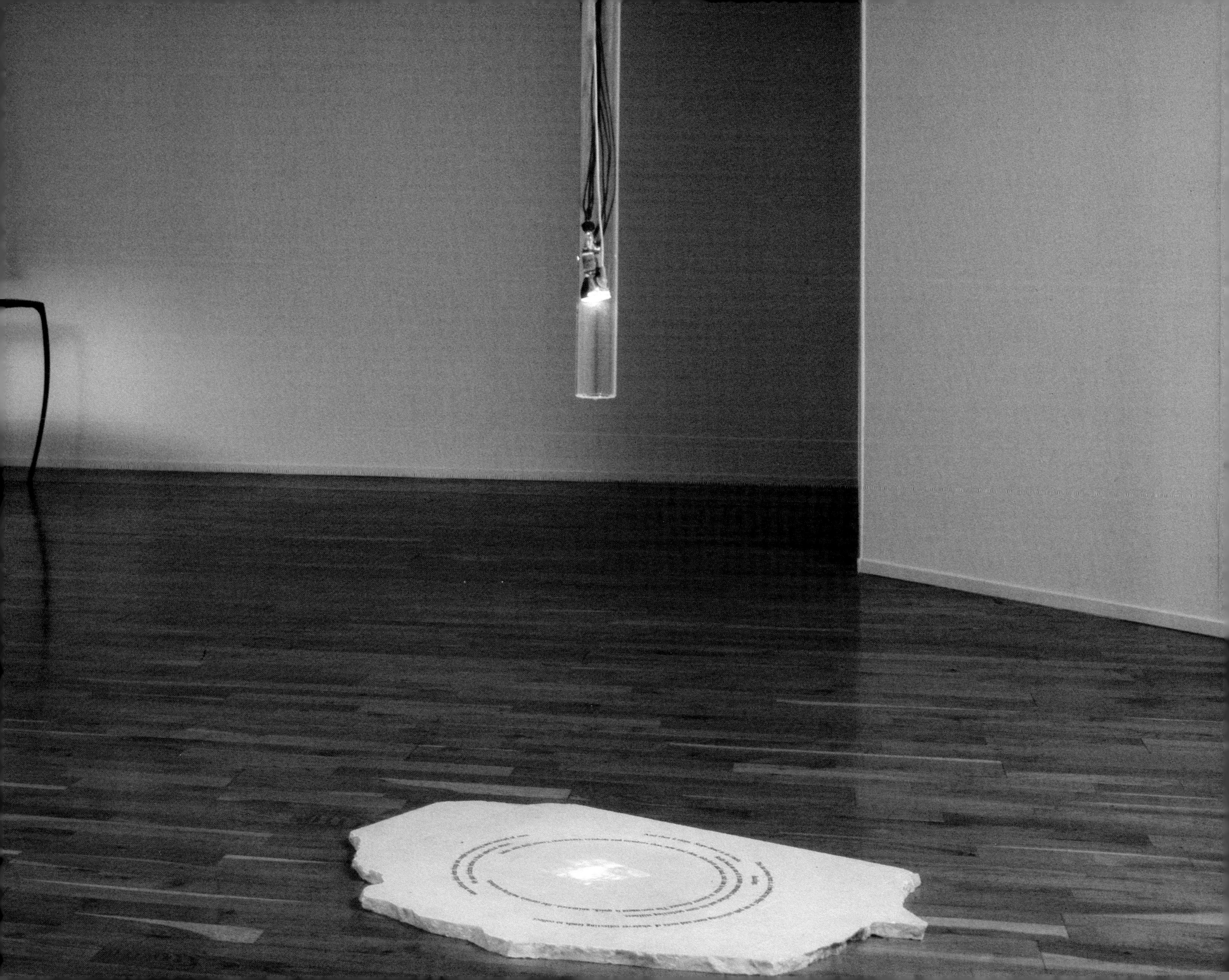

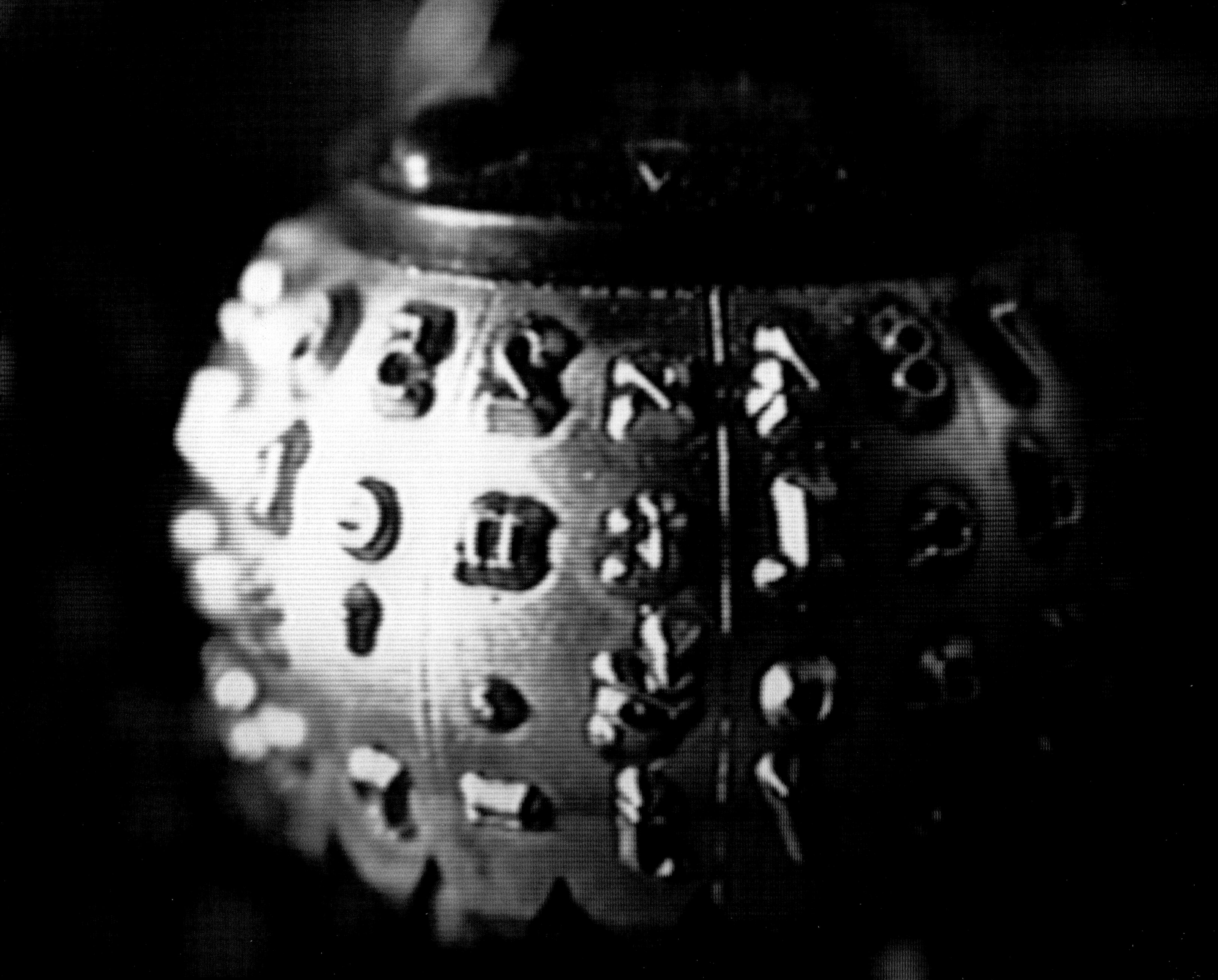

Deja Vu and Deja Lu

(already seen et already read)

Bruce W. Ferguson

At some point in the late 1970s several quasi-independent social and intellectual forces seemed to coalesce dramatically, acting to destabilize and, eventually, undermine the traditional modernist understanding of the role of the artist. This long-standing allegory and institutionalized creation myth of the artist lost some of its (already exhausted) credibility. The forces that weakened its authority (although its day-to-day resurrection can still be found everywhere art journalism exists and commercial art flows) were a combination of new politics (feminisms and post-colonialisms), technological developments ("third-generation" machines and new information orders), and intellectual critiques (structuralism, poststructuralism, cultural studies, and German critical theory, etc.).

I Believe It Is an Image in Light of the Other, 1991-92 (detail)

Although this is an abusively and absurdly foreshortened synopsized history of a much more complex and subtle process, for the purposes of this essay it will have to do as a symptomatic register of the radical shift from a nonfigurative, handmade, existential experience of art making and interpretations based in intentions, to a figurative, systems-derived, culturally based production of art with an orientation to audience engagement and semiotic interpretation. All of which is just a way of signalling that the motivations, culturally inflected understandings, and means of production of an artist of Gary Hill's generation and of his work in particular cannot be seen within a straight set of "artistic" developments. Rather they have to be seen against a different horizon of understanding and a different environment of cultural politics.

In Hill's case, his work has particularly developed in relation to the key intellectual arguments around the role and meaning of language (linguistics, semiotics, and discourse formations) as it inflects within texts and contexts (within culture itself, in other words). The questions of representation, which are questions of the ability of language and image to construct reality, were brought into the forefront of artists' concerns in a move which is often called postmodernism. Hill's brilliance, in the sense of both ingeniousness and lightness, has been to put technological systems of telematic communication—systems of machine "languages"—to full and fufilling aesthetic use by providing a pliant position on both the codes of language and the human body, as they are expressed through wordings and imagery in this new cultural environment. His role in the so-called "crisis of representation" which is the general category for the above-mentioned historical shift is to have devised phenomenal ways in which to *wonder* word to the world and the world to the word. Play prevails and seriousness is entertained, as a result.

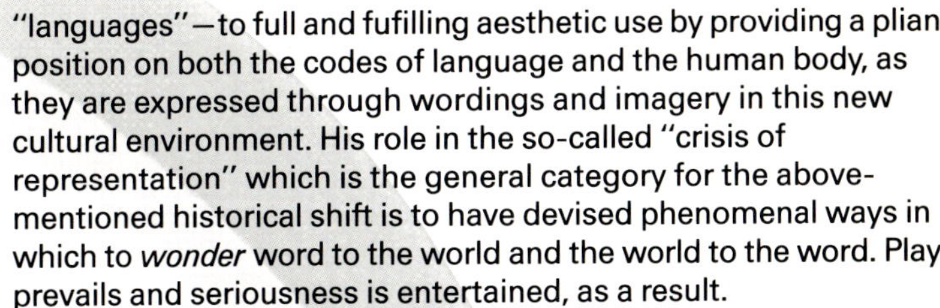

I continued to question the world's limits, seeing the wretchedness of anyone who is content with it, and I couldn't bear the facility of fiction for long: I demanded its reality, I became mad.

Poetry was simply a detour: through it I escaped the world of discourse, which had become the natural world for me; with poetry I entered a kind of grave where the infinity of the possible was born from the death of the logical world.

Georges Bataille, *The Impossible* (translated by Robert Hurley) (San Francisco: City Lights Books, 1991).

Specifically for Hill, which accounts for his reception into the European art scene sooner and more influentially than in America, it was French writing in and around textuality which had a bearing and a density for his work both as emergent reference (i.e., the use of Blanchot's texts) and as interpretive scaffold. Which is not to say that Hill's views were determined by theory as other academic artists often are, but rather that such theoretical and literary work provides the central and controlling community of thought through which his work performs. It is his "horizon of reception," his parallel universe of kinship and affiliation.

This virtual genre of modern French writing includes works from the artistic avant garde as well as purely intellectual or strictly academic texts. They are marked by a forceful anger positioned against the very conditions of literature itself. Or, it might be said, this modern writing rails and writhes and pitches restlessly against the limits of written language at the same time as it uses it; striking out oedipally at its very own privileged and partrilineal heritage. These texts attack the perceived structures of language's grammatical and ideological codes and play against their consensually recognized strictures by trying to disobey them, dislodge them, rupture and elide them in a kind of aspiration for radicality, albeit only textual (a condition which might better be called "readicality").

Knowing language as written down, in opposition to oral uses,

Opposite page
from ***And Sat Down Beside Her,*** 1990

WHEEL Solid cylindrical surface intersected by six rectangles passing through the surface's axis, resulting in six sixty-degree sectors.

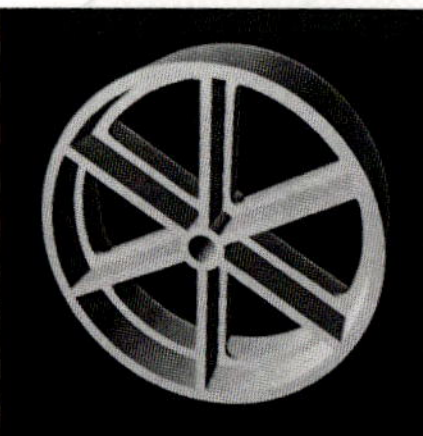

(technical descriptions of images by Caspar R. Curjel with Gary Hill)

to be a self-consciously self-reflexive activity, these French texts exude a resolved class of rage at the betrayal of language to *not* be able to capture completely and accurately the world as it is known through experience. To be (monstrously) contained by inescapable metaphors (endless relays of substitutions of one thing for another in the way that Barthes describes metaphor as making "...an infinitely ambiguous object out of a simple, literal object"). To only know "presence" by virtue of an absence (the always and forever unlocatable referent, which is why photography and death are their determining tropes, sharing the melancholy of the ill-fated binarism of absence/ presence as well). Yet, such texts try to overcome their conclusiveness; try to shift the tide of their historic destiny. Their history is a trajectory of the text's willfulness against a perceived conformism and even authoritarianism within language. This nameless French discourse is about language, but it differs from other similar discourses by consistently refusing to embrace abstraction in art as its corollary. By refusing to avoid the problem of representation as a key dilemma of any analysis of art or politics.

When Gary Hill speaks of the "physicality of language," a "single word's time" and "making something that is already immaterial lose its identity even further," he carefully measures his entrance into this paradoxical discourse. But importantly, Hill's disturbance is created not from the vulnerable tissue of the page but rather from the sinewy depths of embodied technological systems.

Michel Foucault detected the essential dilemma of incompatibility between writing and the world by a summation which he called "the infinite relation between things and words." His was a more hopeful restatement of Samuel Beckett's anguished concern in his theater piece *Malloy* for "thingless words and wordless things." Both writers, of course, wished in dissimilar ways to preserve or even extend this contradiction while at the same time identifying and working against it. The inability of language to completely apprehend circumstance acts as writing's exotic "Other" to the main summons of represention within language (and in this projection of "otherness" is its affiliation with ethnographic writings and surrealist texts in creating a masculinist position which defines and controls its "loss" through a projection of figures of stability).[1]

With Foucault or Beckett, the incongruity of all attempts to

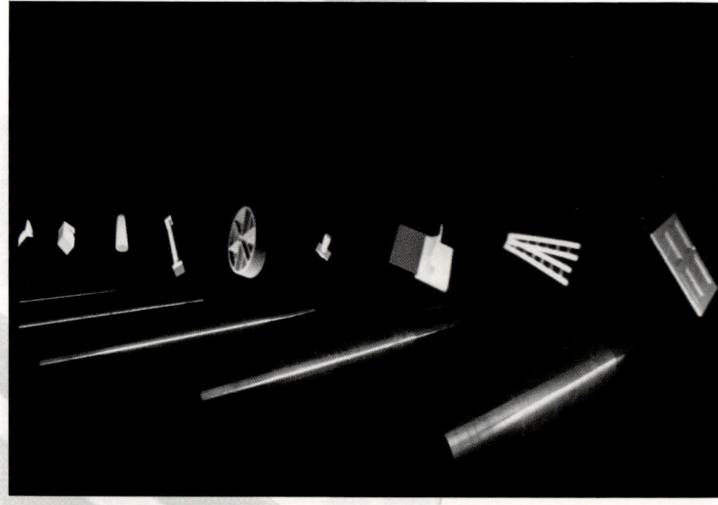

Some Times Things, 1992

I Believe It Is an Image in Light of the Other, 1991-92 (detail)

1. Stephen A. Tyler, "Post-Modern Ethnography," in *Writing Culture: The Poetics and Politics of Ethnography*, ed. James Clifford, George E. Marcus (Berkeley: University of California Press, 1986). Tyler, emphasizing Innis' and other's insights writes..."To represent means to have a kind of magical power over appearances, to be able to bring into presence what is absent, and that is why writing, the most powerful means of representation, was called *"grammarye,"* a magical act. The true historical significance of writing is that it has increased our capacity to create totalistic illusions with which to have power over things or over others as if they were things." (p. 131). For a critique of the whole book for continuing to do the same thing it claims to reproach, see bell hooks, "Culture to Culture," in *Yearning: race, gender and cultural politics* (Boston: South End Press, 1990).

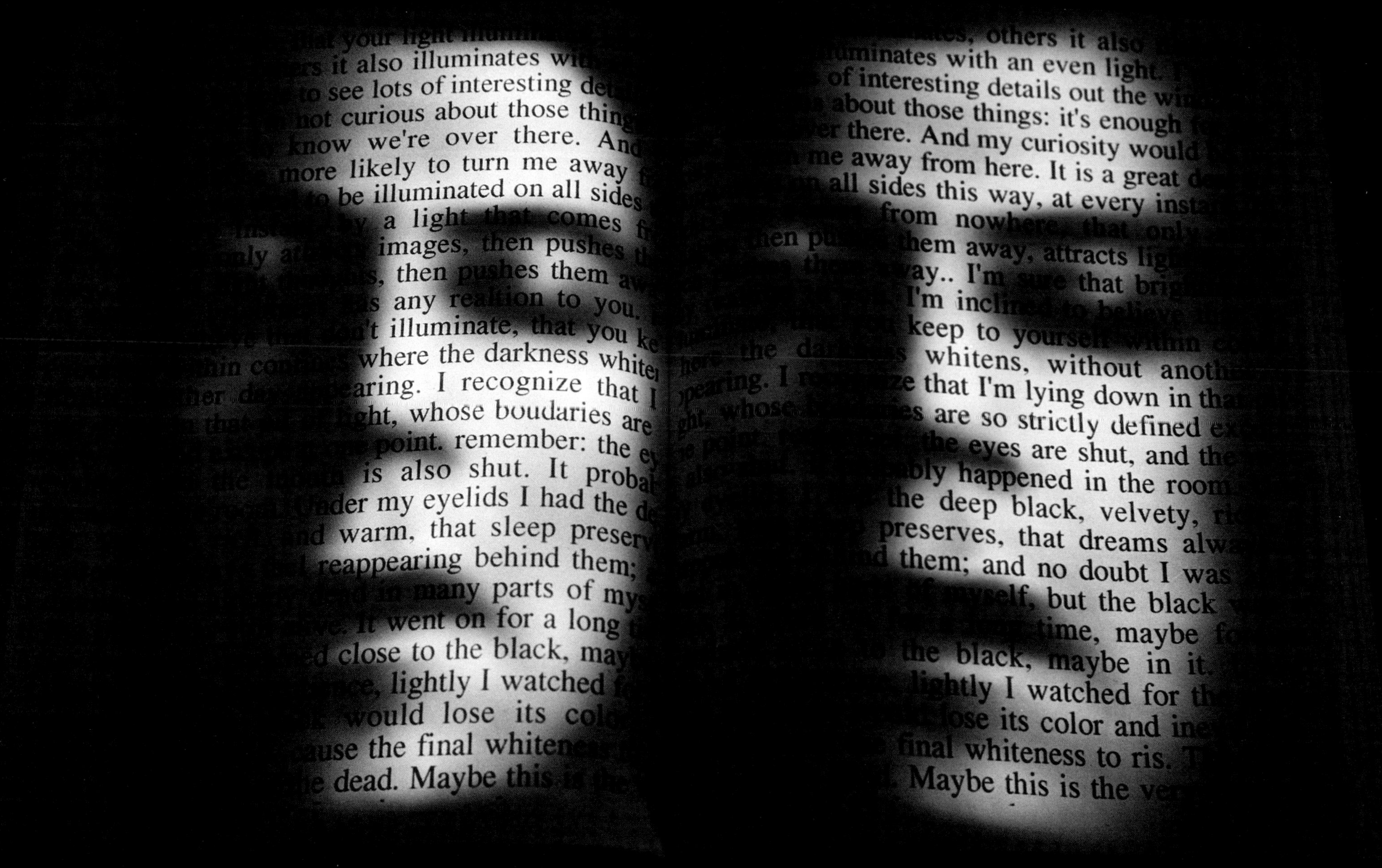

rs it also illuminates wi
to see lots of interesting det
not curious about those thing
know we're over there. And
more likely to turn me away f
to be illuminated on all sides
a light that comes fr
images, then pushes th
s, then pushes them aw
s any realtion to you.
't illuminate, that you ke
where the darkness whiten
aring. I recognize that I
ght, whose boudaries are
point. remember: the ey
is also shut. It probab
Under my eyelids I had the de
nd warm, that sleep preserv
reappearing behind them;
many parts of mys
It went on for a long t
close to the black, may
lightly I watched f
would lose its colo
ause the final whiten
e dead. Maybe this

others it also
illuminates with an even light.
of interesting details out the wi
about those things: it's enough
there. And my curiosity would
me away from here. It is a great d
all sides this way, at every insta
from nowhere, that only
hem away, attracts ligh
ay.. I'm sure that brig
I'm inclined to believe
keep to yourself within
whitens, without anoth
ze that I'm lying down in tha
es are so strictly defined ex
the eyes are shut, and the
bly happened in the room
the deep black, velvety, ri
preserves, that dreams alwa
them; and no doubt I was
f, but the black
time, maybe fo
the black, maybe in it.
lightly I watched for th
lose its color and ine
final whiteness to ris.
Maybe this is the ver

BOOK Two rectangles, gamma/1 and gamma/2 connected by a surface beta. Beta is part of a right cylinder based on a plane curve of variable curvature. The angle between gamma/1 and gamma/2 is variable. Gamma/1 and gamma/2 bound a family of variably deformed surfaces.

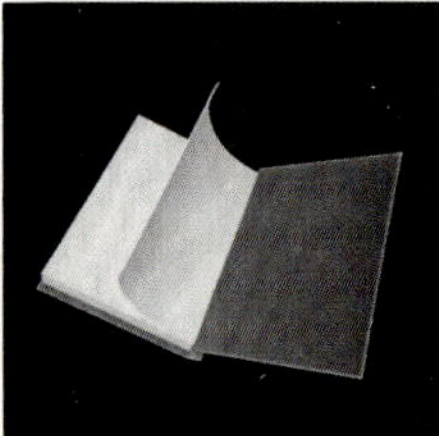

arrest experience in words, a frustration which any writer knows and feels deeply, is made palpable as politicized (and policed) metaphor, as a privileged oxymoronic unit within the rhetorical economy of resistance and frustration. Thingless words or wordless things are presented as an idealized version of a "third" term, a term that might be outside of the binarisms of left/right, colonizer/colonized, master/slave, etc. But, still, such writing is a culturally authorized and, now, institutionalized, *ressentiment,* contributing as much or more to the myth of artistic resistance as to any measure of social engagement.

Reading out from the Bataille quote at the head of this essay it is possible to see immediately the psychic distance between language and its references and the physical world and language's names for it. And how that always produces a coming to terms with any language's inabilities, incompletenesses, and restraints (although the choice is not usually stated as dramatically and hyperbolically, except perhaps by poets for whom words are a working cultural capital). For all writing, it might be said, there is some kind of actual and inevitable *rapprochement* between the word and the world; some kind of understanding of the enfolded relation and the unwrapped difference within the two; some understanding that the resentment of writing is a projection of a fantasy necessary in order to keep writing. The world and the word keep encasing one another in their tautological tension, disappearing into and appearing again on the surface of each other's desperate intertwined skins.

Despite the autonomy of the text, and the divorce from reality which it produces, writers maintain and activate their Sisyphean desire. But, today, in a hyperreal environment of floating signifiers and floating signifieds, of promotional culture and technological highways, the once projected transparency of language which assumed a relation between things and words is now being questioned in all forms and is being extended beyond these intellectual concerns. Far from being just a textual or an intellectual conceit or philosophical issue, with the "decline of the referentials" (Henri LeFevbre's term) at hand, an understanding of this arbitrary, necessary but illusionary relationship has created a new epistemological and social condition. Popular understanding of the divorce between "truth" and meaning causes a fictional and uneasy element to appear in all language presentations, from MTV to E-Mail to political reality.

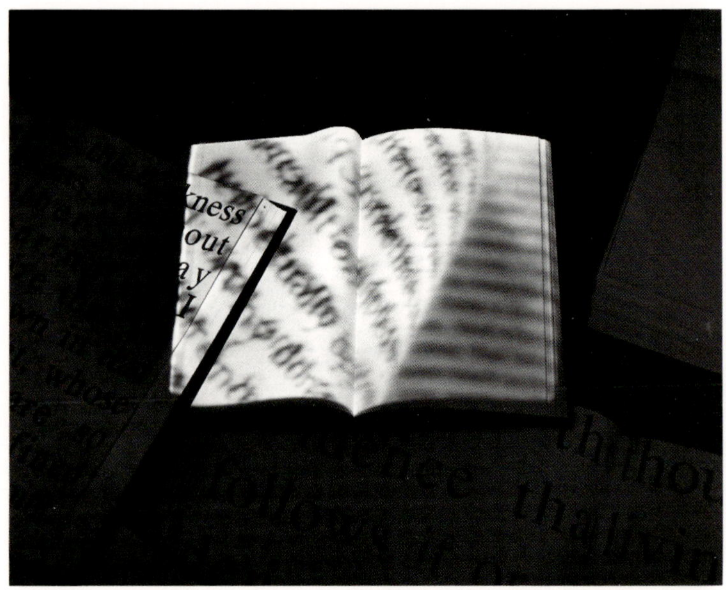

I Believe It Is an Image in Light of the Other, 1991-92 (detail)

BOX A surface S/1 whose boundary consists of four line segments making up a rectangle, and a second surface S/2 whose boundary is congruent to the boundary of the first surface S/1. A tubular solid in the shape of one-half of a thickened rectangle attached to S/1. The two surfaces can be positioned such that they form a closed surface which bounds a solid rectangle.

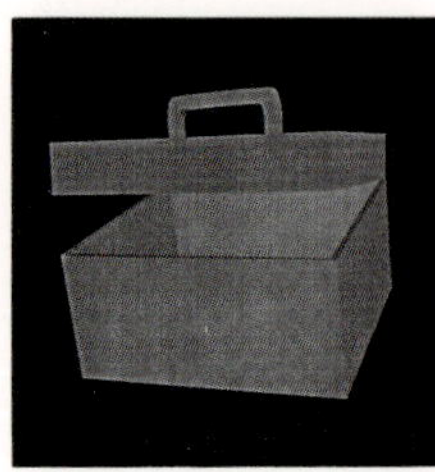

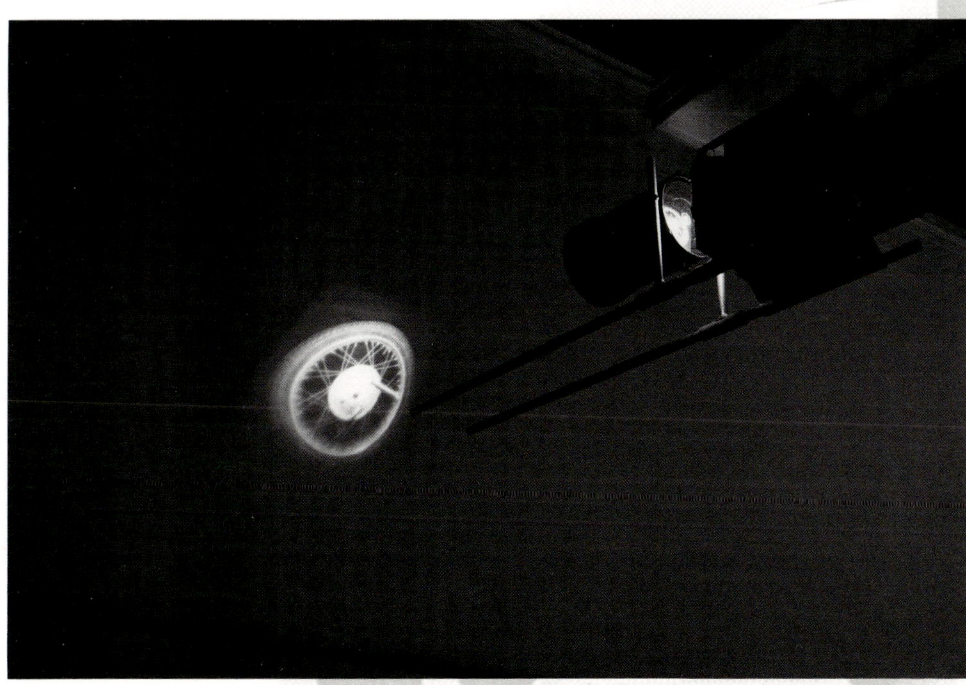

DIG (Mediarite), 1987 (detail)

Geoffrey Galt Harpman has persuasively argued against the idea of language as *fully* determining (which is a subset of this genre of French thought taken up by careerist academics and, often, in America, an uncritical curatorial acceptance of such thinkers as Saussure and Lacan; an acceptance of an idea most forcefully suggested by Barthes when he wrote "Everything is language, or more precisely, language is everything"). In contradistinction Harpman suggests "...as heretical as this sounds, language, too, is inhabited, structured, determined by the nonlinguistic in the form of referents or understanding; the idea of language is incoherent without the concept of the resistant nonlinguistic."[2] The resistant nonlinguistic is what in ordinary language might be called the physical world but it is also the spiritual world, or any world (horror, pain, sublimity, liminality) which resists full linguistic appropriation. Implicitly, to remember the other senses and the other visceralities is an argument for art which is always an erotic body which ceaselessly and carelessly crosses the disciplines defined by language.

This idea is more directly embellished by another North American, Charles Taylor, specifically in relation to the French influence (which some have even called a "tyranny") when he writes, "Indeed for purposes of such diachronic explanation, we can question whether we ought to speak of a priority of language over act. There is a circular relation.... This is a crashing truism, but the fog emanating from Paris in recent decades makes it necessary to clutch it as a beacon in the darkness. To give an absolute priority to the structure makes *exactly as little sense* as the equal and opposite error of subjectivism, which gave absolute priority to the action, as a kind of total beginning."[3] If language and literature are then less privileged, less conspiratorially projected as fully determining, it might be easier to see this influential and mystifying metaphysics in a different light, the kind of light that Hill articulates. As Mark Poster has written, "There are only two social groups in advanced society who by their daily practice are encouraged to regard texts as having transcendent primacy in human experience: orthodox rabbis and academicians in the humanities and some of the social sciences."[4] Part of Gary Hill's aesthetic and intellectual project, in everything from the single-channel tapes to the larger, more phenomenologically precise installations, is to take the fundamental lessons of structuralism and poststructuralist

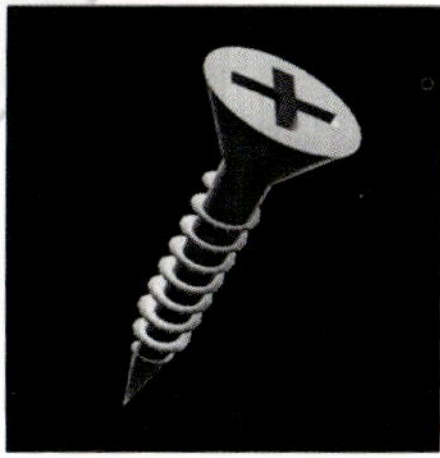

SCREW Rotational symmetry S with respect to a line, except for two perpendicular indentations at a right angle and a helicoid surface of constant pitch and diminishing outer diameter.

2. Geoffrey Galt Harpman, *The Aescetic Imperative in Culture and Criticism* (Chicago: University of Chicago Press, 1987), p. 269. This was stated earlier as more of a tragic dilemma by Theodor Adorno when he wrote "Even the implacable rigour with which criticism speaks the truth of an untrue consciousness remains imprisoned within the orbit of that against which it struggles, fixated on its surface manifestations." *Prisms,* translated by Weber, Samuel and Shierry (Cambridge: The MIT Press, 1981), p. 20.

3. Charles Taylor, "Foucault on Freedom and Truth," in *Foucault: A Critical Reader,* ed. David Couzens Hoy (Oxford: Basil Blackwell, 1986).

4. Mark Poster, *The Mode of Information: Poststructuralism and Social Context* (Chicago: The University of Chicago Press, 1990), p. 80.

GLASS The part of a right circular cone between two planes perpendicular to the cone's axis. A surface consisting of the lateral hull of a cone and a solid circle in one of the two limiting planes. The surface's boundary is the circle in which the cone intersects the other limiting plane. A configuration that is symmetric.

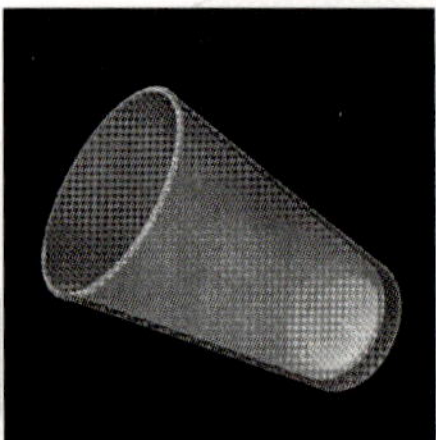

thought about language to heart but also to provide its transformative other as a resistant antidote. To recognize and oblige other corporeal holds on us.

Put more precisely in relation to this modern(ist) French tradition, the writing under discussion is implicitly against *vision* as the privileged sense which determines knowledge. It is vision and visuality which are the unconscious that such writing abhors or at least feels discomfort with when it confronts its own absences. It regrets the fact that vision and all things which are "signatures of the visible," as Frederick Jameson calls this ("pornographic") jurisdiction of visuality, necessarily deny and divorce themselves from the other senses; from the sensuous, from the body as a sensuous whole (the "resistent nonlinguistic"). This penchant for interrogating the visual within textuality was noted in full by Martin Jay in essays where he traced, *à la* Marshall McLuhan, the "scopic regimes of modernity" with their emphasis on "ocular desire" and their moments of disquietude as symbolized by writers among whom might be included Aragon, Artaud, Bachelard, Barthes, Bataille, Baudrillard, Baudelaire, Blanchot, Breton, deBord, Deleuze, Derrida, Genet, Foucault, Kristeva, Lautréamont, Lyotard, Mallarmé, Virillio, et al.; a pantheon of offical writers of the unofficial.[5]

And, if we accept Derrida's premise of the *trace,* in which writing is extended by virtue of its relays in a *mise en abyme* of meanings (the phototext, the text *imaginaire,* the filmic-text, even the oral which is haunted by an already existing text, and so on), then the list could include another partial history of anti-ocularity which parallels and circulates around and with the textual one that energizes French writing. That is the history of images which interrogate visuality. For instance, Surrealism's mostly literary engagement also produced a drama of visuality which also congregated images around and against the privilege of the eye: Dali and Bunuel's cutting of the eye to begin the film *Le Chien d'Andalou,* or Man Ray's *Object to be Destroyed,* a metronome with a cut-up photograph of Lee Miller's eye attached, Magritte's disembodied eyes, Bellmer's eyeless dolls, Duchamp's distaste for "retinal" painting, and Robert Desnos' inventory for the rhetoric surrounding the eye. The eye and its discontents comprise a major imagistic power (in pictures and poems) related to the manikinized and fragmented bodies throughout this work. And of course it is precisely these image/text "traces" that find theory's fatigue reawakened and often rescued from textual hell: Foucault on Magritte, Derrida on Cézanne, Lyotard on Arakawa, Barthes on the illustrative plates of the Encyclopedia, etc., in a set of mirror reversals of language and text/text and language as a bad marriage of inconvenience, but one which at least provides an active narrative.

More emphatically for Gary Hill's work however, the prominence of the strategies and structures of language in French writing may in fact be more an emphasis on the nature of the PRINTED word (as a composition of letters) and thus in reliance on the systematic use of the eyes as precursors to knowledge, a mainstay of (now nostalgic) Western thought. What *homo academius* has wrought to *homo logon echon* is something called logocentrism, the idea that texts have a relation to truth through a concept called rationality. The problematics of the text may just be that—the problem of textualization, the fragility and instability of the making of worlds into words on paper, which was Mallarmé's quintessential issue and positivism's (now) unhappy legacy. It may be that language *seen*—static words under the gaze—is what was so troublesome, so central to the issue of disciplinary activity. To the dilemma of word and world.

And it is Hill's contribution to have understood that video is primarily about time, not vision, and about sound, not vision, and about the choreography of space, not vision, all of which links it more directly and fundamentally to speech (albeit a technologized and distinctly embodied speech). This is simply to suggest that any use of words is bound up in social dynamics and systems which, in the case of the previous historical texts implied here, are already circumscribed to some extent by the linearity, rhetoric, power and institutional circulation of a certain kind of modernist literacy and its visualist assumptions. It is to suggest that language must be considered where and when it is found rather than in any large general theory which only substantiates a much earlier avant garde behavior, an ineffective behavior which has now been inculcated and absorbed by all advertising, television, and filmic codes. It is to suggest that any theory of textuality is simultaneously a theory of history, and of, in this case, a particular and prejudiced history. Any "subversiveness" in such texts, even those which are "anti-ocular" in their frustrated rhetoric, is now historical and historicized. To hold to these linguistic or textual derivations as models would be, at this moment in time, to parody the writers' original socio-political, aesthetic impulses and the usefulness they had at first. And to continue to canonize such texts as "radical" is an aspect of what John Mowitt calls "cloistered vanguardism."[6]

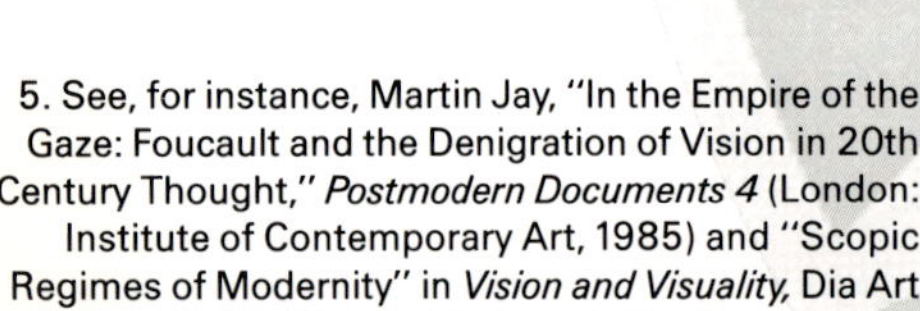

5. See, for instance, Martin Jay, "In the Empire of the Gaze: Foucault and the Denigration of Vision in 20th Century Thought," *Postmodern Documents 4* (London: Institute of Contemporary Art, 1985) and "Scopic Regimes of Modernity" in *Vision and Visuality,* Dia Art Foundation (Seattle: Number 2, Bay Press, 1988).

6. John Mowitt, *TEXT: The Genealogy of an Antidisciplinary Object* (Durham: Duke University Press, 1992). The book provides an excellent history of the emergence of textuality as a subject and object of recent academic concern.

What I am suggesting by too quickly and too unjustly conflating the theoretical, the poetic, the imagistic, and its various strains (structuralist, poststructuralist, psychoanalytic, ethno-methodological, etc.) within a loose narrative of French anti-visuality is that to truly make problematic the question of language, there would have to be a contiguous interrogation of the technology in which the language is found. If such writing is found in print, the whole history of the visual discourse of the printed word from Ong to McLuhan to Ivens to Havelock to Goody, Baudrillard, Virillio, and Poster could be brought to bear to understand that the frustration within the text is also a frustration with the imposed regularity of thought (that myth of Western rationality) which accompanies it. This is, as a tribute to Hill's work, to make a case for understanding the body from which language emerges, whether it be the gut and the mouth, or the chip and the modem. As Poster has written, "The stability and linearity of the written word help to constitute the subject in reason, a confident, coherent subject who spoke the language of realism through signs whose highest ideal was the discourse of natural science."[7] But, it is precisely this subject, this rational distanced author or reader whose natural world is displaced in an environment of radicalized information exchange and data politics. It is this subject who is dislocated by the very radicalization of language by systems of technology which create of identity a fiction, a node in the system of language, a writerly reader. And it is this subject who is literate only to the degree that she or he is jacked in to the information system of language machines as well as the semiotic play of literary textuality.

Gary Hill has taken seriously the discourse surrounding language and representation but, and herein lies his difference from philosophers, academics and most other artists, he has also taken seriously the discourse of technological systems as they come into being and into consciousness. It is his project to "interanimate" (to use Mikhail Bakhtin's term) the cultures of both, the codes of both, and the tongues of both to produce a truly embroiled object, an authentic intertextualized experience (rather than only a metaphor of one). For it is only by creating an actual situation of indeterminacy in which the audience can truly experience the effects of language and technology simultaneously that the possibilities of either can be assessed. And that their poetics may be felt.

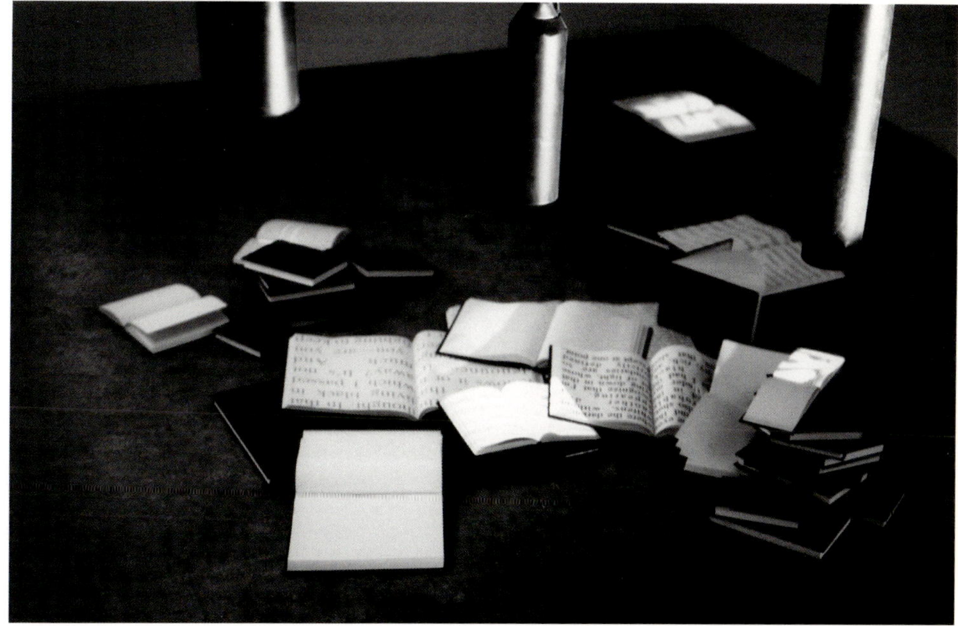

I Believe It Is an Image in Light of the Other,
1991-92 (detail)

7. Mark Poster, op. cit., p. 61.

Bruce W. Ferguson is a freelance curator and critic living in New York. He was most recently curator of *Dress Codes* at the Institute for Contemporary Art in Boston. He writes for numerous publications on the arts.

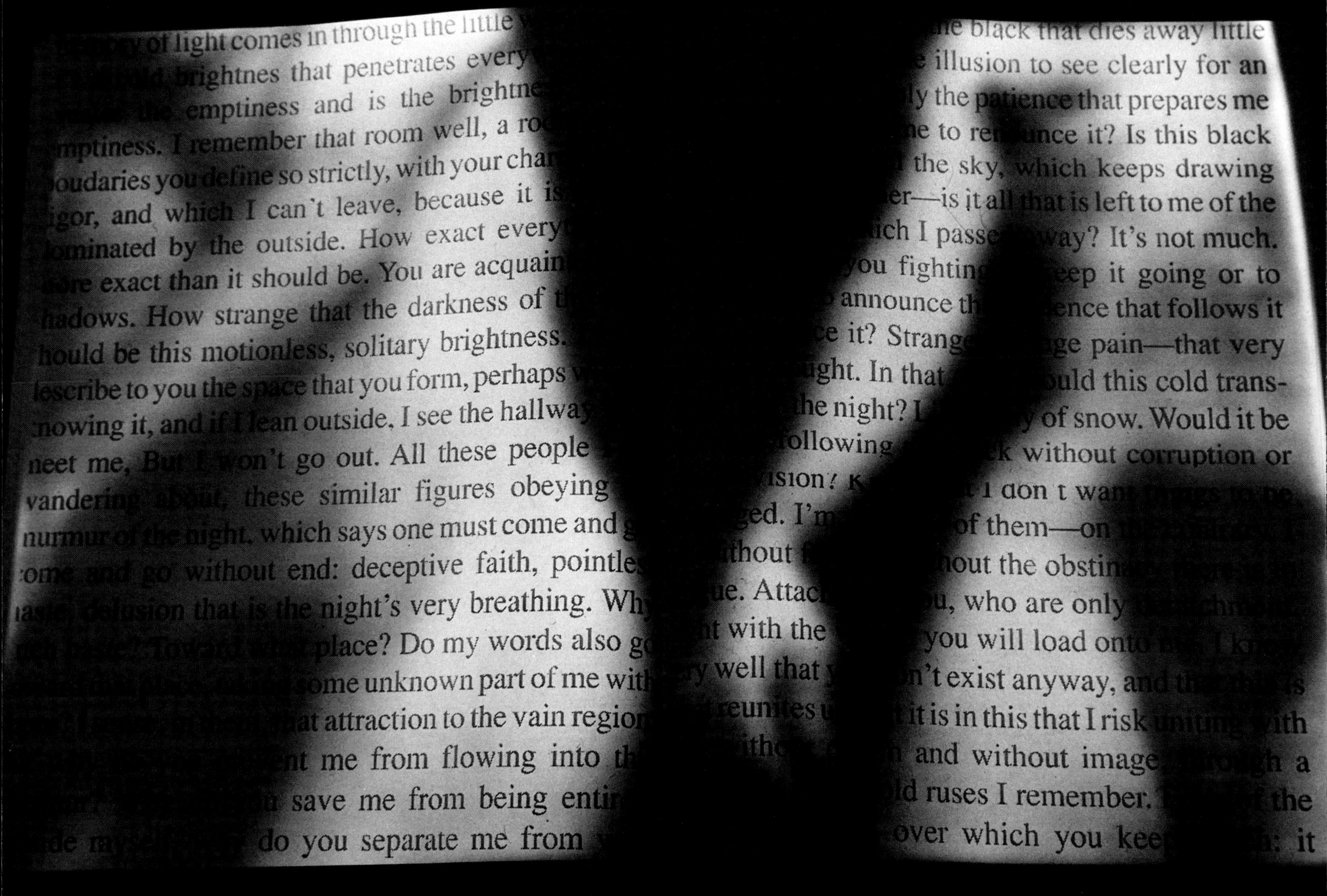

…y of light comes in through the little
…brightnes that penetrates every…
…emptiness and is the brightne…
…mptiness. I remember that room well, a ro…
…oudaries you define so strictly, with your cha…
…igor, and which I can't leave, because it is…
…ominated by the outside. How exact every…
…ore exact than it should be. You are acquain…
…hadows. How strange that the darkness of t…
…hould be this motionless, solitary brightness.…
…escribe to you the space that you form, perhaps…
…nowing it, and if I lean outside, I see the hallwa…
…neet me, But I won't go out. All these people…
…vandering about, these similar figures obeying…
…nurmur of the night, which says one must come and g…
…ome and go without end: deceptive faith, pointle…
…delusion that is the night's very breathing. Wh…
…place? Do my words also g…
…some unknown part of me with…
…at attraction to the vain region…
…nt me from flowing into th…
…save me from being enti…
…do you separate me from…

…he black that dies away little
…e illusion to see clearly for an
…ly the patience that prepares me
…ne to renounce it? Is this black
…the sky, which keeps drawing
…er—is it all that is left to me of the
…ich I passe… way? It's not much.
…you fighting… eep it going or to
…announce th… ence that follows it
…e it? Strange… ge pain—that very
…ught. In that… uld this cold trans-
…he night? I… of snow. Would it be
…following… k without corruption or
…vision? … I don't want…
…ged. I'm… of them—on…
…thout… hout the obstin…
…ue. Attach… u, who are only…
…t with the… you will load onto…
…y well that… n't exist anyway, and…
…reunites… it is in this that I risk uniting with
…and without image… a
…ld ruses I remember.… the
…over which you kee… it

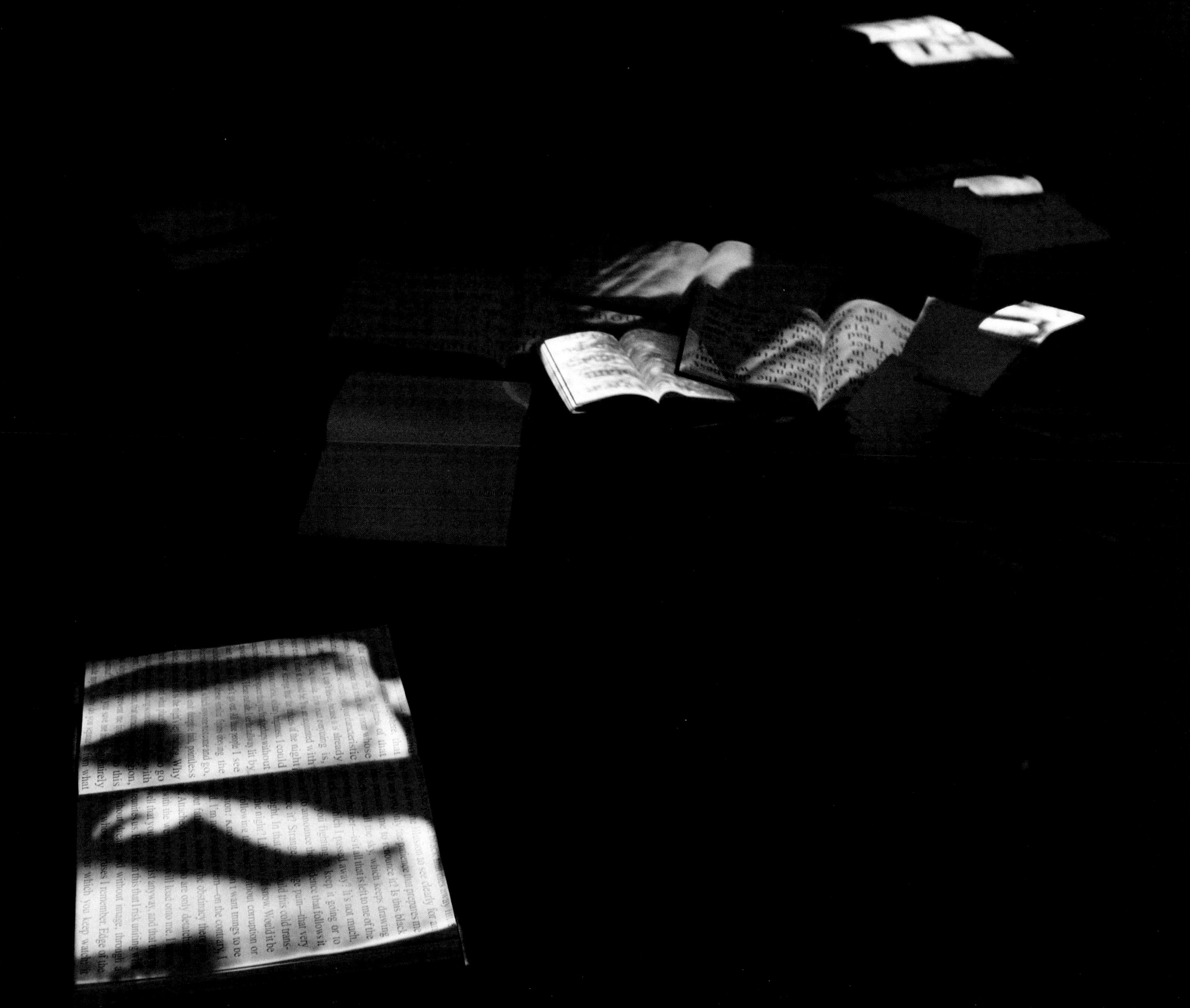

BEACON (Two Versions

Always I become snared in this text of a work. Is it a forward or an after(word)? Is there anything to be gained by description—a walk through with words? Is it to remind the viewer who has already seen the work of what they saw? But wouldn't this be a trampling of their memory, a false recollection, a mere outline of their fascination; a coarse approximation as to the nature of their adjustment to the light (or was it the darkness)? And what about the viewer-to-be, can they be forewarned, foretold (their witness foreshadowed by original intent)? These uneasy viewerships passing through the text, one coming the other going, might just as well be the two versions of the imaginary. No—let us imagine that nothing is imagined...that BEACON is suspended off-center in a darkened room. It is a motorized object: an aluminum tube, fifty-four inches long with a six-inch diameter, capped with lenses at either end, the innards consisting of two four-inch TV monitors facing out in opposite directions, their screens magnified through the glass. What is it? A device, a machine, a technological apparatus that quickly recedes to its function. It is a projection instrument that turns and returns one cycle per six minutes. (Why is it that the moment we become precise in description the mind withdraws to double-check its memory of time and distance only to come back and find them renewed?) And this object with its emission of light wavers between what might be a searchlight sweeping empty dark nights and a form of organized light of an image: a standing figure that seems to float. We wonder (for the sake of imagination); are they images?—these projections that inch across the walls, the light of which grows trapezoidal as they blur (or resolve) leaving a kind of apparition of images behind. One sweep catches a child's face and transports it as if it were in a carriage of light. The viewer is caught up in the fascination of her gaze and follows it across the room where it meets the gaze of a woman (mother?) projected from the opposite end of the beacon. Perhaps one forms the Other's projection across time: mother when child—child when mother. The duplicity of the source, an object, whose beam reveals and inevitably confronts us, suddenly becomes aggressive—a telescope with its terrifying optics of harsh mirrors and polished cut glass—eclipses the viewer, penetrates the eyes, interrupting the passive gaze. An "arc" occurs between the nodes of origin and destination, between light and image, awakening the mind's eye from its stupor, our melancholy for image. The pupils contract from the directed beam of light that only moments before was seen passively from within the peripheral scape as that which clothed darkness and held fast our fascination of image (with the image of fascination) suspending our thought. "After the object comes the image. 'After' means that first the thing must move away in order to allow itself to be grasped again. But that distancing is not the simple change of place of a moving object, which nevertheless remains the same. Here the distancing is at the heart of the thing. The thing was there, we grasped it in living motion of a comprehensive action—and once it has become an image it instantly becomes ungraspable, noncontemporary, impassive, not the same thing distanced, but that thing as distancing, the present thing in its absence, the thing graspable because ungraspable, appearing as something that has disappeared, the return of what does not come back, the strange heart of the distance as the life and unique heart of the thing."[1]

of the Imaginary)

Someone asks, "Why Blanchot?"[2]
Blanchot asks, "Why fascination?"
One might ask Blanchot, "Why text?"
It is perhaps not only the song of the sirens but ironically the enchanting light of the beacon that seduces and leads to a shipwreck of consciousness.
What will you do when you are in the light?

1. Maurice Blanchot, *The Gaze of Orpheus* (Barrytown, New York: Station Hill Press, 1981), pp. 80-81. One of several excerpts used in *BEACON (Two Versions of the Imaginary)*.

2. Raymond Bellour, *The Last Man on the Cross,* translated by Alison Rowe from the catalogue *OTHERWORDS-ANDIMAGES: video by Gary Hill* (Copenhagen: Video Gallerie/Ny Carlsberg Glyptotek, April-May 1990), pp. 20-26.

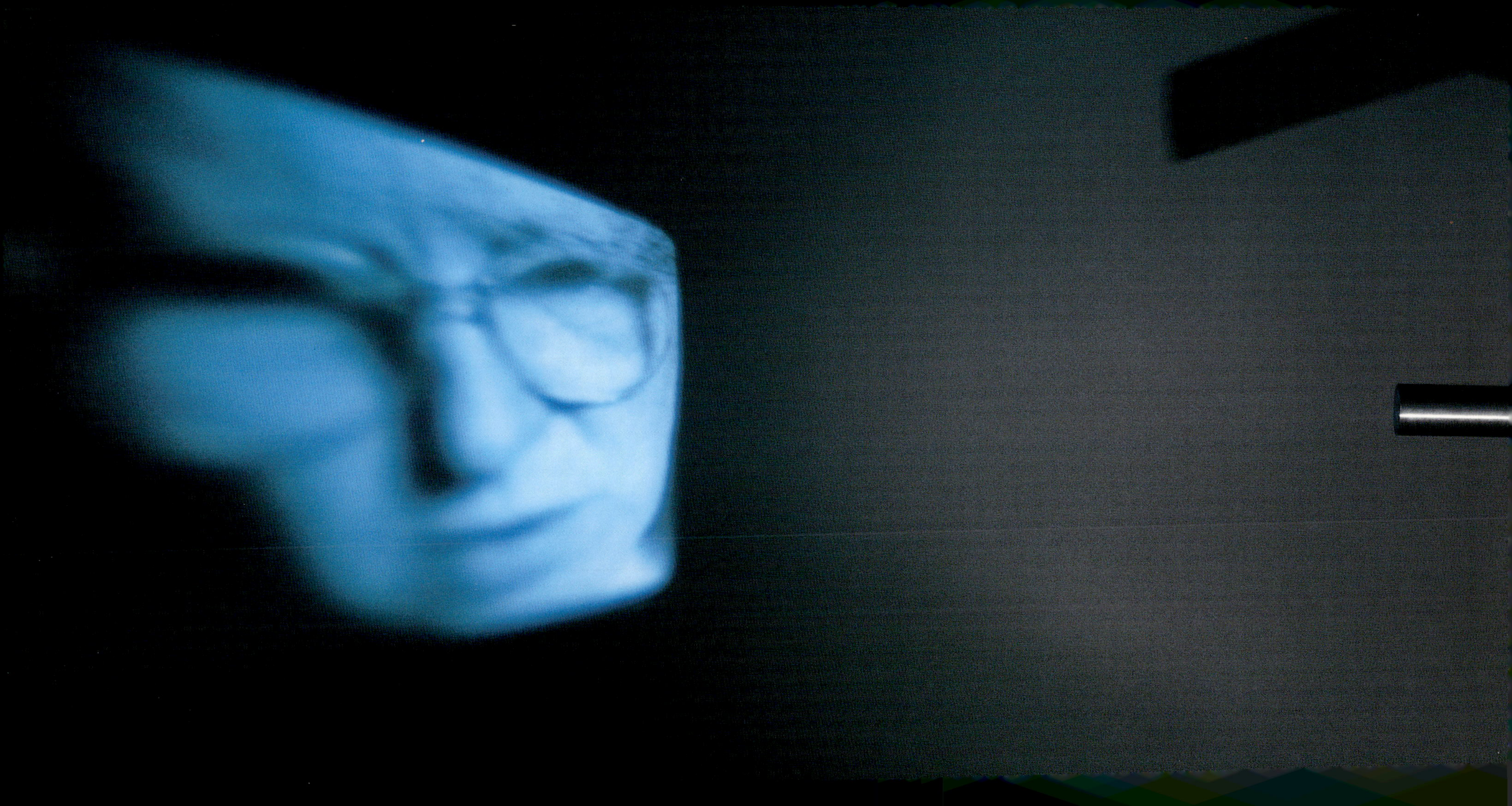

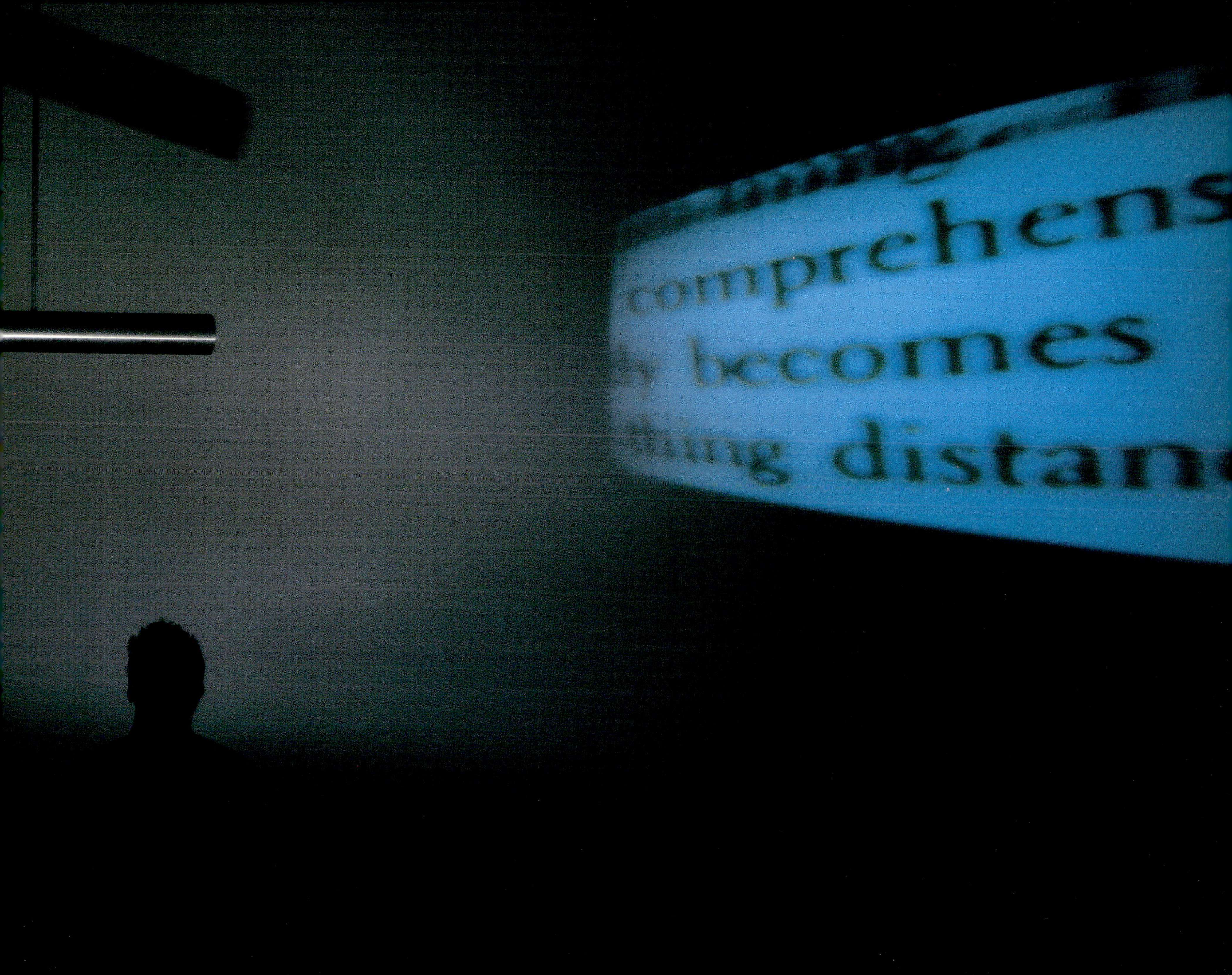
comprehens
becomes
distan

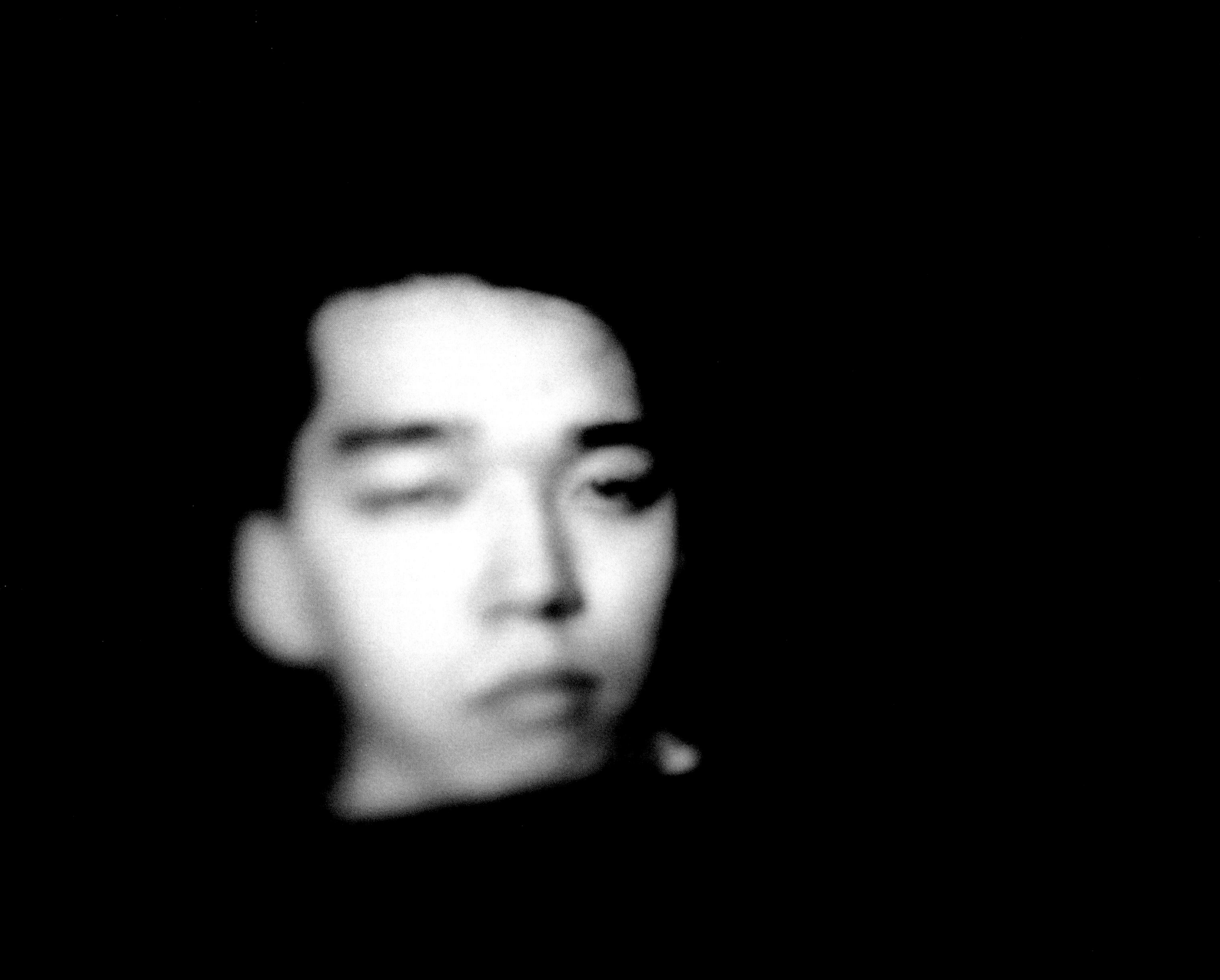

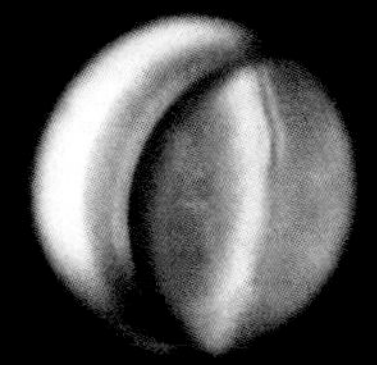

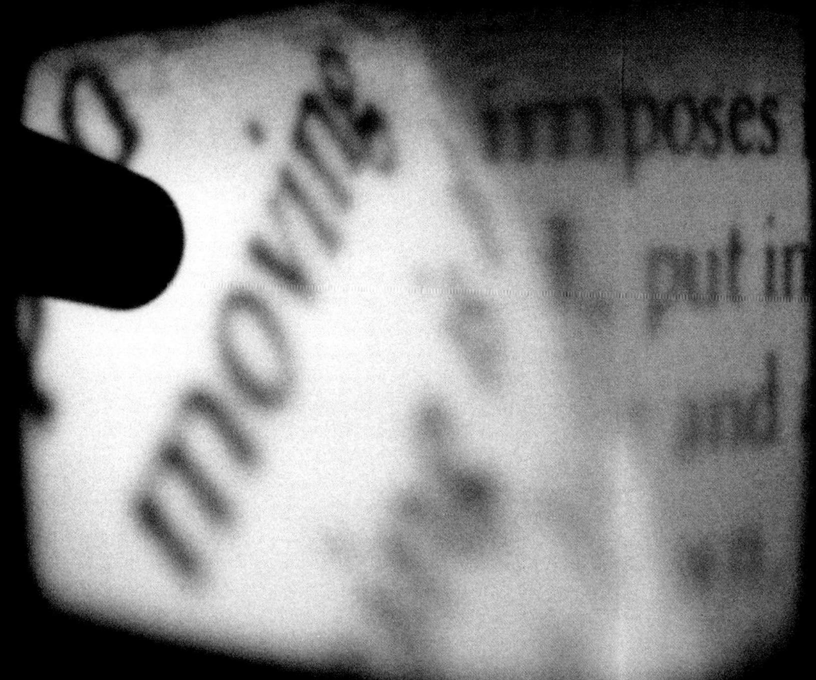
imposes
and

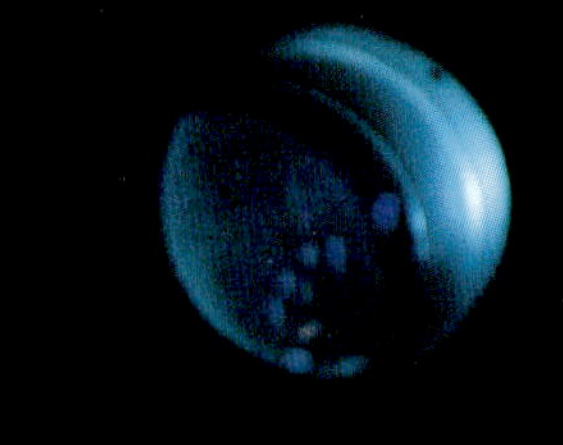

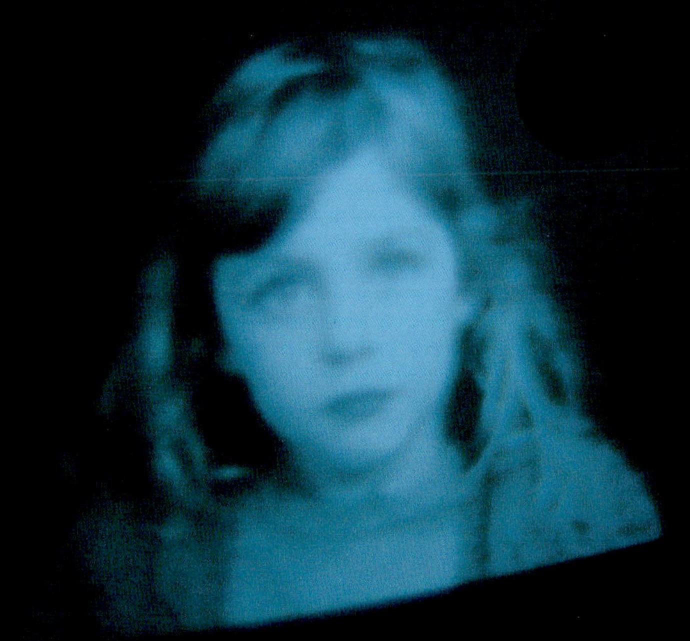

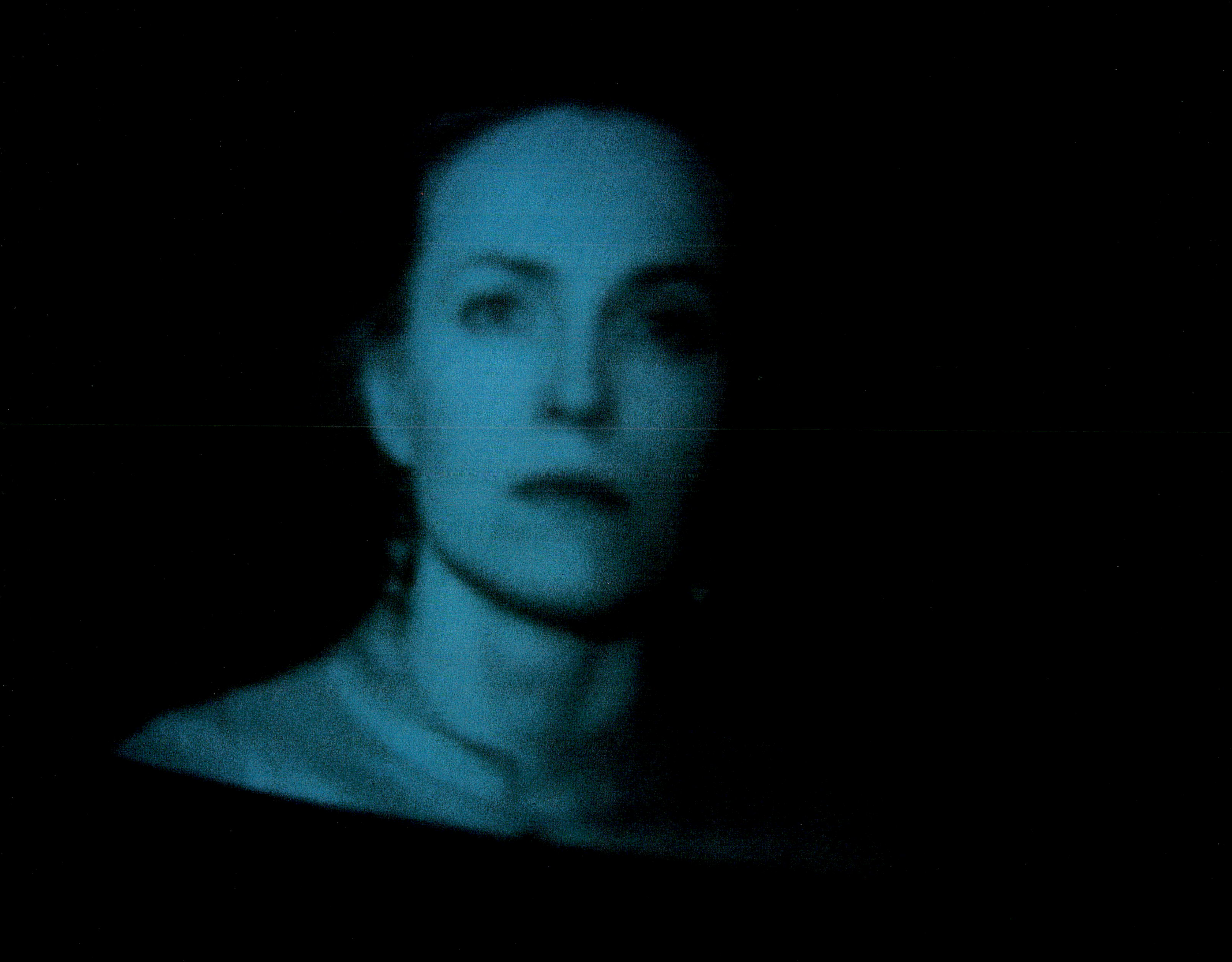

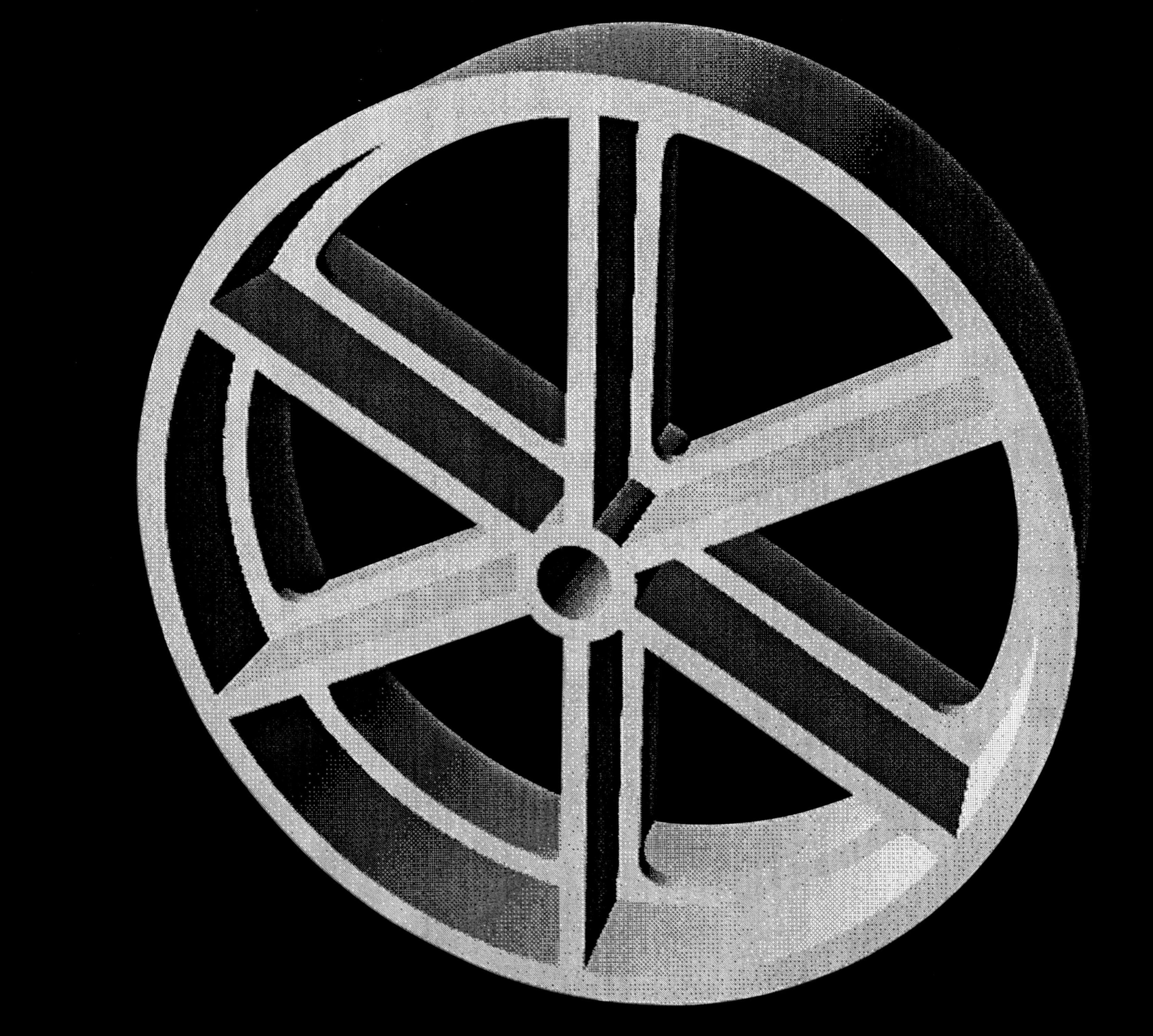

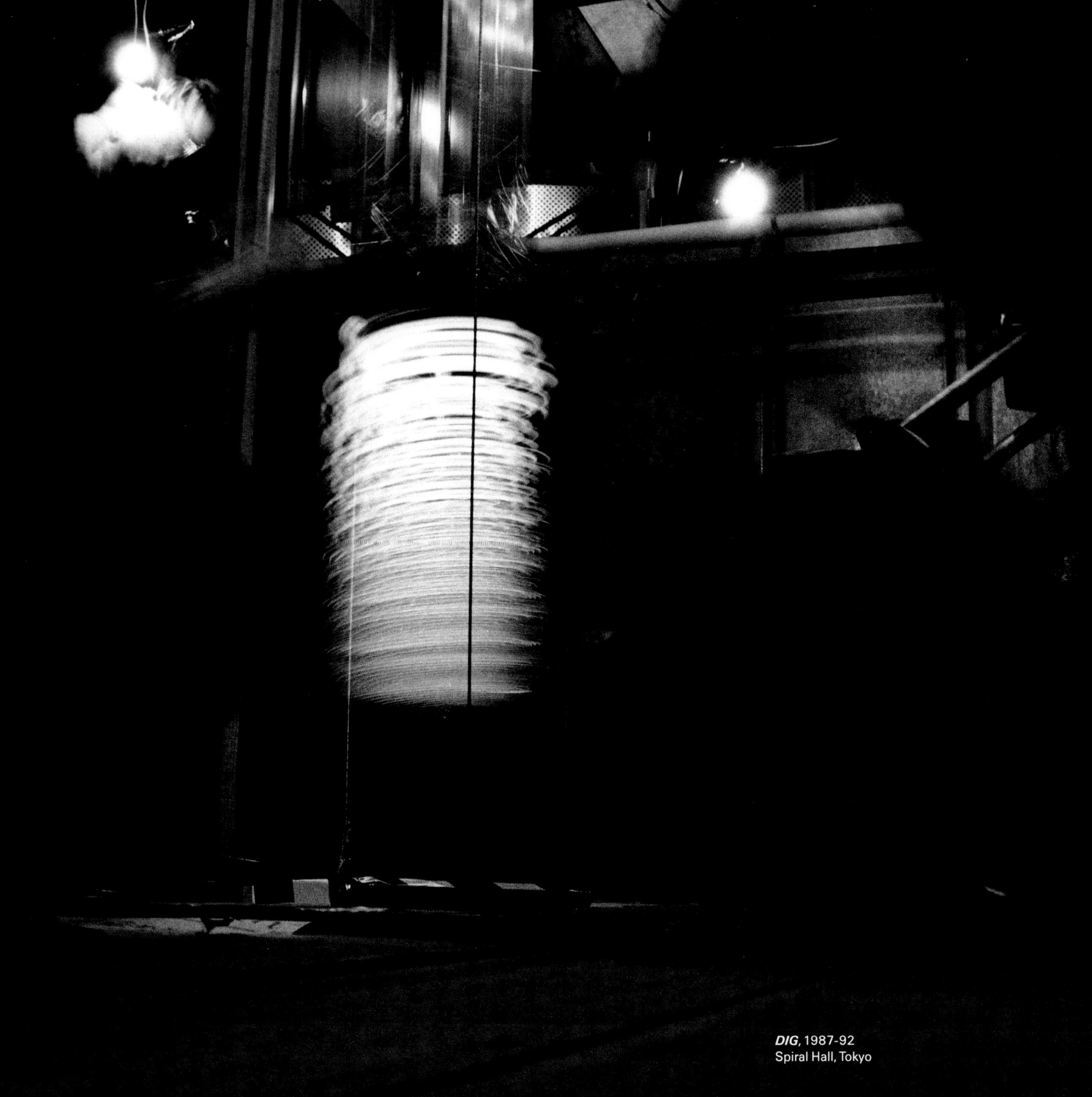

DIG, 1987-92
Spiral Hall, Tokyo

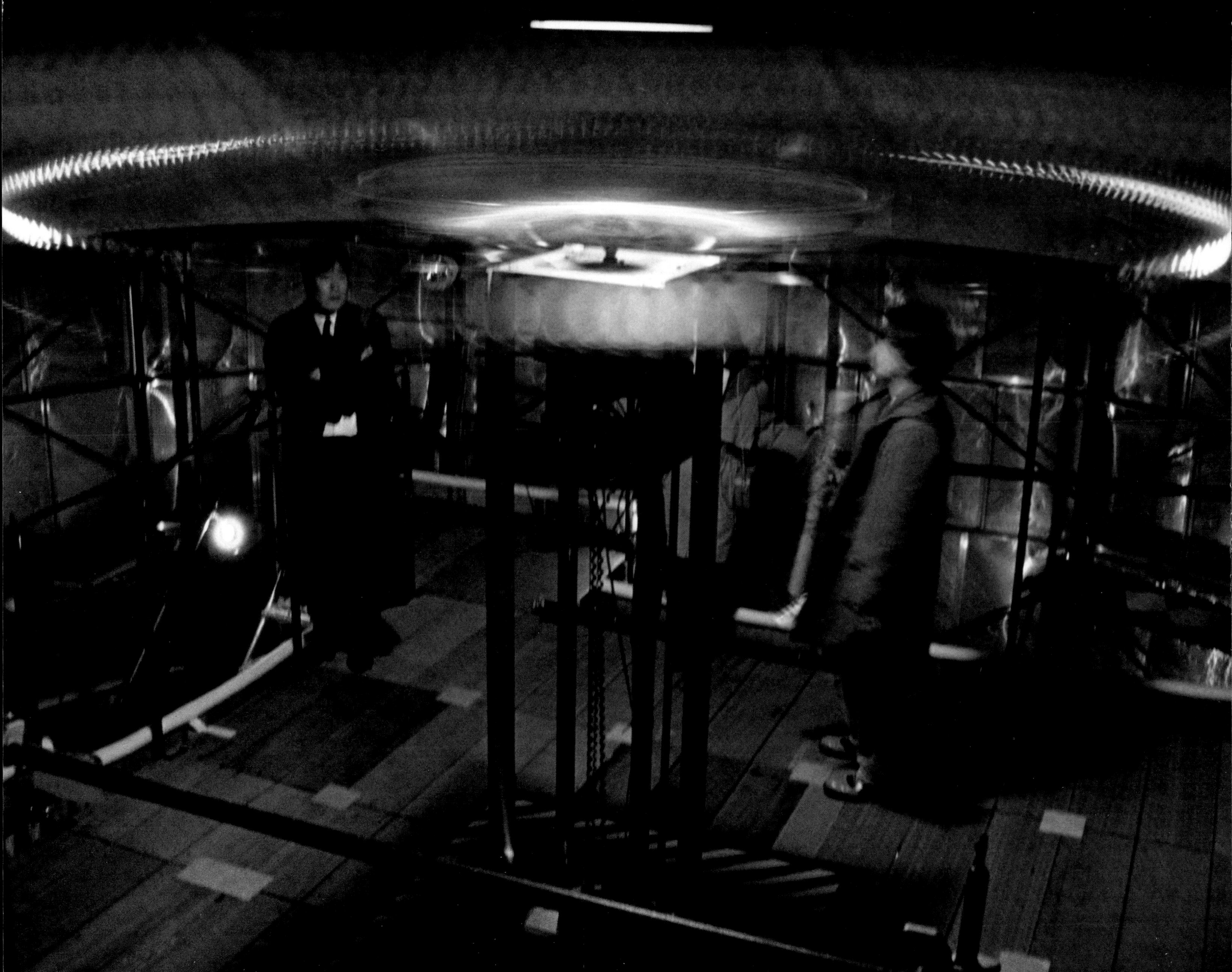

"...Could there have been a specific day, an exact time, a moment, a pause between the sewing of idioms, a burr in the twine...."[1]

In the Process of Knowing Nothing

(something happens)

Chris Bruce

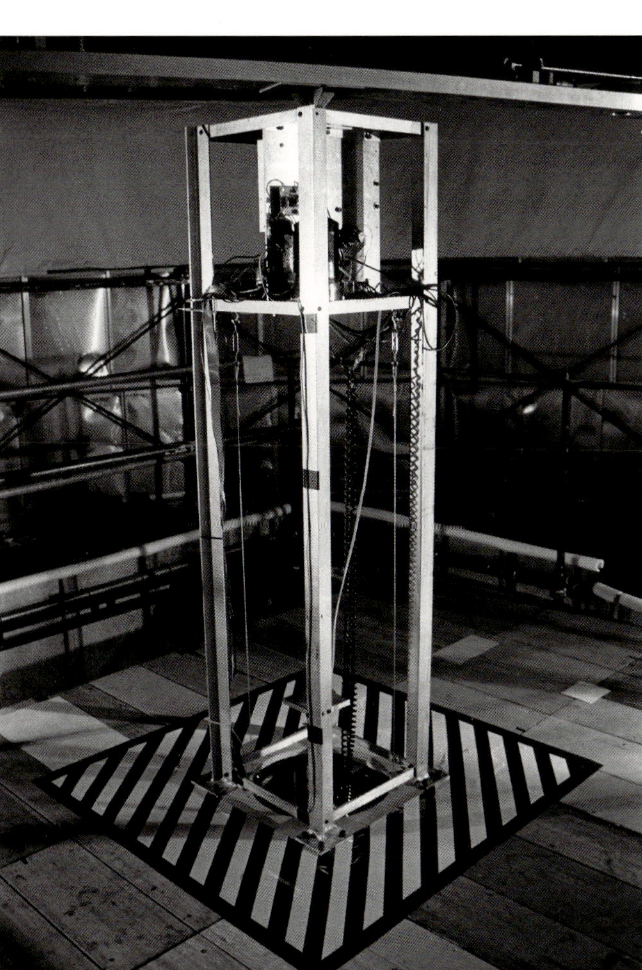

Above and opposite
DIG, 1987-92

Gary Hill's art has at its root a visceral asking of what occurs between events. His video tapes and installations have often been identified with issues of image and language, and clearly these are the parts which fit best the frozen form of publication. More accurately however, one might say that he works *in* time *with* time as the actual space of the encounter with meaning, *using* time to split open seams in moments of consciousness. Titles begin to give this away: *CRUX, Why Do Things Get in a Muddle (Come on Petunia), DIG, Happenstance (part one of many parts), Site Recite (a prologue), Suspension of Disbelief (for Marine), Between 1 & 0.* The works give themselves up less easily, for as the artist admits, this is not an easy place to be. For Hill, meaning, consciousness, and the very act of seeing are full of ambiguity, their only existence tied to the physicality of the body. Indeed, it would seem that in Gary Hill's art, nothing is given except the very space that his works are created from, that being one of extreme openness to process in a medium defined by a simultaneity of presence and absence within the milleu of cybernetics. This is a situation that tends to float, preferring to identify itself only in flux. To me, it is the equivalent of early dawn or the slash bar between either/or. And yet it is from this space that he has created a large body of diverse and entirely idiosyncratic artworks, through a stunning sculptural clarity and an ability to work at the edges of electronic technologies. In a medium (video) that is particularly fluid, Hill works toward subjects (meaning, consciousnes) that are elusive, in a way that seems as basic and mysterious as the way an object enters the eye and becomes cognitive thought.

Recently Hill told the story of driving in the car one night with his daughter, who was at an age when she was just talking. There was a half-moon in the sky, and Anastasia spotted it through the window, "The moon!" They continued driving, turned a couple of corners and came upon the moon again. "Look!" she called out, "There's the other half of the moon!"[2]

This story certainly illustrates an "unknowing" mind and the wonder of direct perception, but part of the sequence that enabled it was the trans(portation) of a car. The innocence and pre-formed logic Anastasia expresses is in part dependent on the machine that changed her frames of reference. Similarly, among Hill's remarkable achievements is his ability to utilize technologies that normally function as distancing agents, and to use them to crack the veneers of human awareness. His art and in particular his installations, thus create sites for ingress through the cracks. I would like to consider two works that precede the time of the core focus of this exhibition,

1. Gary Hill, "Site Re:cite," printed in *Camera Obscura* No. 24, San Francisco, 1991, p. 126.

2. Public talk by Gary Hill, Donald Young Gallery, Seattle, August 4, 1993.

All quotes by Gary Hill, unless noted, are in conversation with the author, July and August, 1993.

DIG (1987-92) and *CRUX* (1983-87), as being particularly clear examples of Hill's sculptural and structural interests, not so much as theoretical constructs, but as architectural fictions that allow the exploration of what consciousness and selfconsciousness mean.

DIG v. tr. 1. To break up, turn over, or remove with a spade, the hand, or the like; excavate. 4. To learn or discover by careful research or investigation. Often used with *up* or *out.* 6. (Slang) To comprehend, appreciate, or enjoy. —v. intr. 2. To proceed along one's way by or as by digging. Used with *through, into,* or *under.* —n. 3. An archaeological excavation.[3]

DIG is one of Hill's most imposing architectural pieces, and it calls on our associations with drilling sites or archaeological digs. As much as anything, *DIG* presents us with a way to see what it looks like to think about thinking.

Raised platforms, railings, machinery, and a high circular armature signify something of consequence, a desire to *get* something or *protect* something. In *DIG,* these desires are inevitably tied to the exposed video monitor, which is sheltered and guarded like some robotic Delphic oracle; fragile, naked, and light-emitting. The monitor is the container of imagery, buried centrally within a complex, derrick-like mechanism and a multilevel constructed site. Like a 19th century tintype set in an elaborate frame, the role of the monitor is so completely supported by other material it is all but reduced to a subservient status. Ostensibly, it is a mere tool by which image is drawn into the projection system. And yet, it is also the objective of our circuitous journey through the labyrinthine structure of *DIG.* This is a complex piece, so I want to describe it in some detail.

One enters a tall (approximately sixteen-foot), circular outer structure to arrive in a space that contains an enclosed, two-level construction. The initial section of the piece is reached by climbing a set of stairs to the upper platform, which serves as a kind of viewing deck. Located at the center of the space and mounted to the floor is the aluminum derrick which houses a piston-like pole that moves slowly up and down through a hole in the floor. On top of the derrick and perpendicular to it is a beam of aluminum channeling, like the outstretched arms of a robot. The beam is motorized so it can rotate over the space. There are two small black and white monitors mounted at the ends of the beam and they too are motorized to spin. Extending out beyond the ends of the beam are aluminum rods upon which are mounted large lenses. From this vantage point, images are apparently pulled up through the floor from the level below by the monitor, and then projected through the lenses onto a circular viewing surface which surrounds the space. The arms of the apparatus reach out over the space at a height of just over six feet, spinning gradually and erratically from a dead stop to a maximum speed of sixty revolutions per minute. The mechanism exerts a powerful control over the space, which

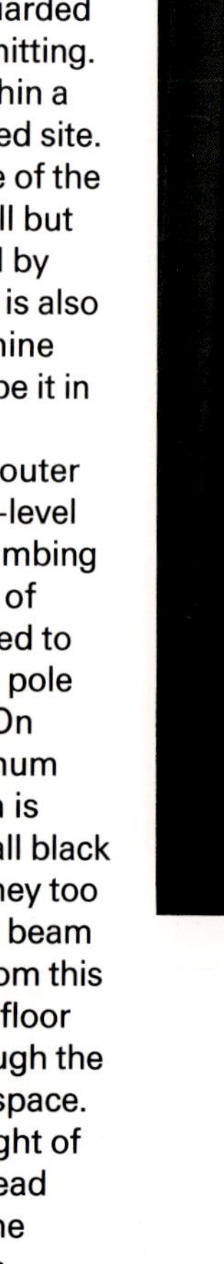

DIG (Mediarite), 1987 Henry Art Gallery

3. William Morris, ed., *The American Heritage Dictionary of the English Language* (New York: Houghton Mifflin Company, 1969), p. 368.

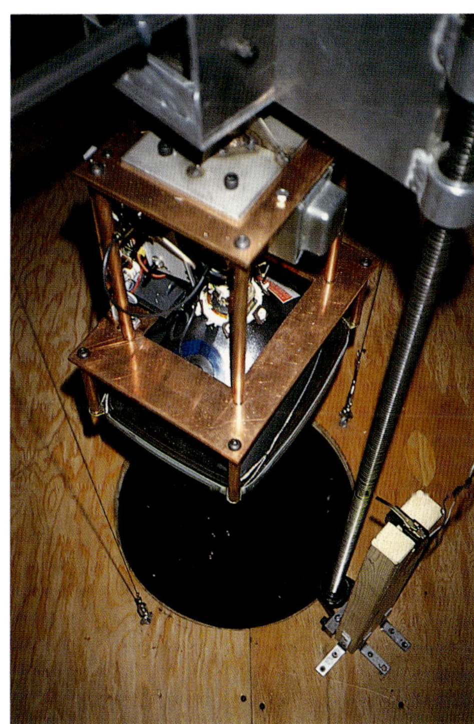

DIG (Mediarite), 1987 (detail)

becomes even more menacing with the tight choreography of the computer-synchronized projection of a wheel, which spins, warps, and finally wobbles out of control in direct relationship to the variable speeds of the spinning arms.

All in all, it is a dizzying experience that encourages exploration below, if only to escape the blade-like projection-arms. From this upper space a second stairwell descends to the dark, enclosed lower level which has a ceiling height of about four feet, forcing one to bend or kneel. A hole in the floor, directly below the hole in the upper level, contains a black liquid that appears to continue underneath the lower floor and have unknown depth. The shaft that supports the TV monitor rises from hole to hole. The monitor is in an open frame construction made of copper and is also motorized to rotate, mimicking the movement and torque of a drill. The bulbous shape of the tube, which is positioned face down, can be easily viewed by looking up at it through the upper hole or down at its mirror-like reflection in the black liquid. Also cut into this floor and mounted vertically are short black pipes. These pipes, or "taps," are actually focused on very small areas of hidden color video monitors, magnified to reveal the individual pixels of video image. They disclose the level beneath the lower level, and take the piece into a realm that does not end.

DIG was initially developed in 1987 at the Henry Art Gallery as part of an exhibition called "Mechanics of Contemplation."[4] The concept of the exhibit encouraged process by allowing the artists the time of the show to work on their installations, even during public hours. Of the six artists, only Hill used the entire two months. Since his studio was compact and essentially given over to video production, Hill used considerable time to concentrate intensively on site issues.

Originally entitled *Mediarite,* it has undergone several changes in the years since, especially concerning the soundtrack and projection imagery. Although the piece was operational for only a short time at the Henry, Hill finally decided on the projected image of a wheel that spun around the coving in the walls. As it was briefly materialized, the imagery was a direct play with the spinning mechanizations of the monitor and projection apparatus.

In Japan in 1992, Hill had the opportunity to develop the work further. At this time it was retitled *DIG,* and although the structure and mechanics remained essentially the same, it became more "time specific" in terms of current events, and the projection image changed slightly to that of a single automobile tire. The exhibition coincided with President Bush's ill-fated visit, which also included representatives of the American automobile industry. The tire image became a reference to the "car wars" between the two countries, an interpretation compounded by the imagery in the soundtrack that included fragments of Bush-speak ("Promises / Problems / The Undisputed Leader / Class / Super Power / Mystery / Back Then They Were / Freedom...."), imposed over traditional Japanese Gagaku court music (the screeching sounds of various reed instruments seemed to parallel the turning metallic machinery, and plucking string sounds and drums complemented the liquid dripping from the rising monitor). The spoken text, warped and speeded up, was heard forwards and backwards as the tire projection changed speeds and directions. All together, the sound, image, and movement formed an orchestrated presentation of sense and nonsense—"meaning" spun, retreated, and raced forward.

As it was presented in Japan (and considered in relation to its original title), one could have concluded that the artist was involved in a dialogue with media. But Hill's art has, for the most part, not been about the politics of media nor about reformulating the context of television. Rather Hill, resisting the envelope of media critique, has decidedly remained within a poetic space of becoming, attempting to enliven a philosphical art through the use of complex media forms and processes. I would add that Hill considers questions of thinking and perception as radically political. He has extended video art through his poetic and philosophic investigations *inevitably,* by using the tool as a means that allows him to work in time, and cross static bounds of space and image freely.

Through these two incarnations, Hill came to realize *DIG* as more about how an idea *becomes* than about the multiplicity of images to be found. Topical references have been eliminated in favor of the simple image of the wheel as a universal symbol of thought as well as the first tool to "move forward." Details such as the striped yellow and black floor graphics, which clearly conveyed "danger zone," have been abandoned, freeing one to see the piece less literally as a construction site and more as a site of the mind. As Hill has cut closer to the core, the piece has become a broader metaphor of the process of uncovering knowledge.

There are two parts to drilling a successful well: drilling into a rich material pool and capping the well so you can access its contents purposefully, that is, harness the raw material so it can be used. In *DIG,* the wheel functions as something of a cap to the well of possibilities. It allows *DIG* to contain (and avoid) details of information in favor of *being:* rather than acting to simply channel

4. The exhibition "Mechanics of Contemplation" took place August 3–October 4, 1987, and included the following artists: Mowry Baden, Michael Brewster, Mineko Grimmer, Gary Hill, Norie Sato, and Laura Sindell.

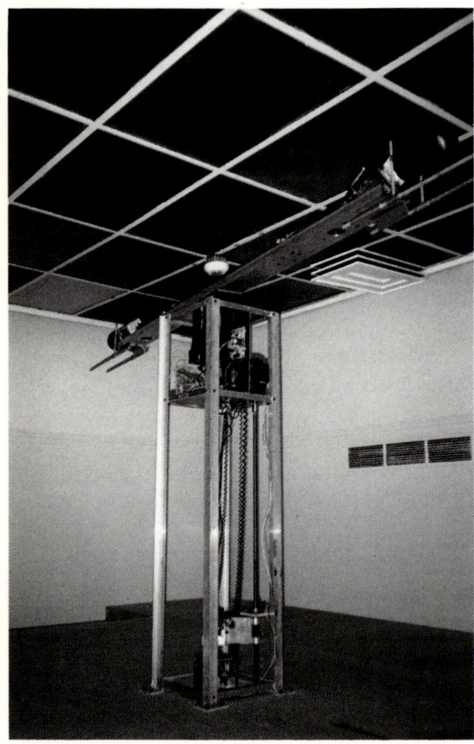

DIG (Mediarite), 1987 (detail)

image flow, the artwork is a site of potential and becoming. This image of wholeness allows *DIG*—like some mythic fountain of knowledge—to be self-perpetuating as long as it remains free of more specific content. The hitch is that this perfect image time after time falls off axis and spins out of control, even as it tries to complete the mechanical apparatus with its meaning. It's like a dragon chasing its tail, a system that cannot complete itself. And then it tries again, and the trying is part of the endless cycle. "It's obviously not about mining for something; rather it's a kind of closed loop that illustrates the fallibility of systems, whether they are mechanical or purely conceptual."

The fact that a change in imagery should alter meaning is hardly surprising, and seems to confirm the importance of image in Hill's work. I would suggest that these changes equally demonstrate the flexibility and importance of the overall site as a manifestation of Hill's interest in the structures of thought and the elusiveness of meaning.

As an alchemical metaphor of uncovering the source of knowledge, there are distinct stages within the loop: above and below; public, private and hidden; standing, crouching and kneeling; projected light, reflected light, and video light. These stations are much more clearly identified—less seamlessly merged—than one normally sees in Hill's work. What is held paramount in the normal hierarchy of art (i.e., image) is undermined and seeps into the whole set of relationships. In fact, *DIG* hides its key elements in the lowest level of the site, where visitors must crouch and therefore "de-volve" in order to encounter the image pool. Of course, children can approach this source effortlessly.

Seen from the lower level, the monitor comes down the shaft and begins to slowly rotate, or "drill" into the opening in the floor. It continues down until the screen is actually submerged and stirs the liquid ("stirring up an image"). The green phosphor light of the monitor combined with the polished copper structure that holds it becomes a tool that "transforms matter" as it moves between the two worlds of above and below. As the downward-facing monitor pulls out of the pool, liquid drips into the reflected image. It is a beautiful moment, indeed one of the few pauses in a complex cycle that has been set up to focus on levels of consciousness rather than on aesthetic ends per se.

The final layer of information, perceived through the metal pipes, extends the piece indefinitely. To peer through the pipes, the already crouching visitors now must get on their hands and knees. The metal pipes expose the "ground" of red, green and blue electronic video dots, thereby allowing a still closer approach to another more hidden pool of data that Hill identifies as "the image/information flow below ground—that which is raw, unprocessed, unmanipulated, untelevised." What we had thought of as the bottom level (the aqueduct), we discover is *not* bottom and, in fact, opens into a vast electronic space. As Hill says, "There's always a further ground below ground—the 'underground.' There's always another way of seeing from where you're standing, from where you are positioned, from your present vantage point." While the dragon chases its tail above, the pipes tap into the dancing light of unformed possibilities, and we encounter our most profound moment of humility as we imagine there is perhaps no end to the succession of ascending thoughts we might have.

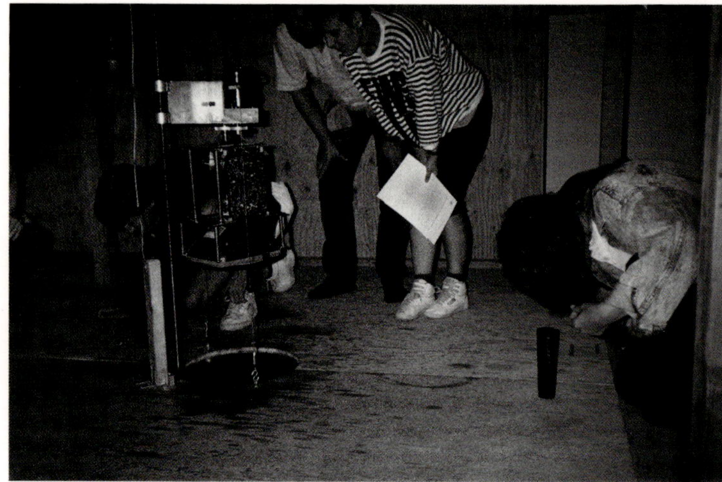

DIG (Mediarite), 1987 (detail)

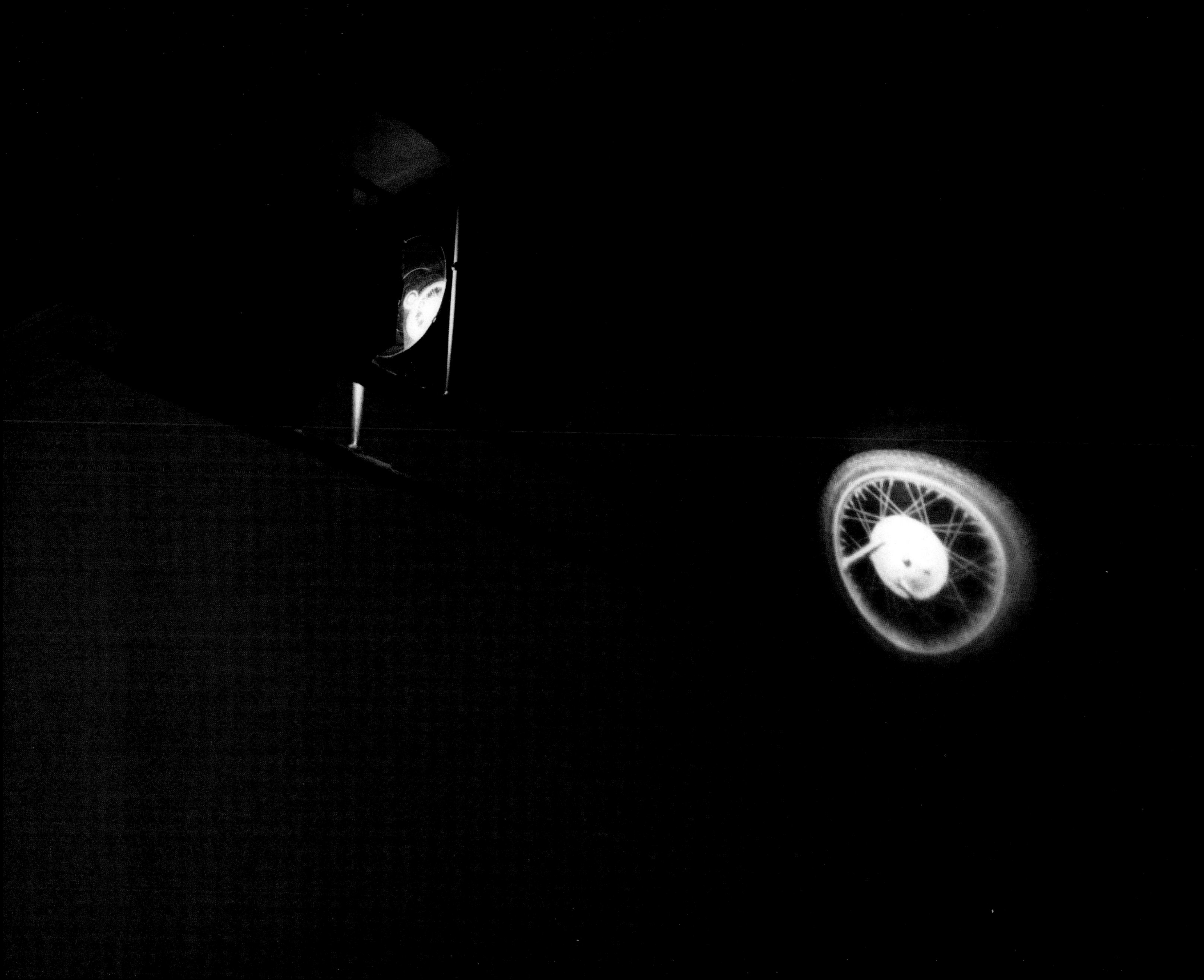

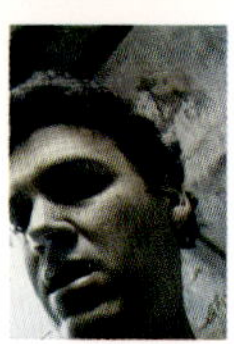

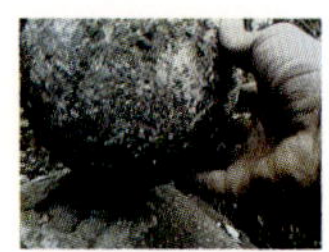

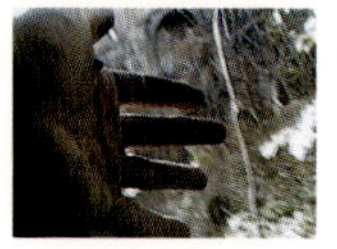

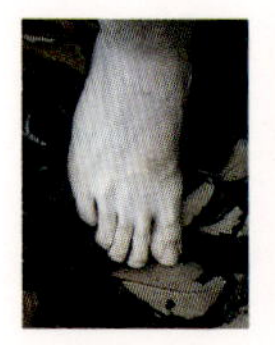

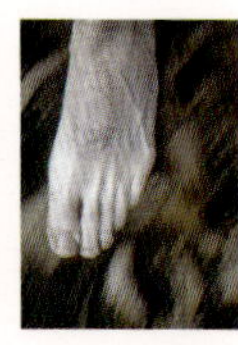

CRUX, 1983-87

"Becoming conscious of the body's capacities is a kind of mechanization which leads to pleasure, which is itself viewed mechanically. . . . The giant metal man abounds in riddles of naturalism: is it more naturalistic to have him talk through his mouth than it would be to have the moan come out his feet?"[5]

If *DIG* suggests a quality of perpetual motion, *CRUX* expresses a paradox of mobility through the constraints of self-consciousness. *CRUX* may be Gary Hill's most straightforward installation work, a twenty-six-minute "performance installation" which consists of five monitors mounted on the wall, positioned to suggest the configuration of a cross, each presenting video imagery of head, hands, and feet in synchronous motion.

Initial real-time recordings were made as Hill strapped a camera and microphone to each wrist and ankle so that images of his hands and feet are centrally framed in each screen. A fifth camera/microphone—aimed at his head—was fastened to a brace that positioned the camera out in front of the body so that the camera was looking back, seeing the face. Performer and camera operator were thus merged.

The results are played back on five color video monitors and loudspeakers, where the extremities are displayed as separate realities, or points of attention, each mindful of its own particular course of action and location.

In effect, [my] body films its own absence, metaphorically pinning or nailing its extremities to the cross with the camera's "objective" view, (dis)embod[ying] the "video". . . . Only the extremities of the body are seen, a body crucified and impassioned by the cameras that have entered it.[10]

These parts, versions, shards, titles, de-scriptions, sutures, occlusions, excerptual reverberances, quotations and all the other

Hill conceived of *CRUX* in 1983 while he was living in upstate New York, and actually made some trial runs for the piece while in Japan in 1985. It was finally taped on Bannerman's Island on the Hudson River in the Fall of 1986 when the Museum of Contemporary Art in Los Angeles provided some funds for production for its premiere there in the spring of 1987. Now an abandoned ruin, the castle-like building on the island was used as an armory from the turn of the century to the 1960s. These days, one would most likely encounter the island from the train that runs along the Hudson, which is how Hill first saw it.

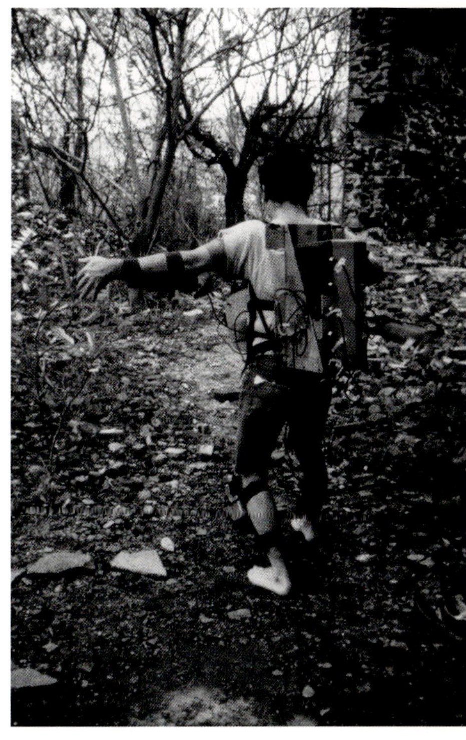

Gary Hill, ***CRUX*** (in process, Bannerman's Island), 1986

From the train, you can only *project* yourself into the landscape. In the train, you can't stop and pull off the road; you view the passing scene through the slight reflection of yourself upon the glass that separates sound and weather from your position inside the metal-enclosed space that moves through the landscape. The view of the castle and the island lasts seconds, but lingers in a dream-like bubble that foreshortens space to the thickness of the glass of the window, the joining space where the thought of the castle inevitably takes over. In other words, the view of the island is an internal one, no longer about nature.

5. Robert Harbison, *Eccentric Spaces* (New York: Avon Books with Alfred A. Knopf, Inc., 1977/1980), p. 80.

In *CRUX,* the crossing of terrain is presented with such visceral intimacy (through the artist's hands, behind his head, against his feet) that the totality of the landscape is obscured. It exists more as a series of ambient glimpses than extensions of Hill's body. As witnesses, we wonder at the strange setting the body traverses, what the rubble and ruins might mean, and yet we fix on the effort of the body. With the exception of the song of a few birds and a distant train passing by, the soundtrack is composed of Hill's body encountering the world around him: broken twig, crunching gravel, splashing water, breathing. The fragmented landscape is presented as archetypal, the body/pilgrim moves from inside ruins, into darkness, through thickets, over rubble, and finally to the water, as if he were returning to some kind of previous amphibious state.

Looking at a photograph of Hill in bondage with his cameras, and then seeing the remarkable results, one reels in consciousness of the collapse between subject and creator, seer and seen. Once, Hill spoke about his work as having to do with "getting inside a very present tense." Similarly, the composer LaMonte Young talks about getting inside a sound—sound as a single wave form—where tuning is a function of time. Hill says, "At that level, sound and space virtually merge as a single event." Seen in this light, *CRUX* was an intensely personal learning experience, more akin to such disciplines of self-awareness as Tai-Chi than it was to an aesthetic undertaking.

As a cinematic event, *CRUX* is a mesmerizing sight to behold, especially at its optimum scale using twenty-six-inch monitors. Clearly, Hill's own body was the original and primary site. It is on this level a profound meditation on understanding the body in space, in a kind of miracle of parts which seem to have whole, independent lives, each with its own "voice." The head is seen from an upward angle, enveloped by a space it is always leaving behind. The hands are focused on as primal evolutionary tools for grasping and picking things up. Framed topologically, showing the details of struggle most acutely, the feet in particular seem almost like animals, burrowing through gravel, hopping like frogs in the water.

Each part becomes objectified in a way, as a separate world that knows itself. Here the void spaces replace the vital organs—only the cognitive tools of the body remain displayed in separate boxes. Through this disjunction, we are brought to acute awareness of the needs and limits of art as something that exists within a frame. The edges of the camera (as receiver) and the monitor (as transmitter) allow us access to the intimacy of *CRUX,* an intimacy that is further coerced by the void of information and the darkness of space beyond those edges, absence informing substance.

It was nearing dusk. Having completed the last walk, we were preparing to leave the island when a late fall storm came in from nowhere. We were left with an either/or decision: to leave at that moment in hopes of reaching the mainland before the storm worsened, or wait it out, hedging it would only be a squall. We took our chances with movement and packed the canoe with our gear and all the tape we had recorded. By the time we entered the water, the wind had worked up a menacing brew of cross-currents and choppy water. Taking the drift into account we headed for the single lacuna in the moat surrounding the island. If we missed it (which felt like a given), there was the risk of shipwreck—the hull would be torn open by the deadheads hidden by the tide. Needless to say, we made it; bodies, equipment

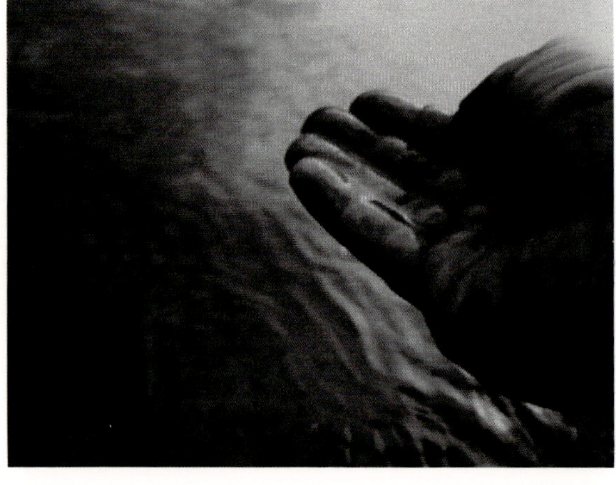

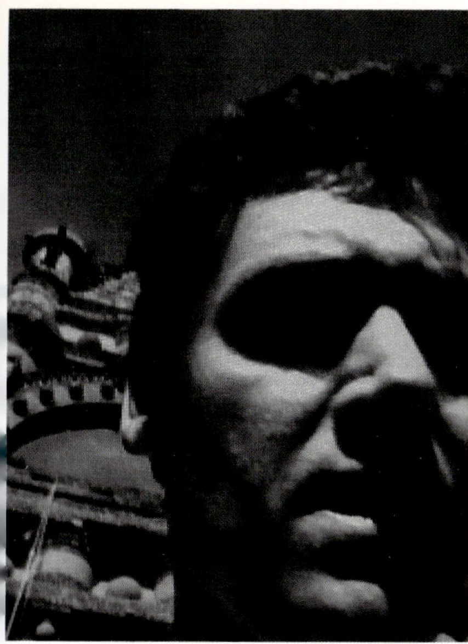

The contrast between such visceral, personal investigation and the grand public gesture of the crucifix form of the monitors could hardly be greater. The crucifix is, after all, the single strongest symbol of death and rebirth in Western culture. Politically speaking, it is the image of martyrdom in the face of a powerful enemy of the people. Thousands of paintings throughout the history of art remind us that the nails in Christ's hands express the transitory earthly might of Rome in arresting the revolutionary message of personal salvation. Stuck on the cross, the harshest and most taunting cry from the crowd pointed out the one thing Jesus could not do: "Save thyself, and come down from the cross."[6]

Considering the mechanics of making *CRUX,* Robert Mittenthal identified the cameras as being the "nails" of this present-day crucifixion.[7] Mittenthal's image wonderfully reorients the point of view, turning the work from a document about body parts to a means of witnessing a process that stakes out territory nowhere more than within the frame of the cameras. The idea of mobility, of a moving image is held in question: the camera lenses are locked to specific focal points, and simultaneously Hill's limbs and head are crucified in those frames.

We need look no further than the controversy surrounding Nicholas Serrano's 1990 photograph, *Piss Christ,* to see that the crucifixion remains a potent image in contemporary art and society. More complex however were the psychological yearnings met by Chris Burden in his 1974 performance piece, *Transfixed.* One of the most shocking, immediate, and "20th century" responses to crucifixion, Burden had himself nailed to the roof of a VW bug whose engine screamed over the artist's own pain. Clearly the daring of the artist has to be acknowledged, but it is the VW that makes *Transfixed* an ironic and contemporary masterpiece. Where Christ's cross is planted firmly in the ground, Burden is rendered immobile atop the familiar little machine that was developed to allow reasonably priced access to personal transportation. Finally, it is the issue of freedom (as movement) that is put in question.

Hill extends this dialogue between stasis and movement by entering the technology the rest of us simply employ from the outside to bring the world to us. Hill takes us on a journey that seems ancient, even primitive; and yet again, it is a journey that takes place in absolutely fixed spaces, first within the cameras, and then the TV monitors. These are the traps of Hill's chosen field of endeavor. This is what it looks like to "carry the cross" of one's calling and to take responsibility for self-consciousness.

6. St. Mark 15:30, King James Bible.

7. Robert Mittenthal, "Reading the Unknown: Reaching Gary Hill's *And Sat Down Beside Her,*" printed in *Gary Hill* (Paris, Galerie des Archives, 1990), p. 28.

CRUX was premiered at the Museum of Contemporary Art in Los Angeles with what was at that point the most fabricated version of the (text in) question. It was foregrounded in the work as a spoken monologue. In describing *CRUX,* Raymond Bellour wrote, "The text that accompanies the gait of this disconnected body is itself a 'blank' text…it is a text of desperation and of wandering, close to some of the writings of the nouveau roman, and in particular to those of Blanchot, whose dislocating and decentering force is [witnessed]. …From this solitary destiny, that in fact isn't a destiny at all because it has neither beginning nor end, the hero bears the cross, alone."[12] It is not only the *neither beginning nor end* that rears here, but in a strangely prescient way, the "blank" text. Bellour wrote this not knowing that the text (in) question had been re-moved from the work prior to his writing. Had he known, how would Bellour have treated this erasure? Or, as it seems, hadn't he divulged the site? Was the text a temporary tool, a scriber,

The viewer/*reader's* primary impetus to engage the work is atypically other than seeing. She/he conjoins with a voice[17] to (dis)cover "their" text (tracks) within a self-reflexive mental terrain of (th)ree-(de)construction. Is a phenomenological experience of thinking possible? Traversing the fold between consciousness and self-consciousness, the viewer reads as he/she writes in the shadows of presence. Here, the linear (author)ity of text, meaning, origin and sight begins to implode. The *viewer/reader/writer* is continually thrown back (to)

Clearly, if martyrdom—or "stoppage"—is the common state of being in question, the medium in each case is an important part of the message. The Burden and Hill pieces complement each other almost perfectly—a mechanistic world view vs. electronic rays of light: Burden's work suggests an extreme commitment to Cartesian thought, while Hill works in technologies that increasingly question such hard forms of knowledge.

No two devices (automobile and TV) have brought about more radical changes in human history, and the new computer technologies threaten to dominate our lives to the extent that it becomes unthinkable that one could live without them (while at the same time a new underclass is identified by its lack of access to the electronic network). If such systems have as much to do with new identities and language systems as they do with new appliances, what does it mean? In *CRUX,* Hill vividly presents the paradox of self-knowledge through machine. As witnesses to the installation/performance, we find the hardware familiar and the images fascinating yet alien. Amazingly, what appears strange is not the machine but the human body.

But to discuss the machine and body in terms of differences, or as a problematic relationship, is to consider the situation outside the intimate territory of Hill's art. *CRUX* is but one particularly direct representation of the reflexive potential Hill has long seen in video and other electronic media. In *CRUX,* the "feedback loop" includes the collapse between recorder and recorded, yet it also exists more generally for the artist as a space where consciousness is accessible. The last line of his tape *Site Recite (a prologue)* (1989) is spoken from inside the mouth, and we view it as we look out through the teeth: "Imagining the brain closer than the eyes." Hill's art leads us to the position where we can encounter just such a visceral, imminently self-reflexive, and inevitable request.

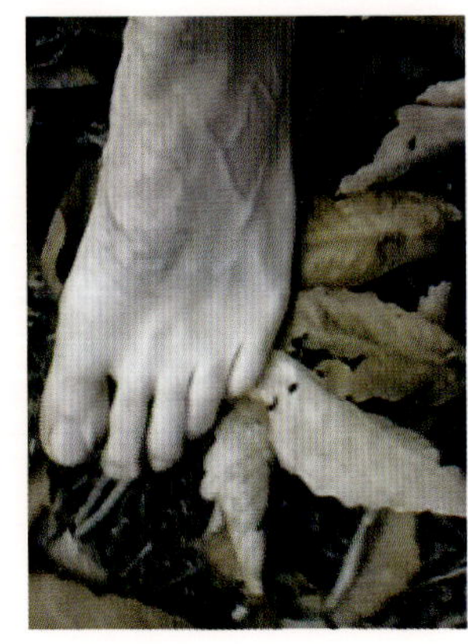

Chris Bruce is senior curator at the Henry Art Gallery, University of Washington. He has organized such exhibitions as *No: Contemporary American Dada; Louise Bourgeois: Works 1943-1987; Myth of the West; Ann Hamilton: parallel lines* for the 1991 Sao Paulo Biennal, and the *Gary Hill* exhibition national tour.

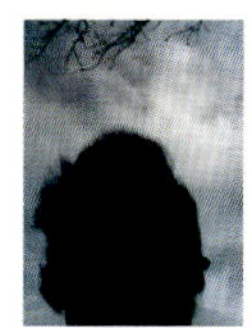

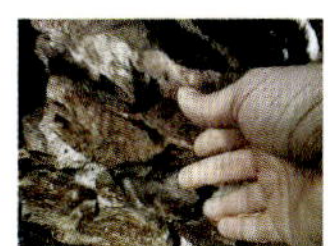

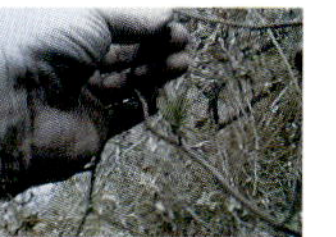

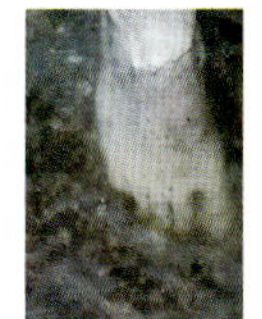

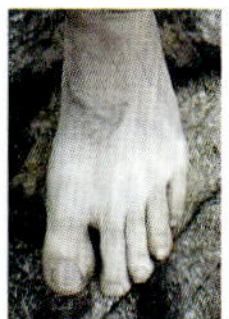

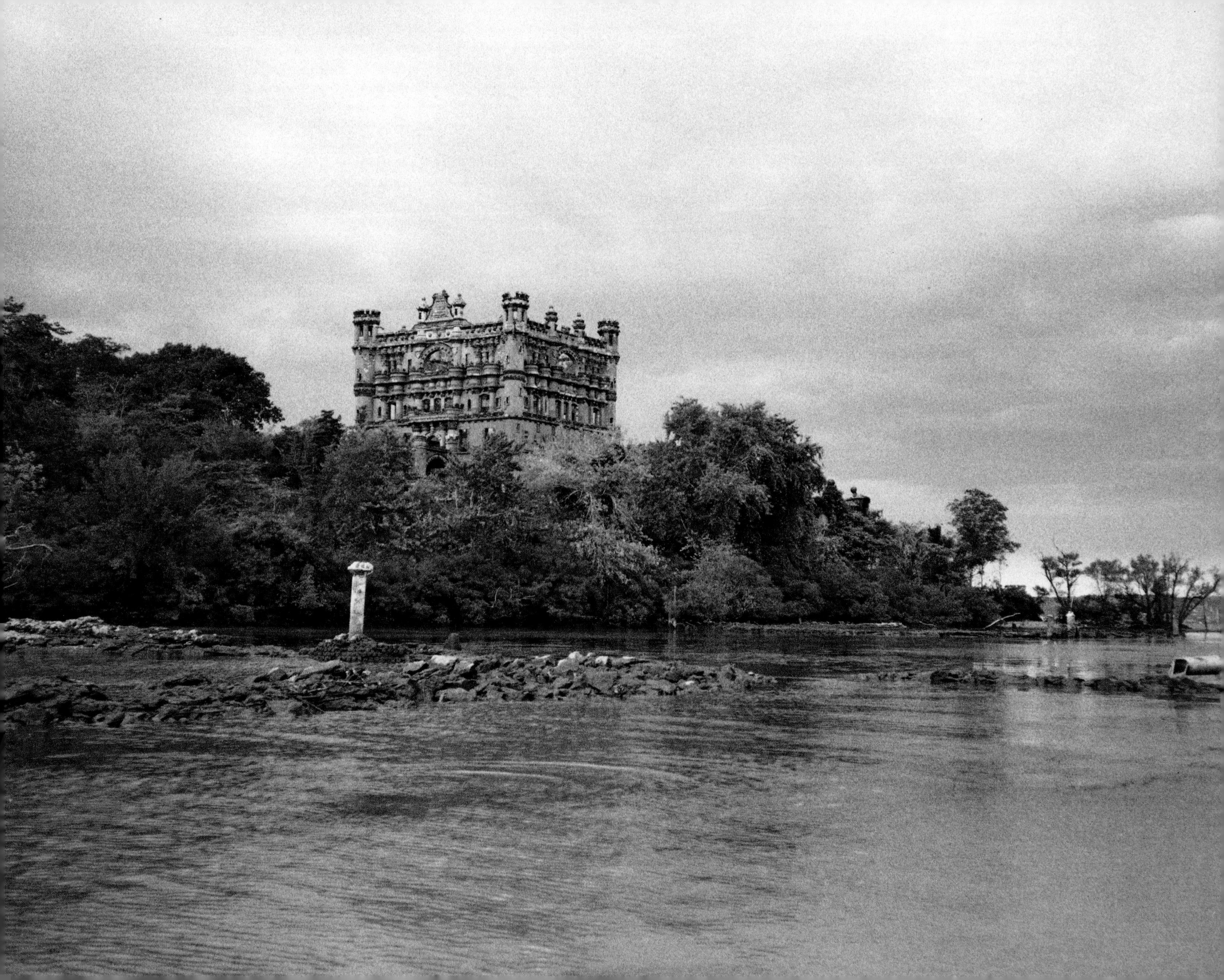

Site Re:cite

Gary Hill

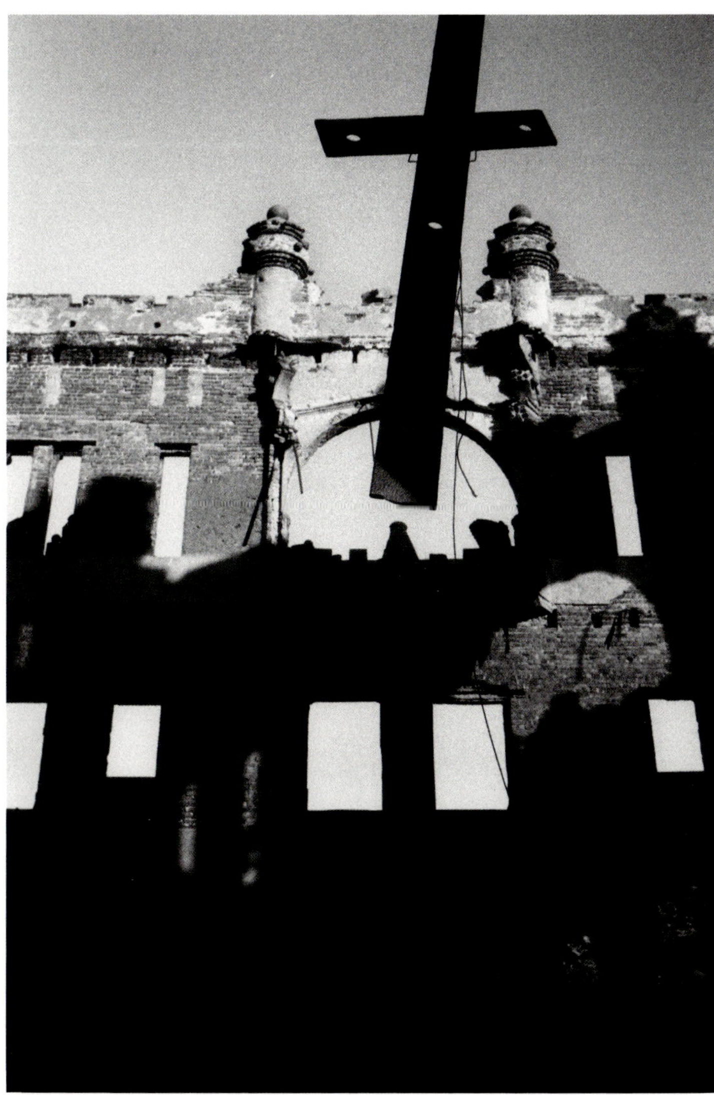

Opposite page and above
Bannerman's Castle, Hudson Highlands State Park, New York, site of ***CRUX***

Site, The place where something was, is or is to be located. *Recite,* from Latin *recitare,* to read out, cite again: *re-,* back, again + *citare,* to set in motion, summon. From the Indo-European root, kei; Suffixed form, ki-neu - in Greek, kinein, to move: (-KINESIS), . . . , CINEMATOGRAPH, . . . TELEKINESIS [kei -: from *Pokorny's Indogermanisches Etymologisches Wörterbuch,* 538]

Herein: bracketed off, framed, safe from incision, a verified moment akin to a photograph, however cropped, of the life (and "little deaths") of a text—a transcription from a videotape entitled, *Site Recite (a prologue).*[1] Why not the epilogue to *Incidence of Catastrophe?*[2] What might it be a prologue to? Is this writing a prologue to it? What am I prolonging? Am I logging on to the text?

The image folded in the double bind of frame and context. Permanence of the act was marginal with a perforated edge of light heartedness. The hand reciprocated with one swift movement. Damage was negligible to the remaining back to back facades.[3]

The transcription (a text in question) is only but a fragment among fragments from a larger textual weave. Perhaps it could be said that it is holographic—any "fragment" contains the whole (the same but not identical).

Moving back words to the text (in) question, *Site Recite* has been seen, heard, recorded, erased, coded, transcribed and published. These "versions" will have existed for reasons other than varied dissemination. They are in fact uneasy outside the hybrid media spaces from which they arose. (Surely there are others in hiding.) The question here becomes how to mark the differences, if there are any, between writing and what I have come to refer to as an *electronic linguistic.*[4]

Notwithstanding the play of the seen/unseen, the traces and (re)remarkings of beginnings & ends, and other intertextual modalities, the scoring here will be along the *trans*textual—how the text is intimately entwined in a process of overwriting itself as it passes between media. Rather than being a referential body for mapping out the evolutionary progression of a "script"—notations of amendments, insertions, deletions, or simply bedded down for a closed reading, the transcription is a momentary flashing, or perhaps, an epistle from a text (in question). One more of however many more re-presentations surfacing in the wake of video. What follows then is a tale of the text, the threads of which are entangled in a briar patch of picture, *The Evil Demon of Images* (Baudrillard). It shall be a reconnaissance to situate the debris, the textual shrapnel in the aftermath of brisance within the garden of inscription. Here then will be a writing work of excavation; pourings at an archeological site, later to be overturned. What kind of cracks and fissures will appear as text and cast separate?

The outline separating the mouth and words was prerecorded.[5]

1. *Site Recite (a prologue),* 1989. Color videotape, stereo sound; 4 minutes.

2. *Incidence of Catastrophe,* 1987-88. Color videotape, stereo sound; 43:51 minutes.

3. *Videograms,* excerpts from *Videogram No. 2;* 1980-81. B/w videotape; 13:25 minutes.

4. Gary Hill, "Processual Video," program notes. *Video Viewpoints* (New York: Museum of Modern Art, February 26, 1980).

5. Excerpt from *Processual Video,* 1980. B/w videotape; 11:30 minutes.

I could say that the progenitor, the mythic seeding of *Site Recite* took place in the midst of writing *Primarily Speaking*[6]... sometime in 1981 or was it 80? *Could there have been a specific day, an exact time, a moment, a pause between the sewing of idioms, a burr in the twine...*

think it over

rattle off a list if that's all that's left

never mind the images **they always return**

if not **new ones will replace the old ones**

it's their destiny

even those permanently lodged

sooner or later

lose their grasp

it's the nature of the beast

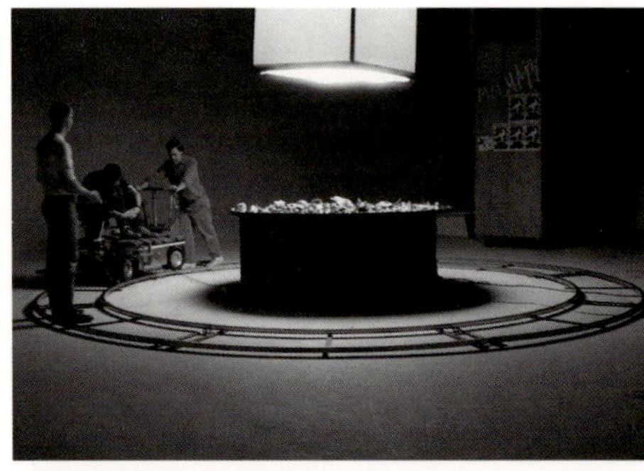

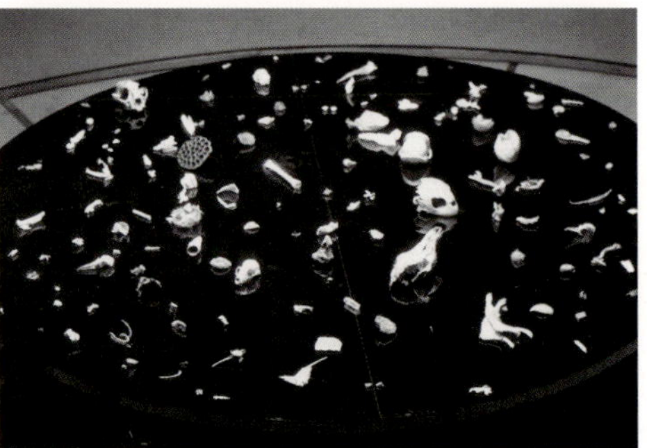

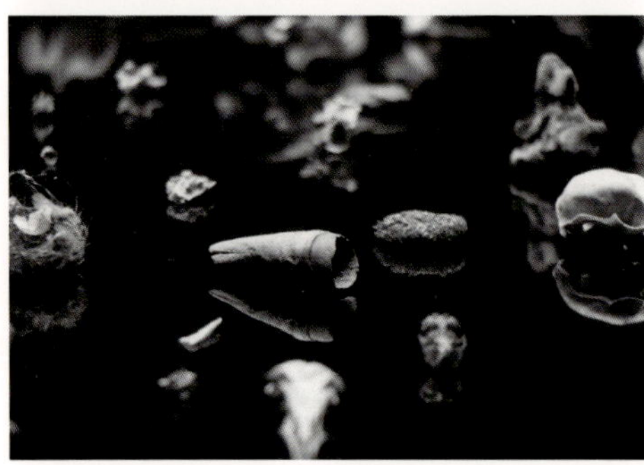

From ***Site Recite (a prologue)***, 1989

6. *Primarily Speaking,* (1981-83), exists as both a single-channel videotape and eight-channel video installation. The text was closer to being "constructed" than "written." I literally surrounded myself with a cinerama-like scroll of hundreds of idiomatic expressions and "watched" them fall together.

7. Gary Hill, *Focus,* Scan Program notes, April-May 1985, Video Gallery Scan, Tokyo.

8. *Why Do Things Get in a Muddle? (Come on Petunia),* 1984. Color videotape; 32 minutes. This work was based on the metalogue by Gregory Bateson published in *Steps to an Ecology of Mind* (New York: Ballantine Books, 1972), pp. 3-8. Curiously, now, in comparing my script notes with the original text, it was I who had performed this mirroring of the text. The original has an additional "pennies" at the end. (Also, *Come on Petunia* replaced Donald in the original text. The daughter used anagrams, Once Upon a Time and Old Dan, respectively, to mix up the father's logic.)

...a phrase set aside, a single word that resonated in the margins—a verbal cocoon, a pinpoint (no-body, not even I heard the needle drop).

The mind can't help but mince and suddenly you're beside yourself entertaining a party of two only to fall back a few steps, a few words gone by, a few instructions on how to get from point A to point B [points known only by the needle that records everything].[7]

From a catalogue statement excerpted from what was then the (text in) question. A marginal thought for the screening of *Why Do Things Get in a Muddle? (Come on Petunia),* wherein an exception to a slippery entropic dialogue comes to mind. After having heard her father explain by enumerated examples why things tend towards chaos rather than towards tidiness, the daughter cites the examples in exact reverse order from the way she had heard them during the course of the dialogue, "Then Daddy, are you saying the same thing about pennies, and about Come on Petunia, and about sugar and sand, and about my paint box?"[8]

What happens with these recitations, historicities, circuitous extratexts that (dis)figure the (con)text? There is a kind of pile up; an exquisite corpse leading a procession of dancing flip-flopping parentheses (Greek: "a putting in beside"). They begin to take on something other than abstract grammatical marks—pliers with unseen handles wiring the syntax with shifting -vexes and -caves tripping the gait of the eye; amassing pairs of upright bows diking the script. Brute metaphors somehow won't do. The heap of language still seeps. The parenthetical is but a meandering line that whispers what one hears, which side is (a)side and which is (be)side?

Site Recite (a prologue)

Nothing seems to have ever been moved. There is something of every description which can only be a trap. Maybe it all moves proportionately cancelling out change and the estrangement of judgement. No, an other order pervades. It's happening all at once, I'm just a disturbance wrapped up in myself, a kind of ghost vampirically passing through the forest passing through the trees.

The sun will rise and I won't know what to do with it. Its beak will torture me as will its slow movement, the movement it invented that I can only reiterate. Too much time goes by to take it by surprise. Bodily sustenance is no longer an excuse. The quieter and stiller I become the livelier everything else seems to get. The longer I wait the more the little deaths pile up.

A vague language drapes everything but the walls—what walls? The very walls that never vary—my enclosure, so glorious from a distance, stands on the brink of nothing like a four-legged table. What is it? An island with a never ending approach? A stopgap from when to where? Something to huddle over with my elbows like trestles without tracks, the bases of which are scattered with evidence of unsolved crimes? The overallness of it all soaks through, runs through the holes in my hands and continues to run amok, overturning rocks that should not be overturned, breaking bread that should not be broken.

So much remains. No doubt it can all be counted. Starting with any one, continuing on with any other one until all is accounted for, a consensus is reached. That it can all be shelved in all its quantized splendor, this then is the turf.

These sightings. This scene before me made up of just so many *just* views (nature's constituency) sits with indifference to the centripetal vanishing point that mentality posits so falsely. Brain, minding business, incessantly constructs an infinite series of makeshifts designed to perpetuate the picture—the one like all others that holds its breath for a thousand words, conversely exhales point zero zero one pictures. This insidious wraparound, tied to the notion "I have eyes in the back of my head," binds me to my double, implodes my being to a mere word as it winds the world around my mouth. A seamless scroll weaves my view back into place—back to back with itself—the boomerang effect, decapitates any and all hallucinations leaving (lo and behold) the naked eye, stalking each and every utterance that breaks and enters the dormitories of perception.

I must become a warrior of self-consciousness and move my body to move my mind to move the words to move my mouth to spin the spur of the moment.

Imagining the brain closer than the eyes.

9. "Video Installations 1983," special addition to *Afterimage,* Vol. 11, No. 8, Dec. 83, unpaginated. Also, the "same" work for a time had the working title, "The Writing's on the Wall and I Can't Stop Reading It."

10. Robert Mittenthal, "Video's Event: Gary Hill's Catastrophe." *Reflex,* Vol. 3, No. 6, 1989.

11. *CRUX,* 1983-87. Five-channel video installation. Collection of the artist.

12. Raymond Bellour, "Video Writing," translated by Alison Rowe. Included in *Illuminating Video,* (New York: Aperture Press, 1990); originally in a separate article, "Le dernier homme en croix," in *Cinq Pièces avec Vue,* exhibition catalogue (Geneva: Centre Génevois de Gravure Contemporaine, 1987), unpaginated.

13. The wait state of a computer works in conjunction with its speed (in megahertz). The lower the number the faster the CPU computes. A zero wait state suggests the hypothetical ideal of no waiting.

14. *Happenstance (part one of many parts)* 1982-83. B/w videotape, stereo sound; 6:30 minutes.

It's Time to Turn the Record Over, was the title of a proposed work,[9] a five channel/screen video installation that would display synchronous recordings of my feet and hands, made by attaching four cameras to my limbs, and my head, recorded with a fifth camera attached to my trunk and positioned out in front of my body looking back at my head. The screens were to be configured as a cross.

In effect, [my] body films its own absence, metaphorically pinning or nailing its extremities to the cross with the camera's "objective" view, (dis)embod[ying] the "video".... Only the extremities of the body are seen, a body crucified and impassioned by the cameras that have entered it.[10]

These parts, versions, shards, titles, de-scriptions, sutures, occlusions, excerptual reverberances, quotations and all the other generic simulacra of text cited above, bled into *CRUX.*[11] During that time, the text developed metaphorically *with* the location and process of making the work: the topology of the site, a river island laden with castle ruins; labyrinthine paths, stairways and rooms through which the body might gain passage; perceptual discovery; moments of abandonment and physical pain were all to bear upon "scripting" the walk. Even the anecdotal seemed to ripple the text:

It was nearing dusk. Having completed the last walk, we were preparing to leave the island when a late fall storm came in from nowhere. We were left with an either/or decision: to leave at that moment in hopes of reaching the mainland before the storm worsened, or wait it out, hedging it would only be a squall. We took our chances with movement and packed the canoe with our gear and all the tape we had recorded. By the time we entered the water, the wind had worked up a menacing brew of cross-currents and choppy water. Taking the drift into account we headed for the single lacuna in the moat surrounding the island. If we missed it (which felt like a given), there was the risk of shipwreck—the hull would be torn open by the deadheads hidden by the tide. Needless to say, we made it; bodies, equipment, tape, sediment intact.

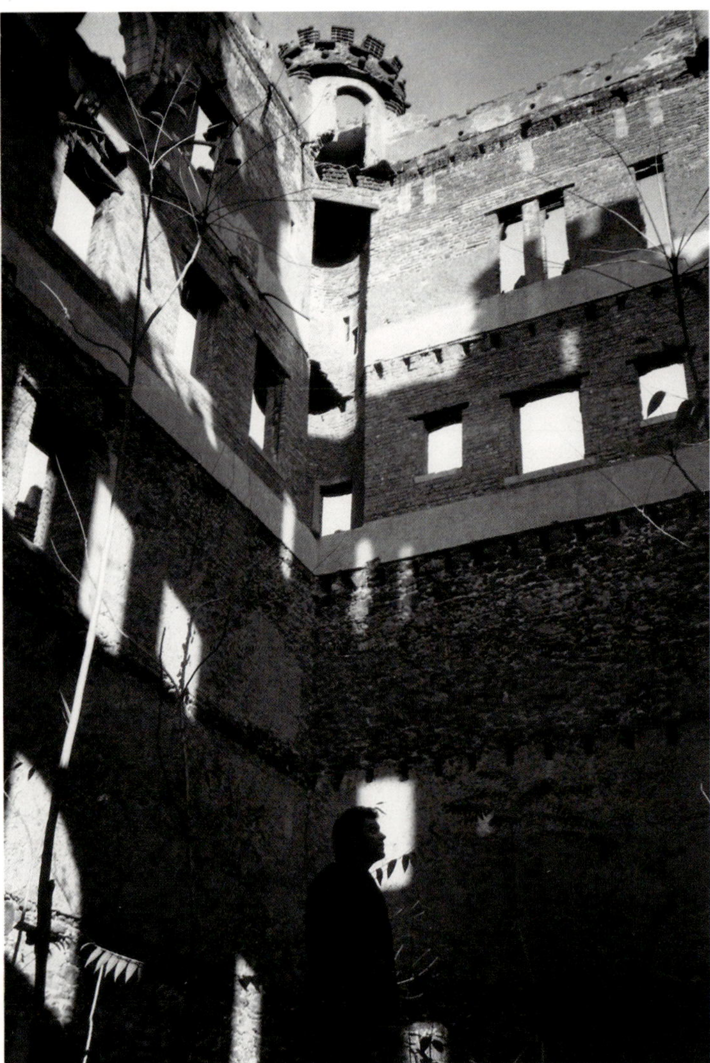

Bannerman's Castle

CRUX was premiered at the Museum of Contemporary Art in Los Angeles with what was at that point the most fabricated version of the (text in) question. It was foregrounded in the work as a spoken monologue. In describing *CRUX,* Raymond Bellour wrote, "The text that accompanies the gait of this disconnected body is itself a 'blank' text...it is a text of desperation and of wandering, close to some of the writings of the nouveau roman, and in particular to those of Blanchot, whose dislocating and decentering force is [witnessed]....From this solitary destiny, that in fact isn't a destiny at all because it has neither beginning nor end, the hero bears the cross, alone."[12] It is not only the *neither beginning nor end* that rears here, but in a strangely prescient way, the "blank" text. Bellour wrote this not knowing that the text (in) question had been re-moved from the work prior to his writing. Had he known, how would Bellour have treated this erasure? Or, as it seems, hadn't he divulged the site? Was the text a temporary tool, a scriber, used to dislodge the image (of flesh); to excavate the site (of absence); to break the spine of the book? Is the absent body the word/image crux? Is it Freud's mystic writing pad, everyone's desire, every ones' death, zEros' wait state?[13]

The crux of the matter... A talismanic depression left over from *Primarily Speaking?* (My mouth couldn't quite fit around the words?)

So far, the traces of historicity have only referred to the public domain of the text (in question). What of that which has been left behind; the sediment that accumulates in folds, files, discs and onion skin. In the margins of one such scrap, I had counted syllables from selected parts. Each part had the same number of syllables. What was this numerological encrypting about?

Decoding my own code, the idea was a kind of möbius interlocutor of speech and writing for videotape. A similar notion was applied, though sparingly, in *Happenstance (part one of many parts).*[14] The text is folded on itself (textual Rorschach); one part is spoken, the utterance of which dictates the other part on the screen syllabically corresponding one to one. Each part

15. One of a collection of essays in *Illuminating Video* (New York: Aperture Press, 1990).

16. Although the images appear continuous (real time), all directional changes—left and right movements, "in" and "out" focusing—are edit points that join separately recorded images. All the segments were recorded for an interactive videodisc project, *Which Tree* (work-in-progress, 1986-??).

17. The spoken text of *Which Tree* will be an electronic combine of a male and female voice. Unlike a simple mix (chorus) of the two, the sound will be a harmonic weave of the two sources that can be dynamically weighted one way or the other at different points in the labyrinthine text.

minding the other—logosfrog and leapscript fraying the play of meaning.

And then there's the forthcoming, where the (text in question), entitled, "And if the Right Hand Did not Know What the Left Hand Is Doing" is the left side of a double sided text and the column between is a meandering crack.[15] Left with these unrelenting beginnings and ends—the unravelings of disembodied text(s)—its "prologue," *Site Recite* paronomastically disturbed, there is little recourse but to enter the current work. *Site Recite* (the videotape) can be seen as a single reading/ writing from an "interactive" videodisc entitled *Which Tree.*[16] I mark this word interactive with its tendency to attract an optimism of infinite possibilities, contrary to the fact that it is not only delimited by if/then scenarios, but thoroughly collapses when the viewer finds his/her self forced to make decisions inscribed by "multiple choice."

To subvert this technocratic illusion prescribed by interactive media, *Which Tree* is an attempt to create a field of play wherein the modus operandi is one of wandering, where one makes way through a metaphorical wood entangled in a web of reflexivity. Description: a single line scribbled on a page makes points of intersection where the line overlaps itself. These labyrinthine intersections (points of "inter-activity") the viewer wanders "through" are embedded in the "paths" rather than announced by signposts. Neither image nor text (the scribbled line) break up into multiple plots, stories or non-sequiturs (collage, montage, juxtapositions, cut-ups, etc.). Rather, by continuous passage through said intersections, the viewer/*writer* unfolds a scenario in real time. No matter which way one turns (wanders), the camera obscura and (spoken) text continue seamlessly, uninterrupted by edits or syntactical quirks.

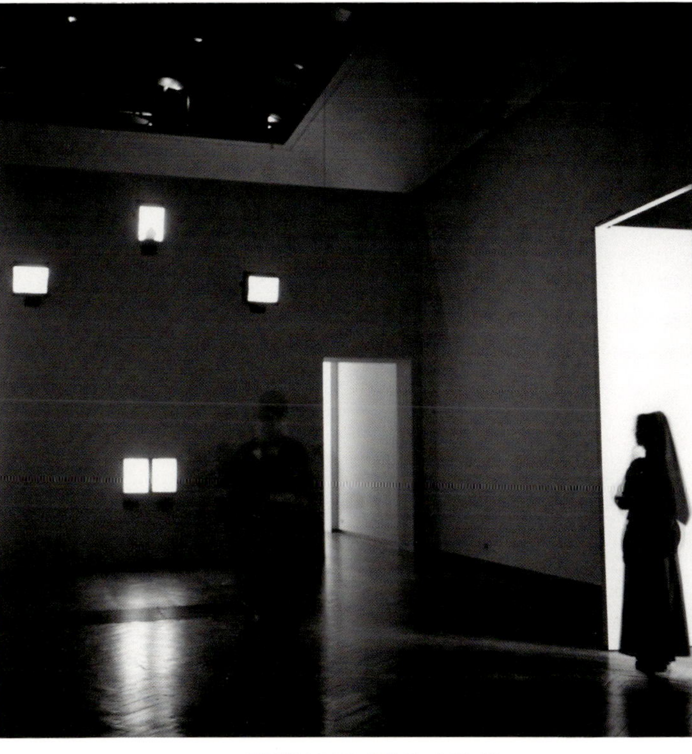

CRUX, (1983-87) Stedelijk Museum, Amsterdam, 1993

The viewer/*reader's* primary impetus to engage the work is atypically other than seeing. She/he conjoins with a voice[17] to (dis)cover "their" text (tracks) within a self-reflexive mental terrain of (th)ree-(de)construction. Is a phenomenological experience of thinking possible? Traversing the fold between consciousness and self-consciousness, the viewer reads as he/she writes in the shadows of presence. Here, the linear (author)ity of text, meaning, origin and sight begins to implode. The *viewer / reader/writer* is continually thrown back (to) incite the text.

Following pages from
Site Recite (a prologue), 1989

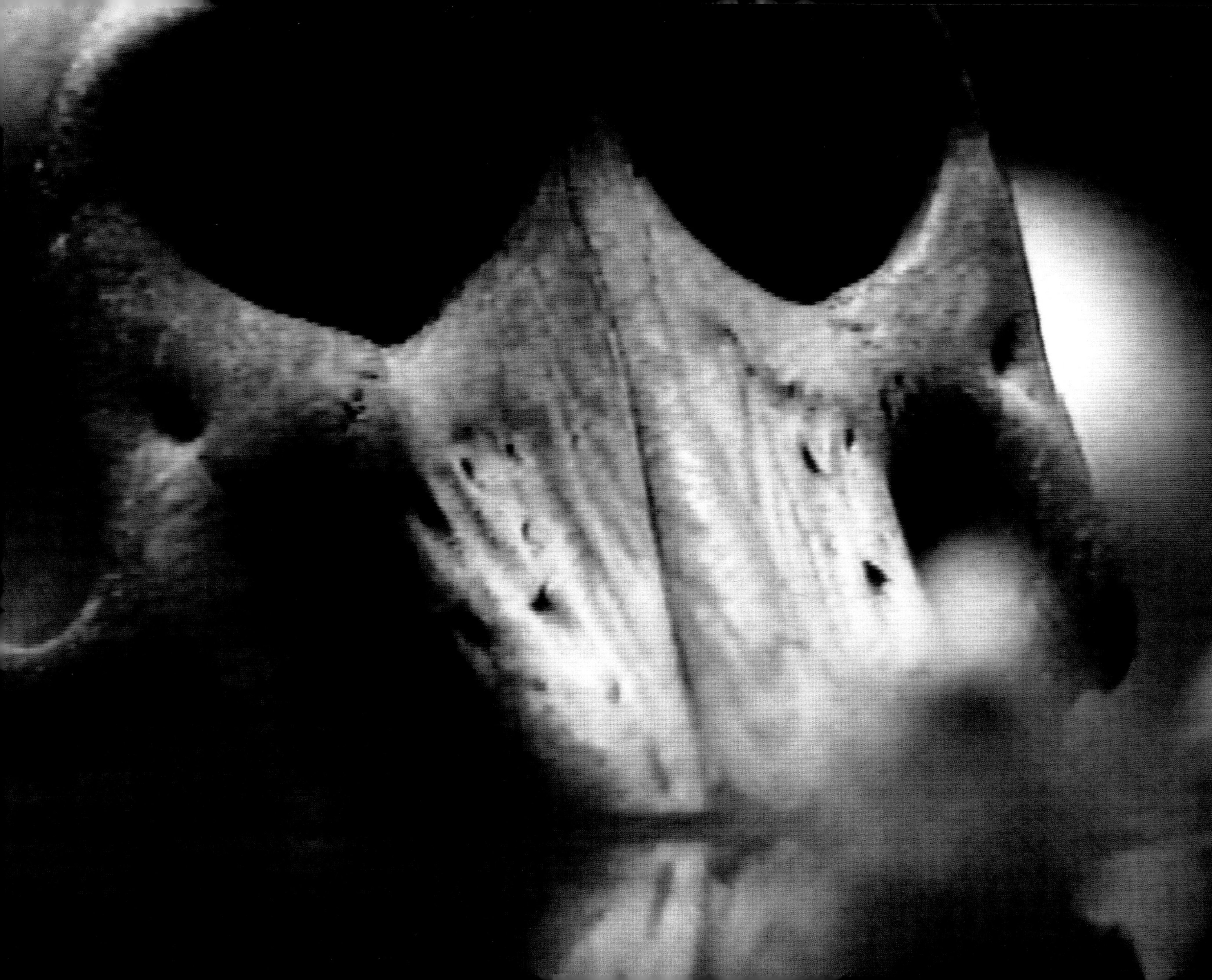

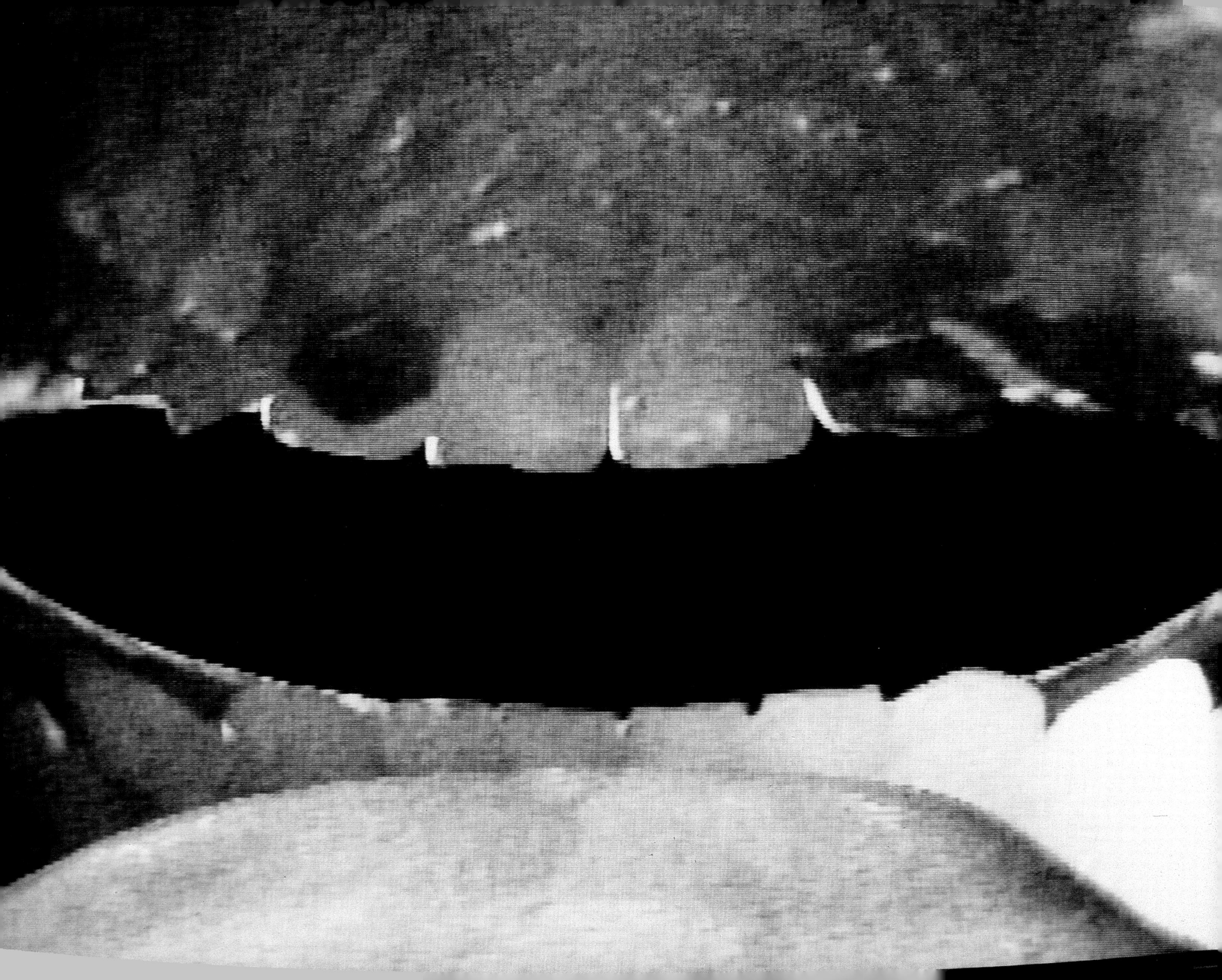

Cut Pipe

Following pages
Cut Pipe, 1992 (details and transcription of spoken text)

sounding an image

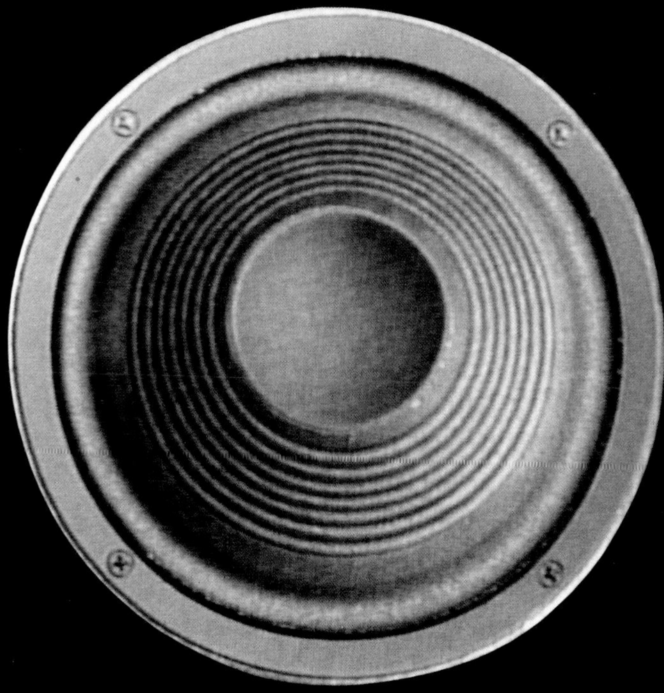

signing a sound

voicing thoughts

between soundings

imaging my voice through an object

the time of my voice

giving voice to an image

tangent to my finger

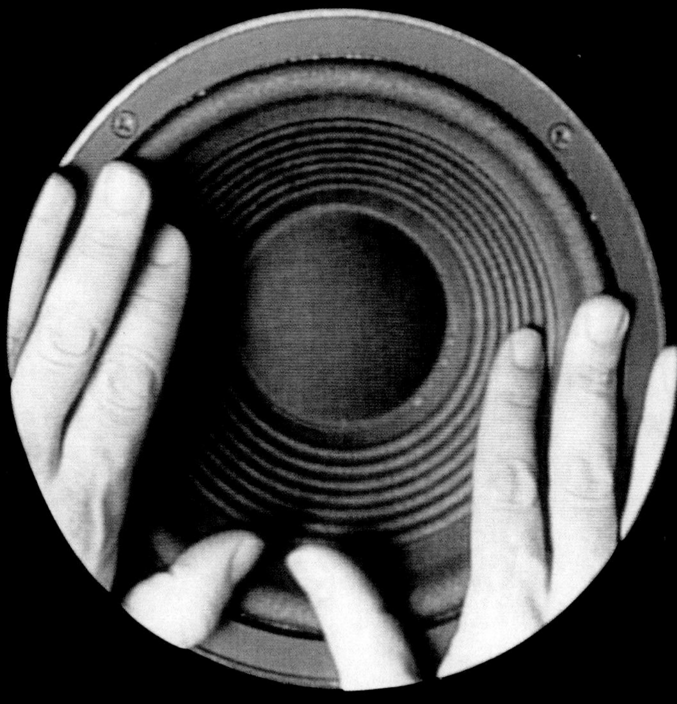

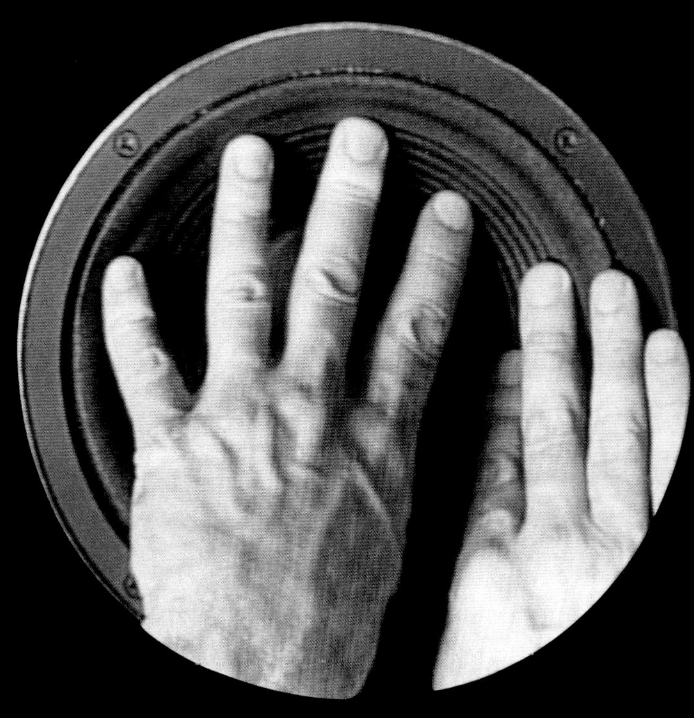

between thoughts

my voice, my finger

following an edge

unraveling speech

two points in the mean

from both beginnings and both ends

my skin its skin forming another skin

around extended periods of time

the skin of myself circulating with self-corrective pressure on its skin forming a skin of space where I voice from

touching down

the skin is always forming and shedding itself

touching sound

I have my finger on it moving it

touching image

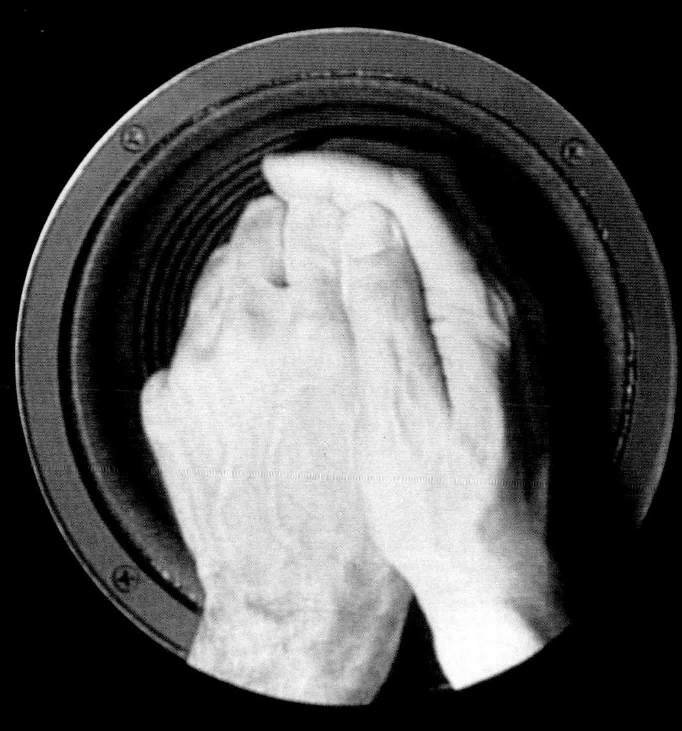

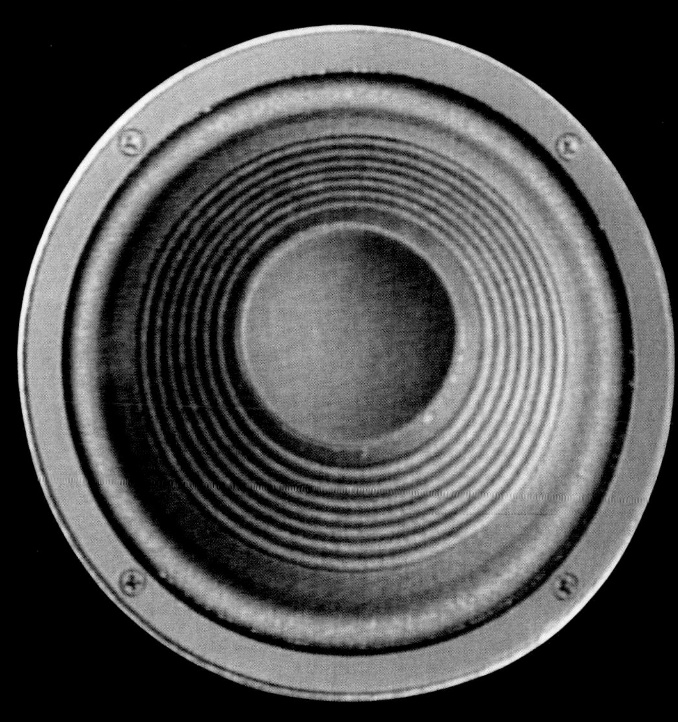

I have my finger on my voice tracking it

voicing thoughts between skins

thinking it

drumming thoughts into a skin

within the skin

to touch your space

continuing a space of

imaging the distance between soundings

playing the meaning

stretching the skin taut

ground the voice to the skin

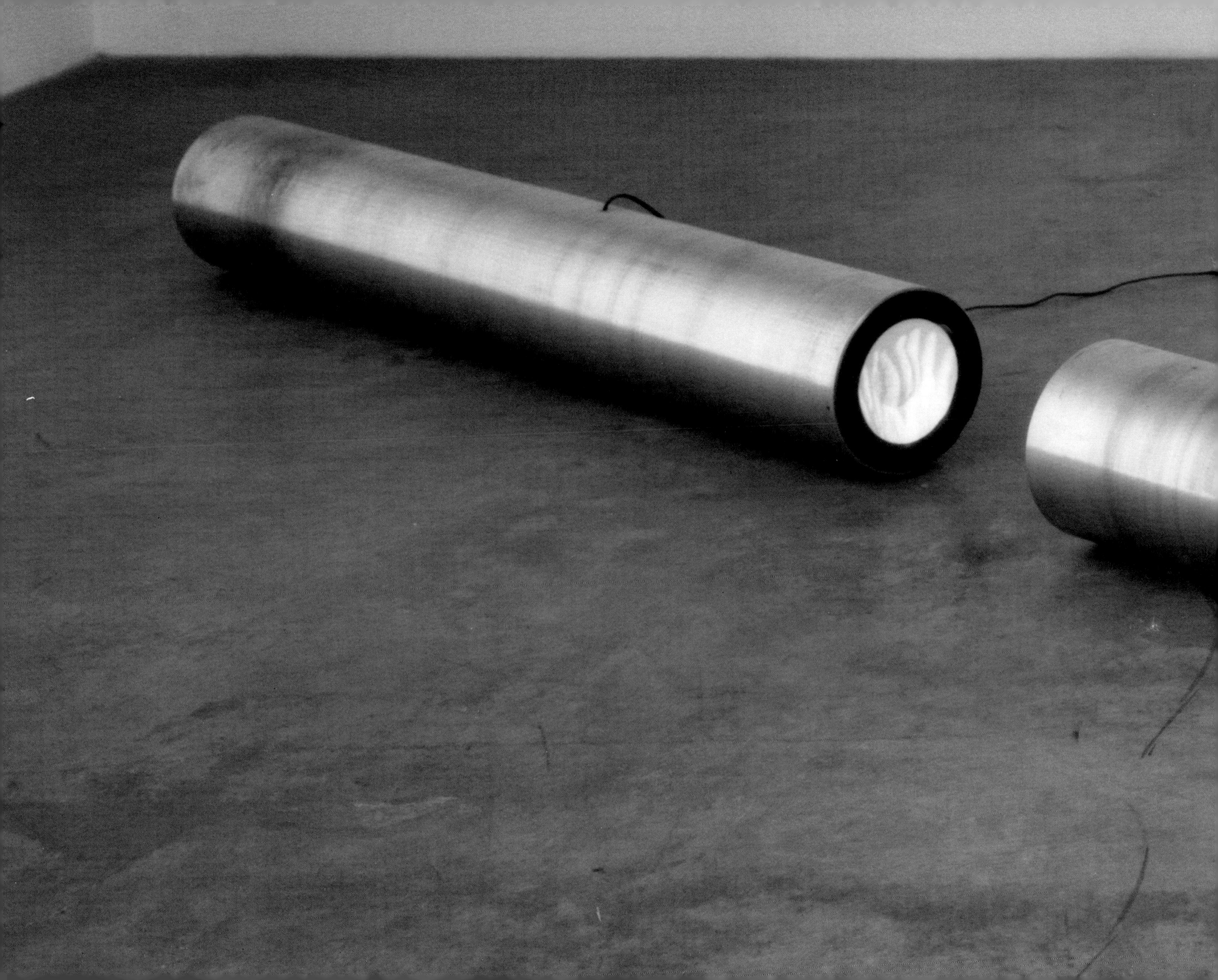

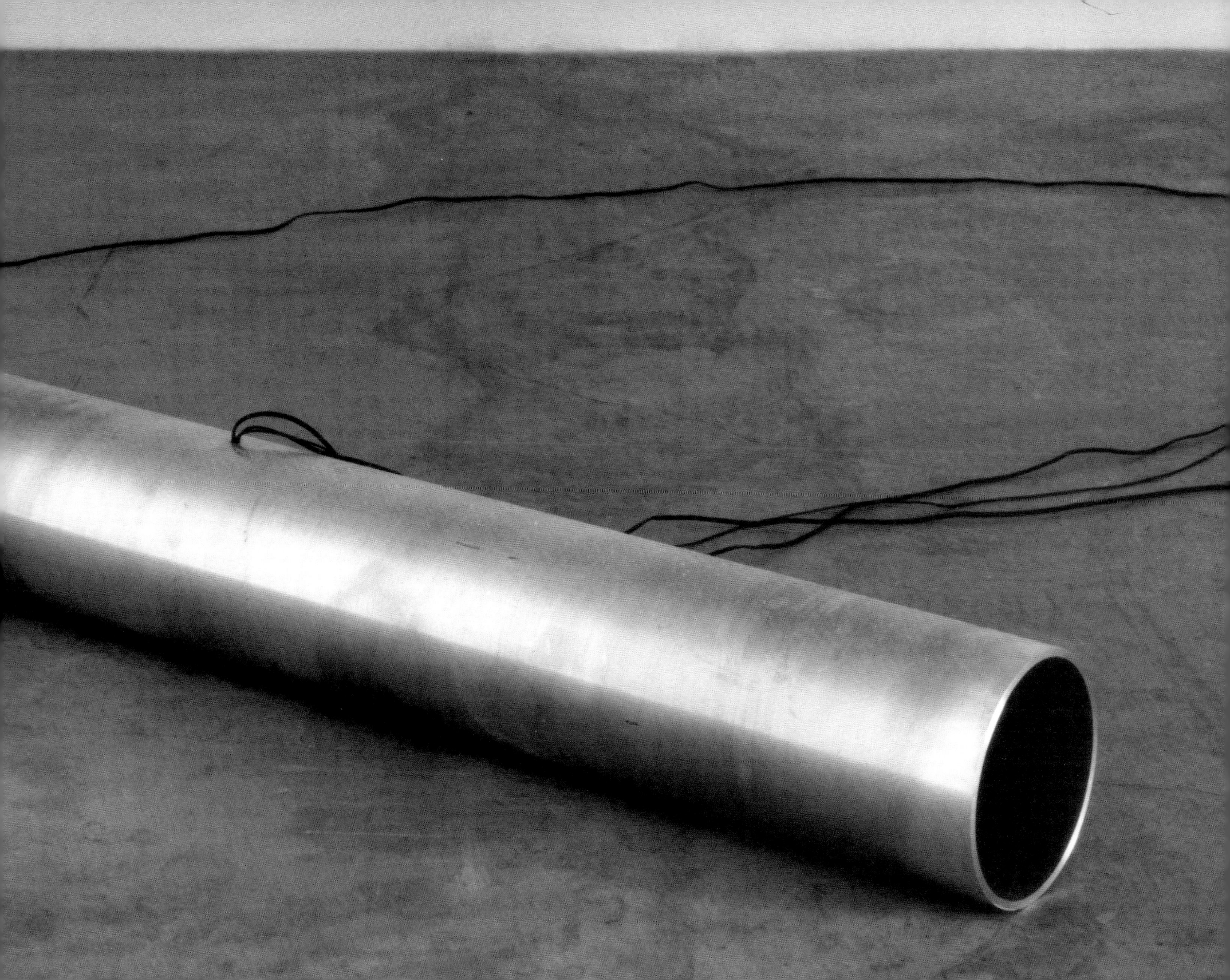

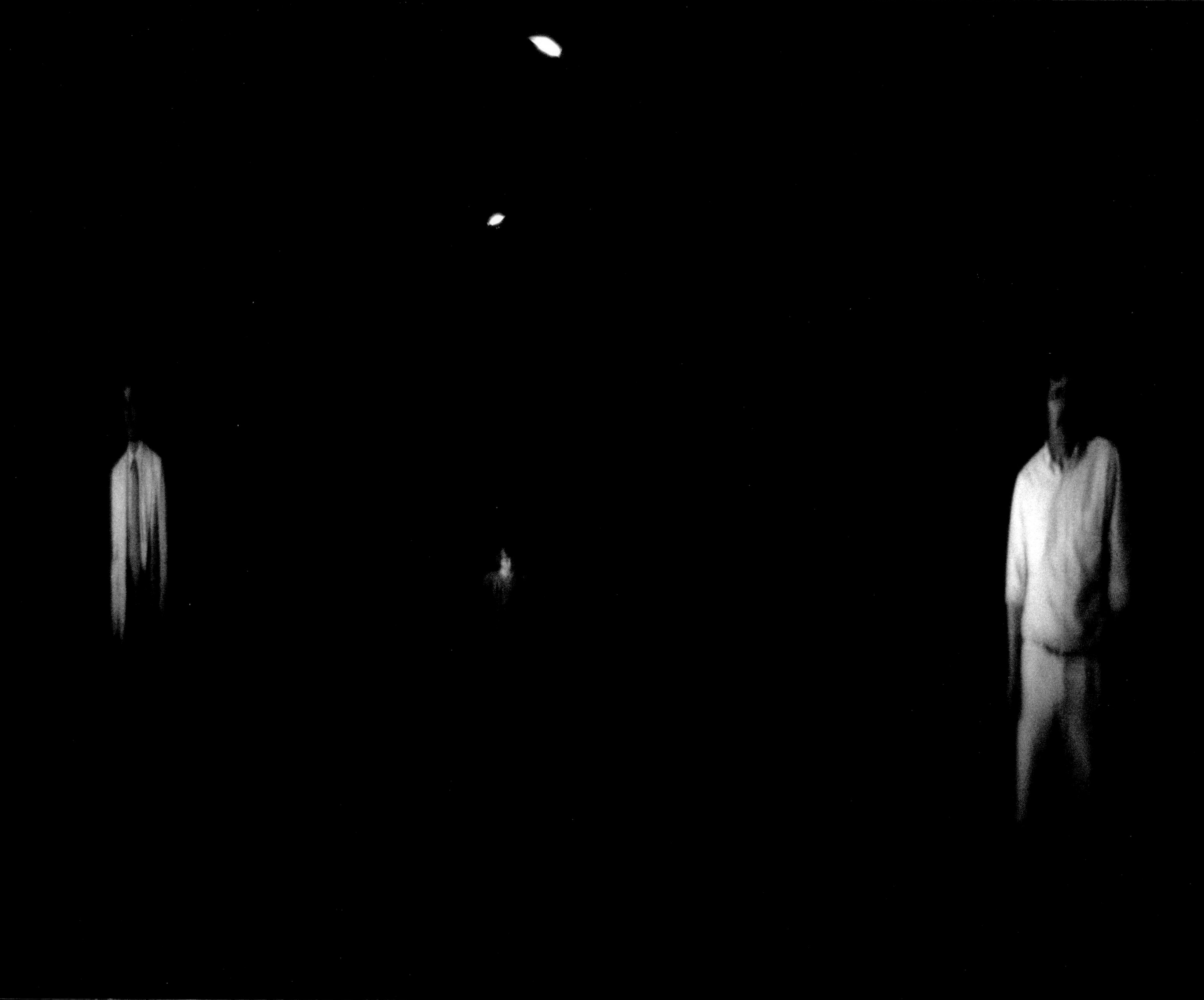

Am I ready to answer the essential question: What is writing? But it presupposes the power to reply and who could possess it?
Edmond Jabes, *The Book of Margins*

Between Language and the Moving Image: The Art of Gary Hill

John G. Hanhardt

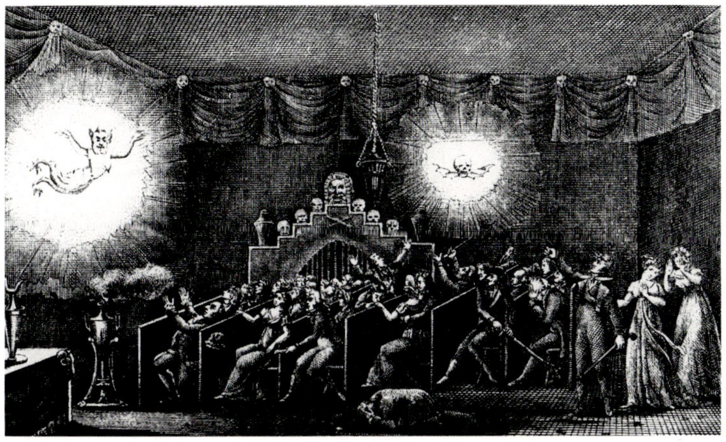

Etienne Gaspard Robert (Robertson).
A Phantasmagorical Seance. 1797. Engraving.

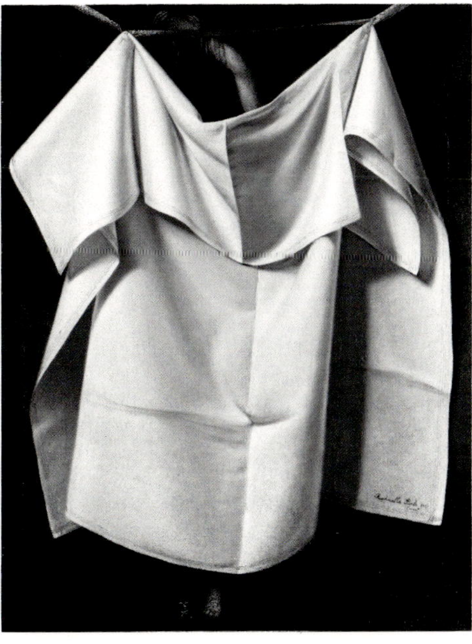

Raphaelle Peale. *Venus Rising from the Sea—A Deception.* ca. 1822. Oil on canvas. 29¼ x 24⅛ in. Courtesy of the Nelson-Atkins Museum of Art.

Tall Ships, 1992 (detail) Whitney Museum, 1993

Central to Gary Hill's project as an artist is the negotiation of the processes that link language to the moving image. His works reveal a fascination with the exposure of the essential relationship between language and our cognitive formation of images, with the exploration of the materialism of writing articulated through video and multimedia installation. This primary concern with the vital power of the word is located in a poetics of language that finds its fundamental expression in the incorporation of the body as an idea and ideal into the aesthetics of the text. Extending this aesthetics, Hill carries the self into the larger context of the public sphere and the history of the word as logos. The irony in his work is derived from the potential threat of the erasure of language within the very technologies he employs in his art making; his aesthetic investigations are based on a philosophy of language and expression that seeks to recode technology through a logos of a poetic language of imagery. This tension between modern technology and the primary philosophical roots of techne as a poetic of language and meaning is the space negotiated by Hill in his art. In this space, by turning the camera upon and into the self and the other, Hill eradicates the traditional boundary between subject and object, body and technology, word and image. With the aim of providing a context for Hill's work in this exhibition, I want to comment on these merging themes by exploring the relationships between a selection of Hill's projects and various other artworks and objects.

The first illustration in this investigation of works connected to Hill's art is a phantasmagoria from the 18th-century Belgian creator, Etienne Gaspard Robert (Robertson). In his pre-cinematic magic lantern demonstrations, Robertson created spectacular installations in which images of skeletons and the dead, projected into the smoke-filled space, floated ghostlike above the spectators. In American artist Raphaelle Peale's *Venus Rising From the Sea—A Deception (After the Bath)* (1823), a similar play with the themes of illusion and reality, desire and spectatorship, is achieved through the trompe l'oeil canvas which masks its presumed subject (the body behind the sheet); Peale uses his uncanny artistic skills to simultaneously hide and reveal the object of our gaze.

In juxtaposing these two works from the late 18th and early 19th centuries, we are faced with the everyday realist style of Peale's canvas and the spectacular illusionism of new technology in Robertson's theater. These works foretell the crisis in representation created by the photograph and motion picture, a crisis being played out today as electronic-image technology

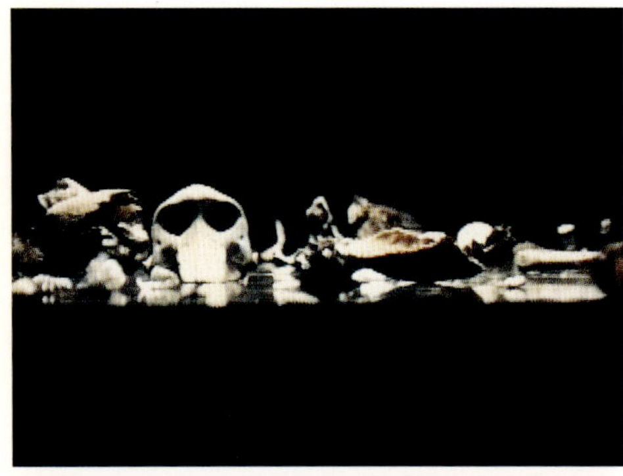

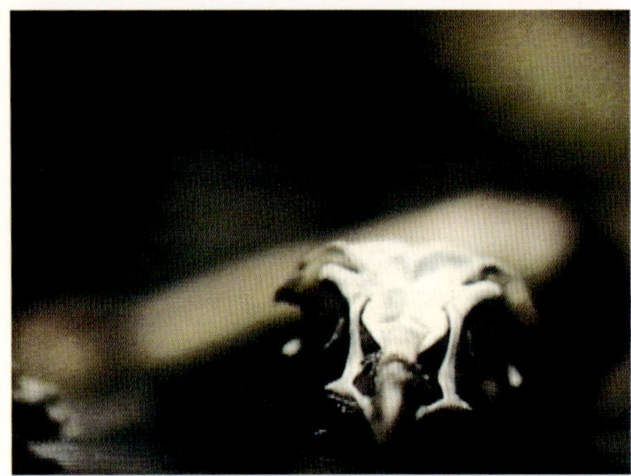

From *Site Recite (a prologue)*, 1989

assumes new dimensions of power in our culture, further diminishing the boundary between the "real" and "unreal." Peale's play with the image that records at the same time it conceals its subject explores the epistemological limits of realism; this type of image has been at the center of the debate surrounding the photographically/cinematographically recorded image and its relationship to the "objective" representation of the world around us. Robertson's theater of illusionism playfully articulates and anticipates the spectacle contained within the projected film image and the later proliferation of television screens and the power they have for creating apparent truth. Both Peale and Robertson are offered here as emblematic texts of the diminishing boundary between real and unreal explored in Hill's videotapes and installations. Hill's vision becomes fittingly relevant at this critical time in the history of art and technology as his aesthetic draws on a variety of metaphorical strategies to revise the relationship between the image and the means of its creation.

In Hill's exploration of these creative and destructive forces of technology, the body becomes a metaphor for language and a means for exploring the spectator's reception of the aesthetic text. His installation *Tall Ships* (1992) and his single-channel videotape *Site Recite (a prologue)* (1989) are particularly interesting in their placement of the body at the center of perception and representation of the spectator's point of view. In *Tall Ships*, images of bodies, hovering in near three-dimensionality on the walls of the dark corridor, approach and pull the viewer into a shared space; there the viewer is engaged in an intimate dialogue of gestures and facial expressions. The silence of the images reinforces their presence while their gestures convey deep longing and an isolation relieved only momentarily as the viewer shares the space with them. Like Robertson's phantasms, Hill's apparitions elicit a strong response from the viewer, who is launched into a sort of primal discovery of the images and recognizes in them the same desire for an intimacy with the moment and with the other.

Site Recite (a prologue) articulates a representation of the Renaissance "wonder cabinet" filled with lost and remembered objects. Upon the screen, images shift in and out of focus as the camera lens becomes an eye recording objects; the sound track, through its unique use of language, layers the experience of perception and reception of the image as a complex text of meanings. Placed on a rotating disc, the skeletons—the shifting signifiers—circle in and out of the camera's eye, which eventually shifts to the dark interior of a mouth, looking from the inside

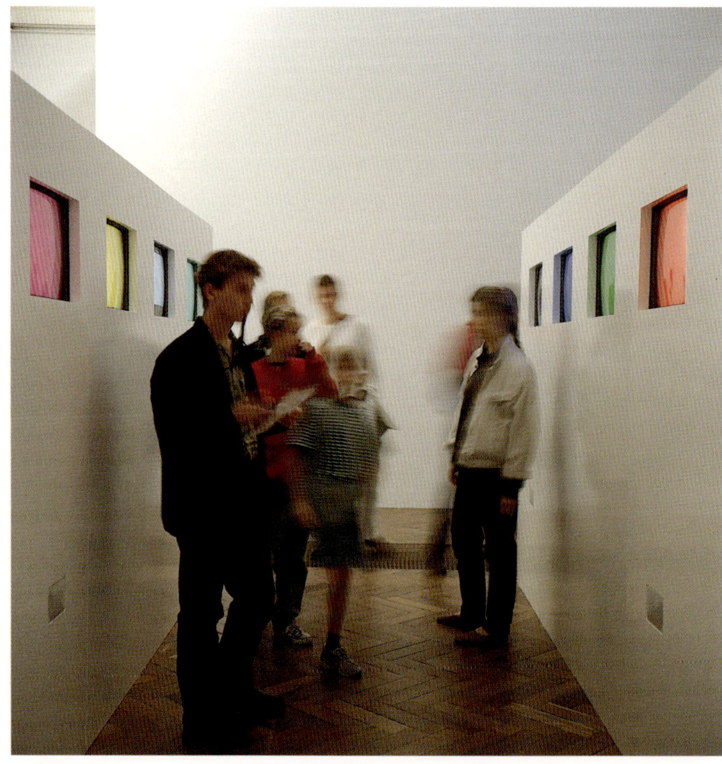

Primarily Speaking, 1981-83

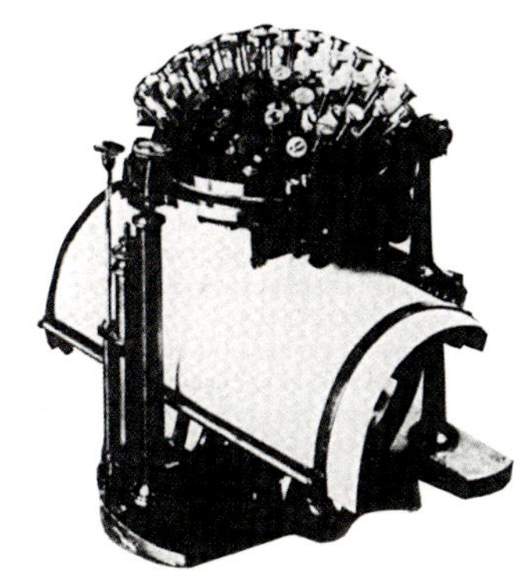

Friedrich Nietzsche's typewriter. c. 1879.

through a web of tongue and teeth, out. The camera develops into a simulacrum of the body as its lens becomes the mouth and the eye, both the articulator and observer of the world, and it approaches a phonetic vision in which image and word are fused. A metaphor for this fusion is the body as both image and articulator of speech, a speech consisting of a language which circles back to represent and ultimately embody the image; here, the language of words and images circulates through the videotape, representing and ultimately embodying the phenomenology of observation. Hill's postmodern spirits, like Robertson's pre-cinematic ghosts, are fused to their technological counterparts, and receive their living breath from the medium even while overcoming that medium in terms of its traditional usage.

The first philosopher to use a typewriter was Friedrich Nietzsche who in 1879 experimented with the rounded keyboard pictured here. Nietzsche's decision was motivated by his increasing blindness, as the organization of the keys permitted a tactile means for an organization of his writing. I use this typewriter, its instrumental embodiment of language, as an instance of technology at once being shaped by and shaping language. In its spatial organization and displacement of language from the mind to the page, it reflects Hill's exploration in his videotapes and installations of how to make concrete the processes of cognition. Nietzsche, the great postmodern philosopher and assailant of the sacred traditions of academic philosophy, began to reshape his discourse through the instrumentality of this first technology for writing: the typewriter, the immediate precursor of the word processor. The word processor further transformed written language, from the typewriter's static sheet of paper to the word processor screen, which allows the easy shifting and reorganization of language. Hill's art, too, reshapes the discourse of the traditional cinematic order of frame sequences into that of the fluid time and space of the video universe; his cognizance of philosophy and the tradition of the word places his writing and image making in the precarious realm between tradition and revolution, written language and moving image.

Primarily Speaking (1981-83), one of Gary Hill's early video installations, plays with the movement of words and images. The installation consists of two long wall units positioned face-to-face, each equipped with four built-in monitors masked to be flush with the surface. Words and phrases are aurally presented and integrated with solid fields of color and images of objects and scenes on videotape. The articulation of images and sounds is

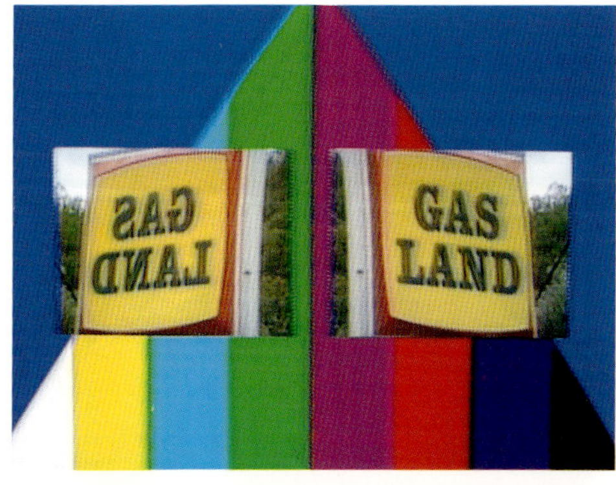

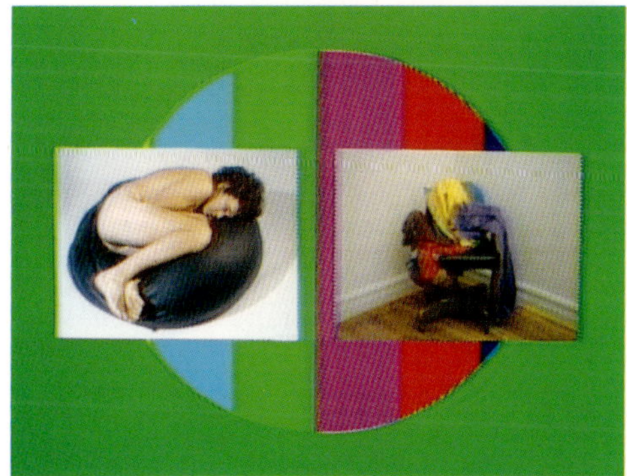

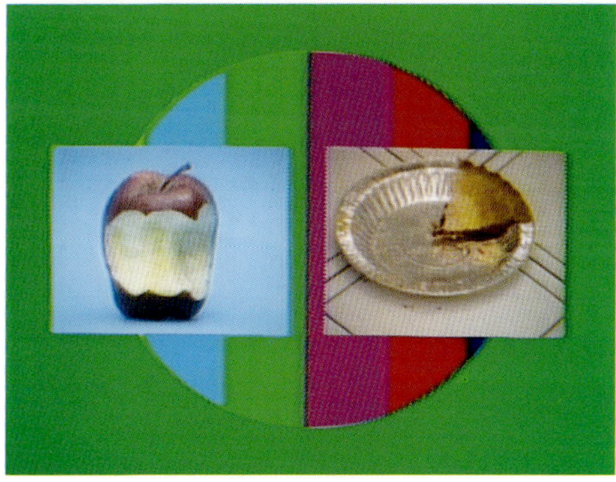

Primarily Speaking, (single-channel version) 1981-83

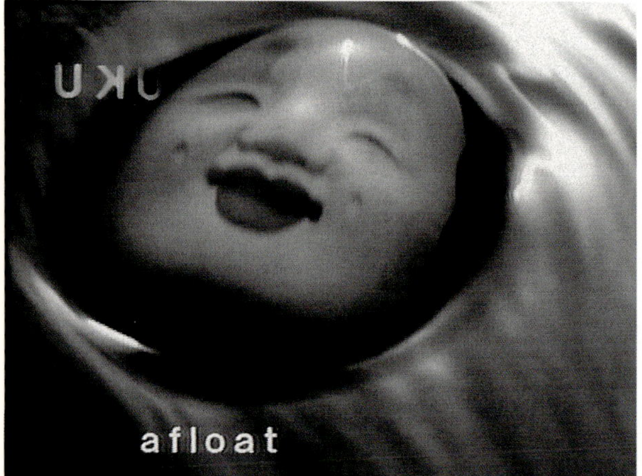

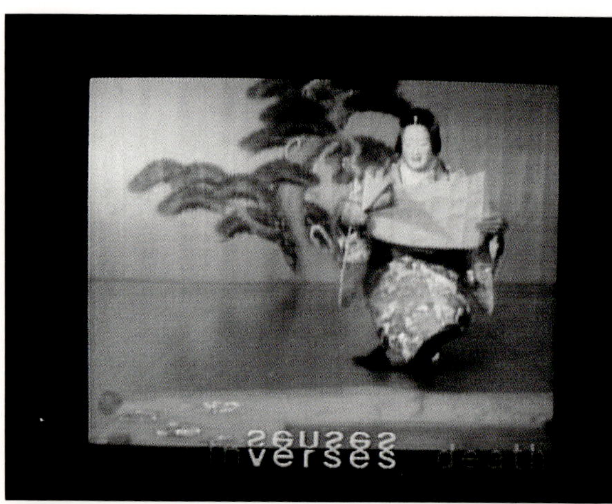

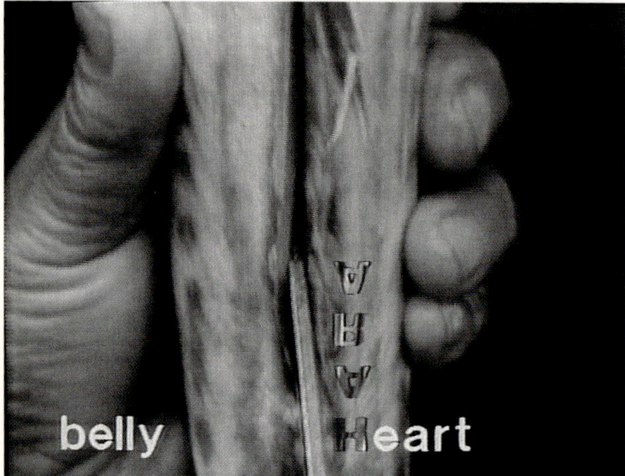

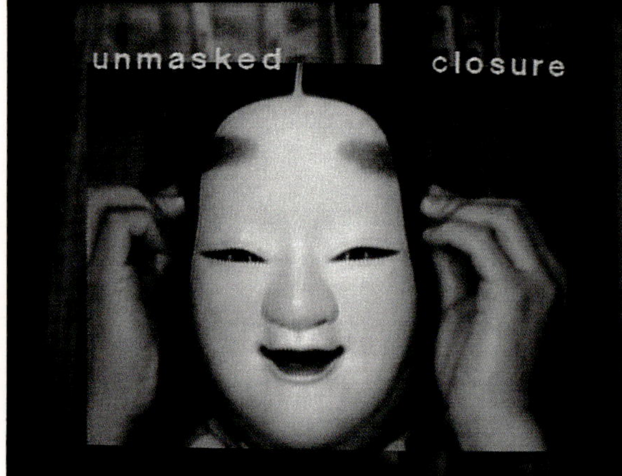

From *URA ARU (the backside exists)*, 1985-86

formed by the changes in sequences of the videotapes and soundtracks between the two wall-like structures. This rapid and precise movement between color fields, images and words, combined with the shifting position of the listener/viewer, results in a proliferation of contexts—and thus the contents—of the various elements.

The physical depiction of semantics in *Primarily Speaking* moved to another more literary level in Hill's *URA ARU (the backside exists)* (1985-86). This spectacular videotape employs formal and rhetorical strategies to explore word meaning in its treatment of a selection of Japanese words as palindromes (words that read the same way both backward and forward and that Hill further breaks apart and reforms). In the tape, which consists of a series of visual-verbal haiku, Hill employs great economy of action and technique; the printed word moves through each scene, echoing the spoken word. The result is the inscription of language into the visualization of its own meaning.

In *Primarily Speaking* and *URA ARU (the backside exists)*, language is rendered *material* as images representative of it extend from the optical enclosure of the monitor and into the installation space, which is the spectator's space as well. Hill's transposition of language into a visual medium reconstructs the language of video art itself. Like Nietzsche's typewriter which made visible the thoughts of the near blind philosopher, Hill's video works make manifest his uniquely expressed view of the relationship of word to image. His understanding of video technology is expressed in his ability to remake these instruments into a supportive complex of poetic interrelationships.

The artist's place within the context of the artwork is a complex cognitive issue. The physical stance—of the painter before the canvas, the writer bent over her paper, the sculptor contemplating his materials—reflects physically the question of where the artist stands in terms of the work, but there are also the spatio-temporal and ideological positions when the work of art is viewed in its social context. Hill's art constructs a variety of metaphorical strategies with which to represent the body's position within society; he achieves this via his rendering of video into a technology usable as a means of individual creative expression.

At the written heart of American democracy is the Declaration of Independence, written primarily by Thomas Jefferson. Jefferson embodied an 18th-century ideal which replaced a narrow view of the self in favor of one of the self as part of something greater, exchanging tunnel vision for a broad multi-perspective stance

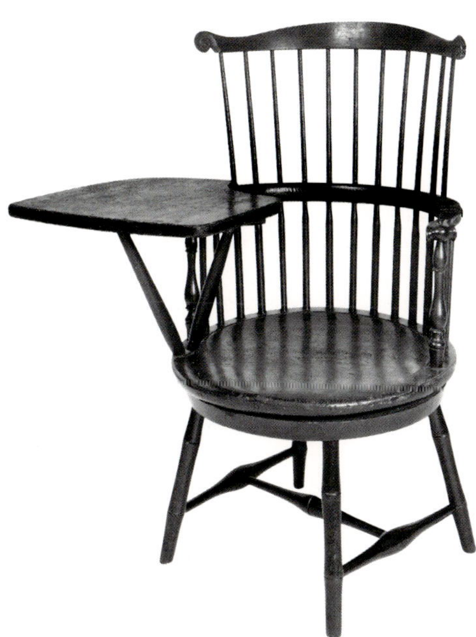

Thomas Jefferson. Swivel Chair. Courtesy of the American Philosophical Society.

toward the surrounding world. Jefferson's Monticello, built on a hill from which a physically broader view was possible, was an architectural expression of that desire, as was his invention of the swivel chair. The swivel chair's arc of movement permitted Jefferson to physically shift his writing body and point of view from the locked position of a single aspect to numerous other ones; this is symbolically fitting as this was probably the chair in which he drafted the Declaration, the written testimony to his engagement with the democratic ideals of the new republic, and with an all-encompassing and less self-interested perspective (a distinctively greater perspective than, for instance, that of Bentham's architechtural panopticon, which afforded society a limited yet controlling view of prison life).

Art—also as architecture and design—embodies ideals and ideology. Hill's videotapes and installations bear a relationship to this distinctively American poetics of expanding the view of the self through an open exploration of language and image making. In *CRUX* (1983-87), this idea of image making Is taken one step further with the image's making of itself, a complex negotiation of the traditional concepts of subject and object as discrete entities. Here, Hill himself controls—via his positioning of them—the five cameras: two focused on his arms, two on his legs, and one pointed up to the face. The cameras accompany the artist as he crosses a ruined building in a rural setting, turning him into the ironic subject. The five video channels thus recorded are played on five monitors suspended against a wall and synchronized to represent the movement of the body over the torn landscape. The constant replay of the installation conveys the sense of a technology open to all, a generous means for the construction of a vision. Hill's remaking of the technology into an instrument of poetic inquiry with the potential to express the quest for an ideal, and not simply mercantile, vision of television and society is parallel to Jefferson's creation of the Declaration, which also was, in a sense, an instrument of poetic inquiry for a nation then just beginning to identify itself. Jefferson's chair, whose mobility allowed for a generous view of the world around him, becomes a physical embodiment of the Constitution's own inclusiveness and support of a democratically viewed public sphere. This is echoed in Hill's new installation *Learning Curve* (1993), in which the old-fashioned school desk and chair embody, in their view of an ocean wave's endless movement, the expanded vision of personal experience and public history that is the necessary foundation of our perception and understanding of the present.

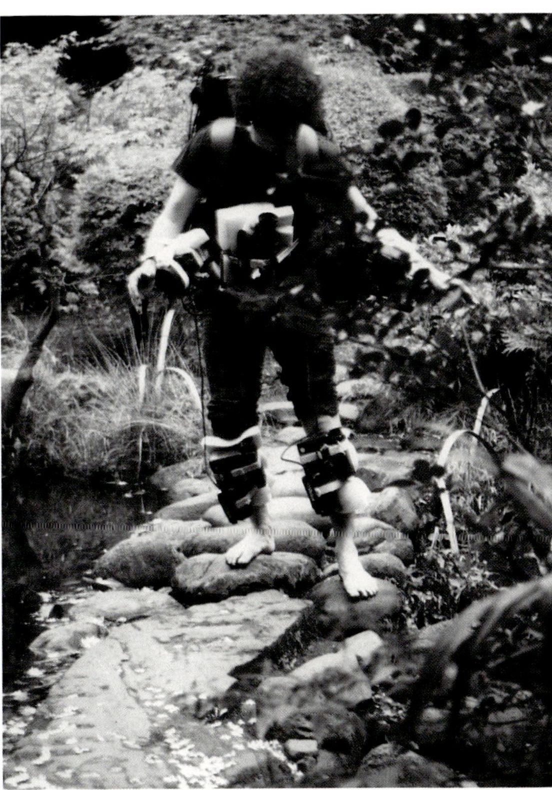

Gary Hill, ***CRUX*** (in process, Japan), 1985

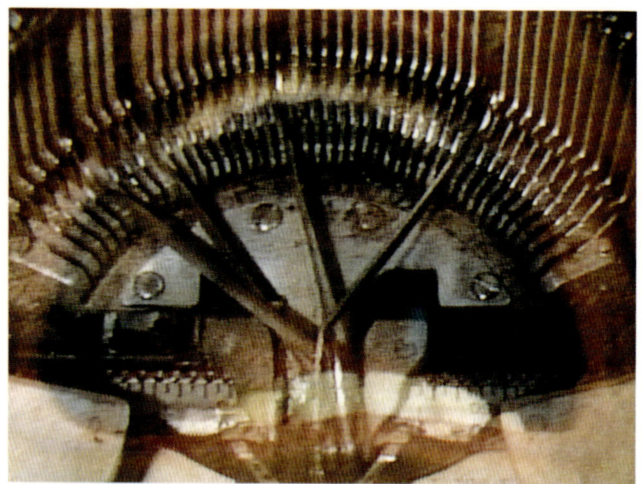

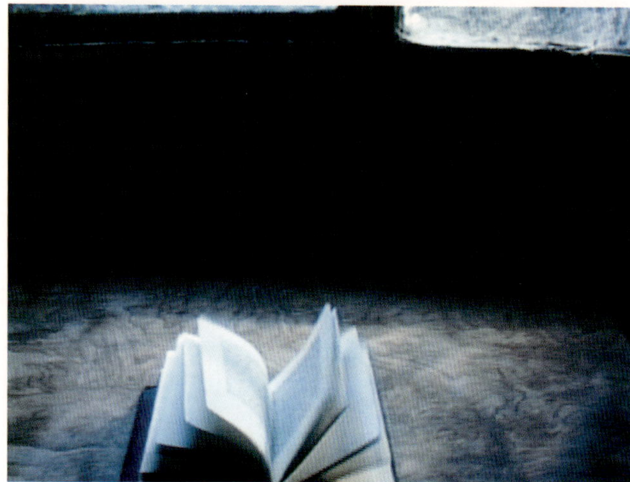

From ***Incidence of Catastrophe***, 1987-88

In the 1980s, video installations moved to the forefront of new expression in contemporary art. Nam June Paik, Bill Viola, Dara Birnbaum, and Gary Hill created large and compelling bodies of work. At the same time the art market and artists' careers were expanding, expressing a new surge of interest in artistic culture, best manifested in the rapid construction of museums during the decade.

Today, the art world is once again in flux; art continues to flourish in terms of abundance but the markets are changing. Anselm Kiefer's extraordinary installation *20 Jahre Einsamkeit (Twenty Years of Loneliness) 1971-1991* is composed of the refuse of the artist's studio, objects related to his artistic past ranging from actual works of art to raw materials and balls of dirt and sunflowers from the place where he lived in Germany. In the installation, the canvases and other materials that distinguished Kiefer's art are piled to the ceiling in a mute and moving testimony to the creative ideals of the previous decade. Kiefer's reflection on the painter's canvas and materials as a kind of detritus of the imagination is an ironic and poignant meditation on the creative process and the materials an artist chooses to work with. His installation lays bare the contents of his studio and is, in a sense, a laying bare as well of a life, of the realization of the self he is today and of the precarious flux of the artistic venture. A space that could have been cold and impersonal is hauntingly personalized.

I am suggesting that Hill's art is itself a meditation on being an artist and the struggle to remake technology into a poetic instrument. Like Kiefer, Hill confronts himself in his art as a thinking being seeking to strip it of the decorative and ephemeral so as to retrieve a sense of self and memory. For Kiefer it is the poetics of a personal history and painting; for Hill, the poetics of language and media.

Hill's art does not face the crisis of a questioned and eroding art form and tradition, but the challenge of renewing tradition and charting a new horizon of possibility. Indeed, he transforms the technology of video, carrying it away from the conventional categorization and usage of art and television and into the intimacy of the artist's studio and imagination. By stripping the monitor and camera of their conventional applications, he recreates cathode ray tubes so they become a contemporary language which allows the moving image to enter into the discourse of sculpture and installation, and of self-inquiry. In this regeneration of the medium through a philosophic strategy of image making, Hill has recovered the place of language and origins of technology in a metaphysics

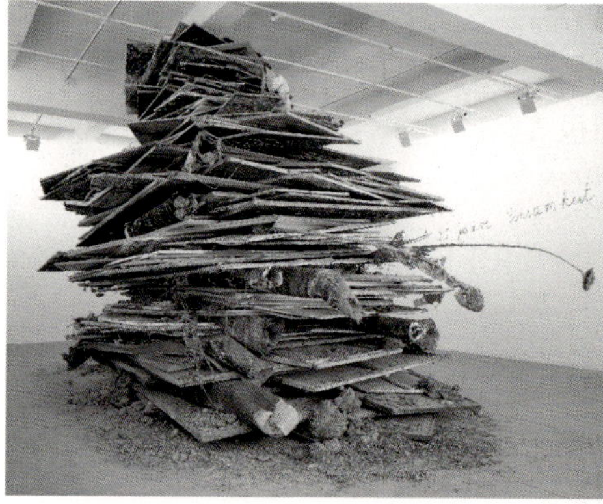

Anselm Kiefer. *20 Jahre Einsamkeit (Twenty Years of Loneliness).* 1971-1991. Installation. Courtesy of the Miriam Goodman Gallery.

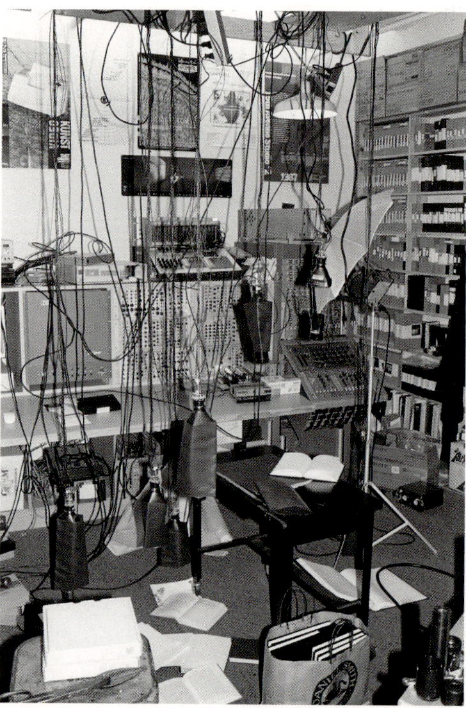

Gary Hill studio, Seattle, 1992

of techne. His installation *Between Cinema and a Hard Place* (1991) consists of twenty-three monitors positioned to create a demarcated space with rows like that of a field. The work adapts Heidegger's *The Nature of Language* into its self-questioning meditation on the marking of space and time, language's earthly roots, and disrupts the mechanics of the cinematic sequence of moving images and spoken text, and thus its own flow, to bare the nature of a technology at odds with itself.

"As soon as we try to reflect on the matter we have already committed ourselves to a long path of thought," Heidegger wrote. Thought is commitment, language, a precious vessel for thinking, images need words in order to be understood. This sequence of demands, commitments of both time and energy, has led to Hill's artistic release of a body of work fragile in construction but strong in its resolve to resist the easy consumption of ideas. This is perhaps most eloquently articulated in his videotape *Incidence of Catastrophe*, one of the handful of major works created within the discourse of single-channel videotape. This work uses as its inspiration the writer/philosopher Maurice Blanchot and his text *Thomas the Obscure*. In this epic work the artist himself is enfolded within the phenomenology of the written/printed text; as his body and eye merge to become one, the screen struggles with the folio sheet, the press-type on the page—with the impression of language on our consciousness.

In his exploration of the age-old debate between word and image, Hill's aesthetic language has retrieved a hope for art. As Kiefer symbolically rebuilds the aesthetic discourse of painting in a Homeric pyre of fragile canvas, Hill, our most visual of new image philosopher/artists, also reconstructs the aesthetics of the video medium with his brilliant solution to the dilemma of being an artist in the *fin de siècle*: the placement of the body at the center of the process that links language to image, poetics to poetry, and the words we speak to the tongues we embody.

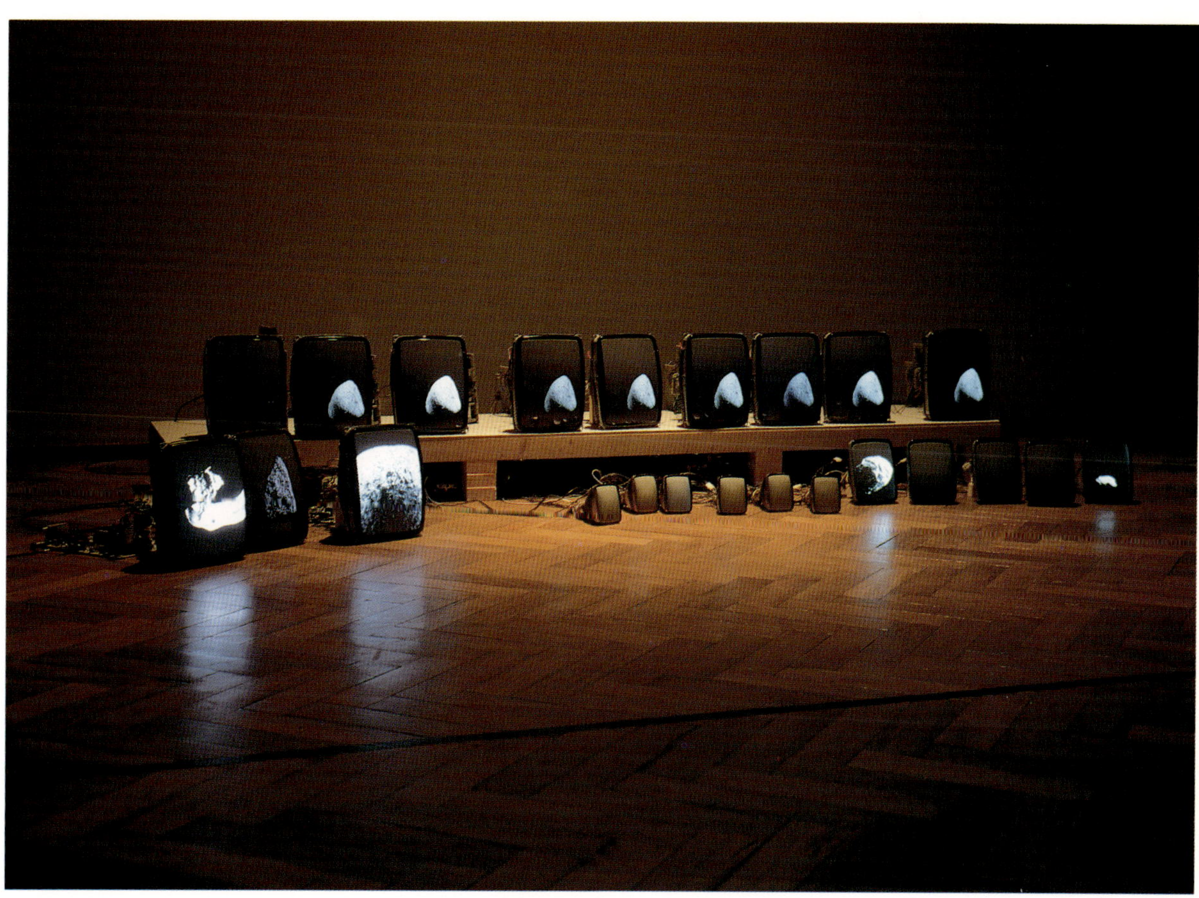

Between Cinema and a Hard Place, 1991 Whitney Museum, 1991

John G. Hanhardt is curator of film and video at the Whitney Museum of American Art in New York since 1974. He has curated many exhibitions including *Re-visions: Projects and Proposals in Film and Video, Nam June Paik, The Films of Andy Warhol,* and has made the film and video selections for ten Whitney Biennials.

Following pages
Tall Ships, 1992 (details)

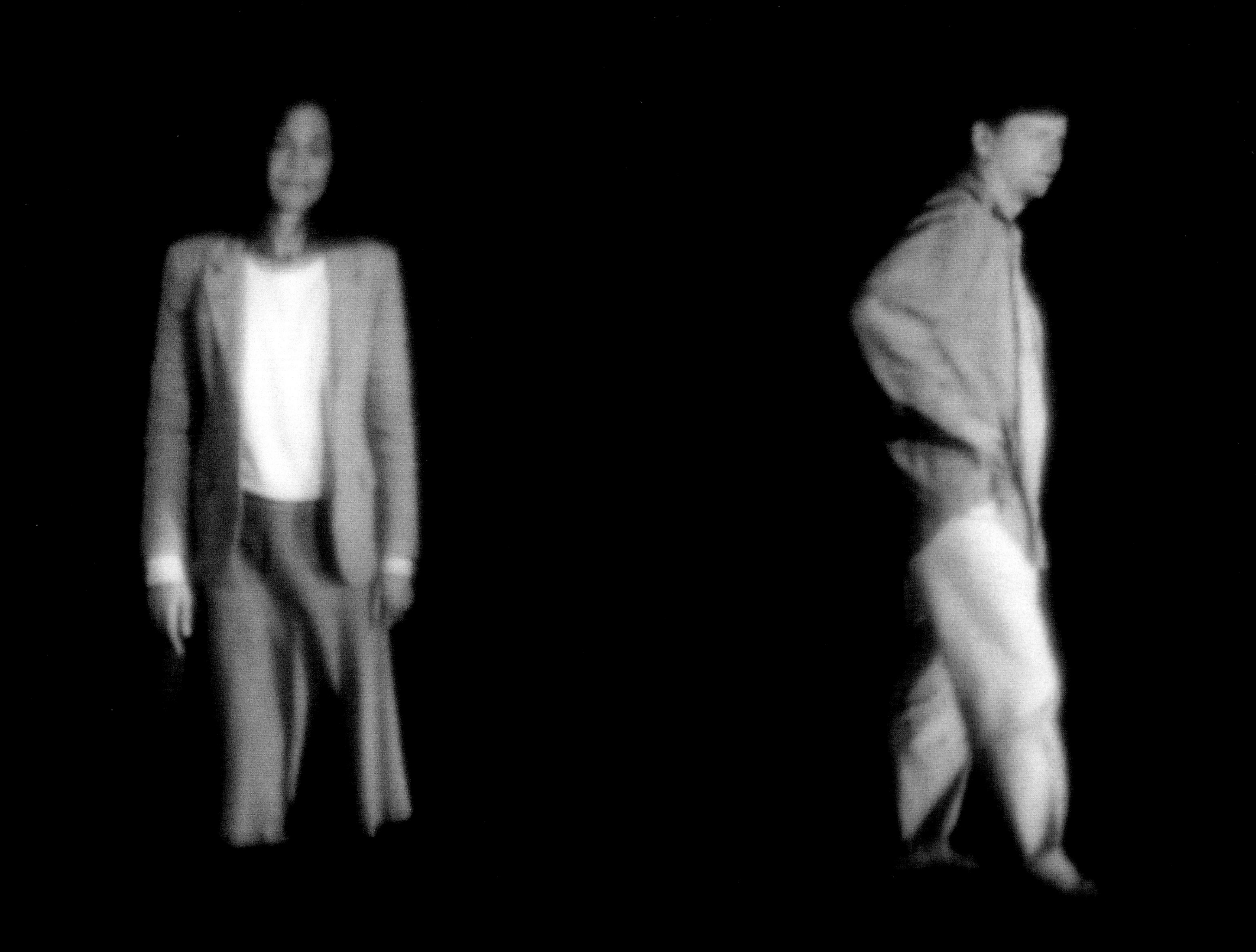

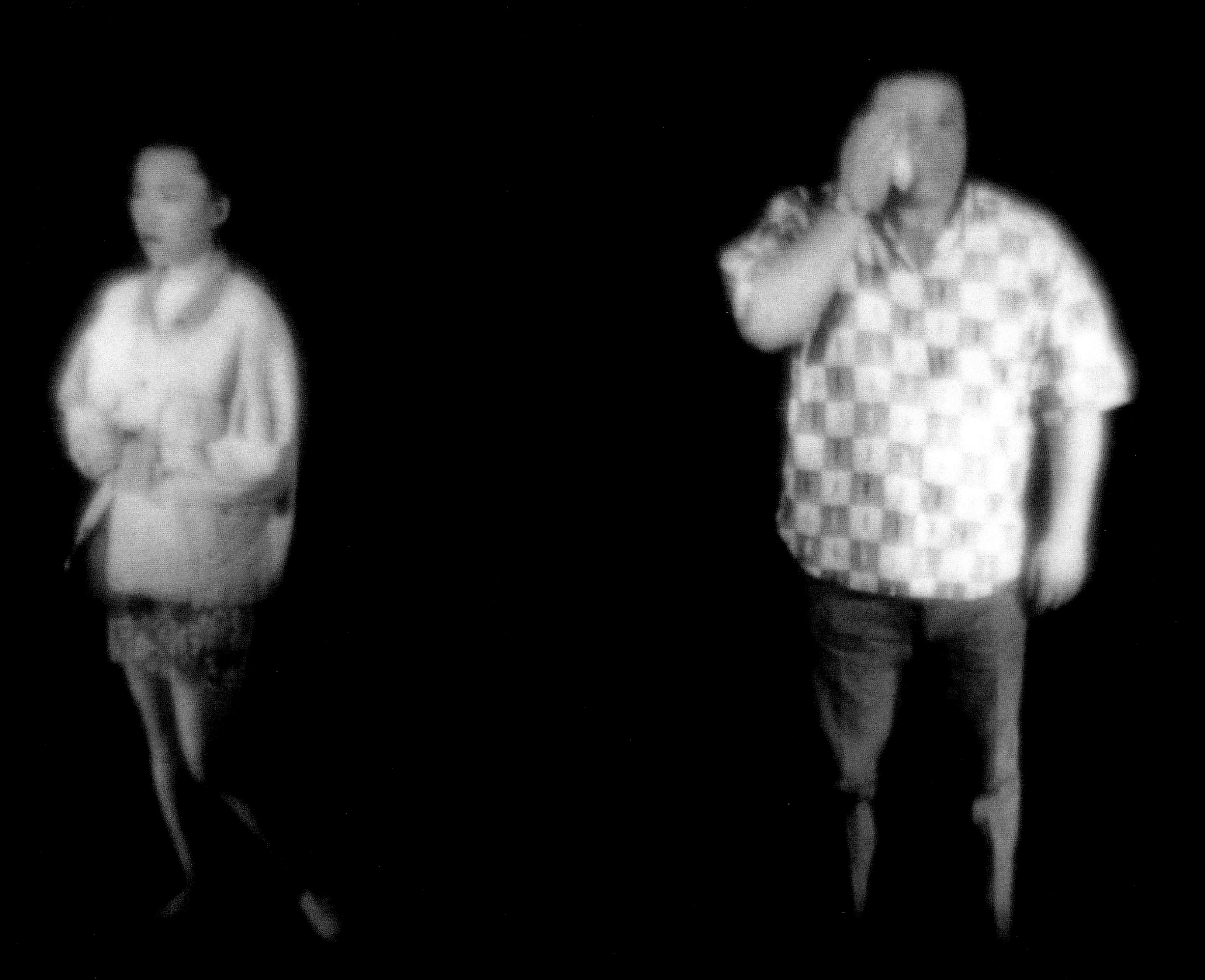

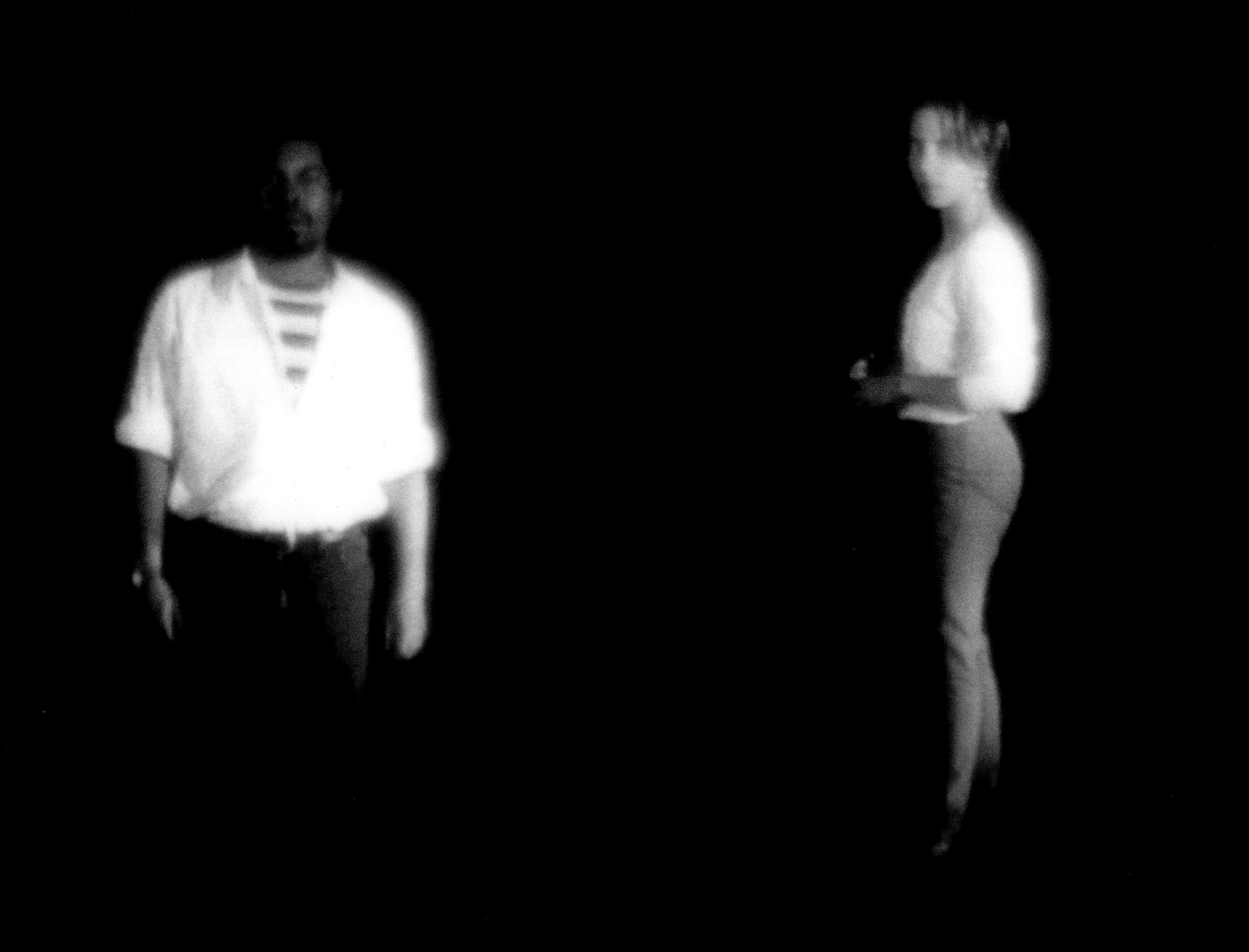

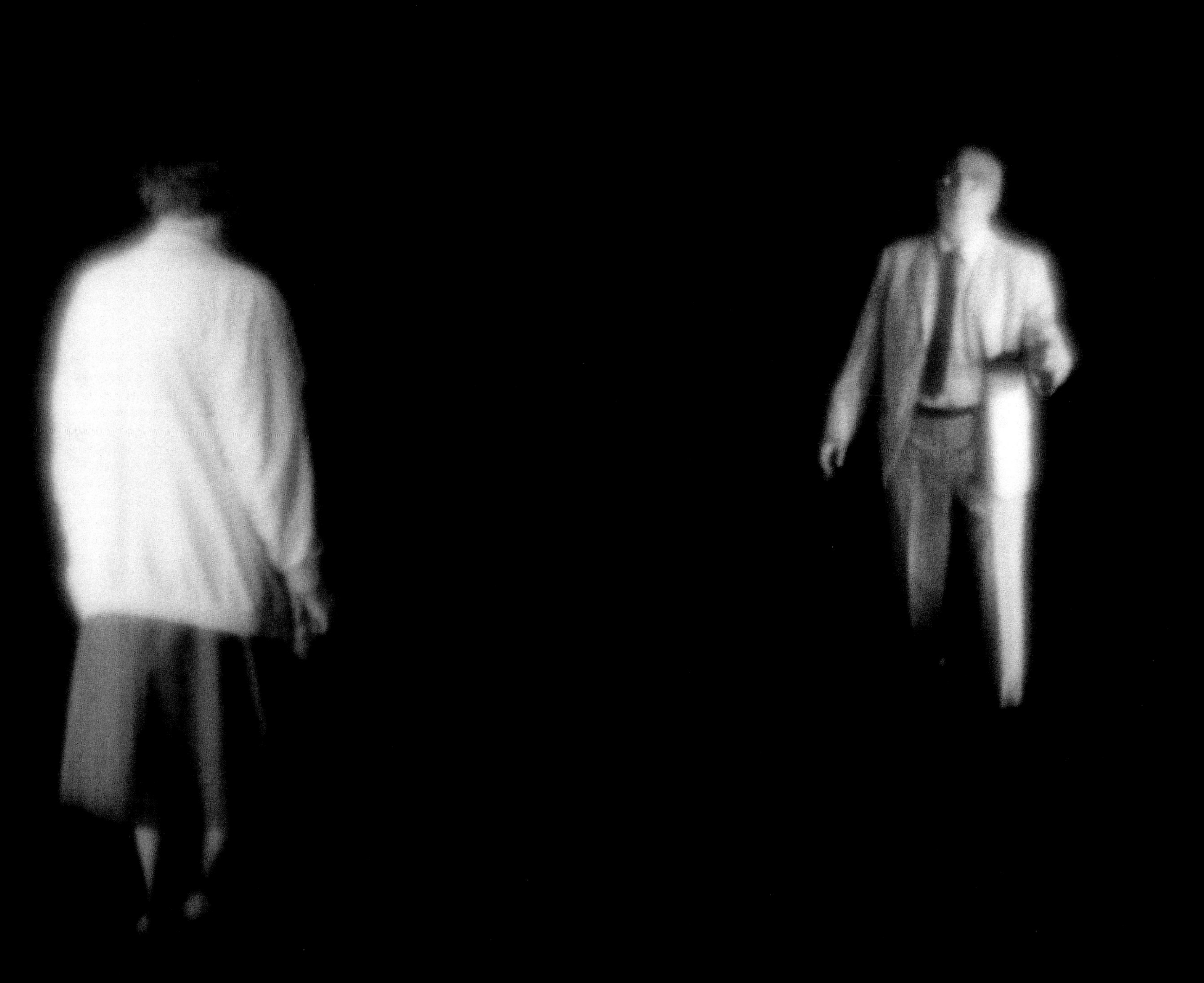

S u s p e n s i o n

o f D i s b e l i e f

Following pages
Suspension of Disbelief (for Marine), installed at Le Creux de L'Enfer, Centre d'Art Contemporain, Thiers, France, 1992 (details)

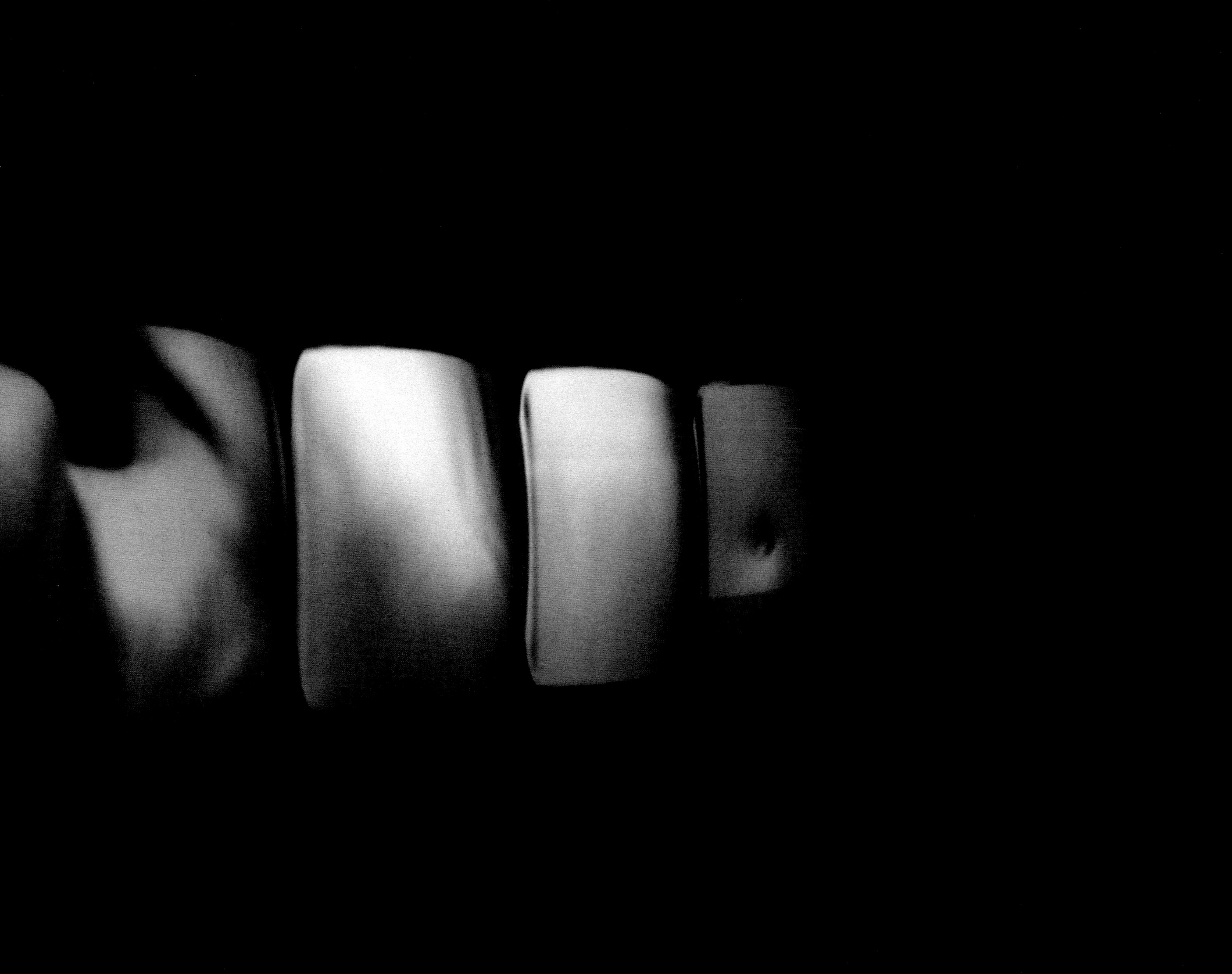

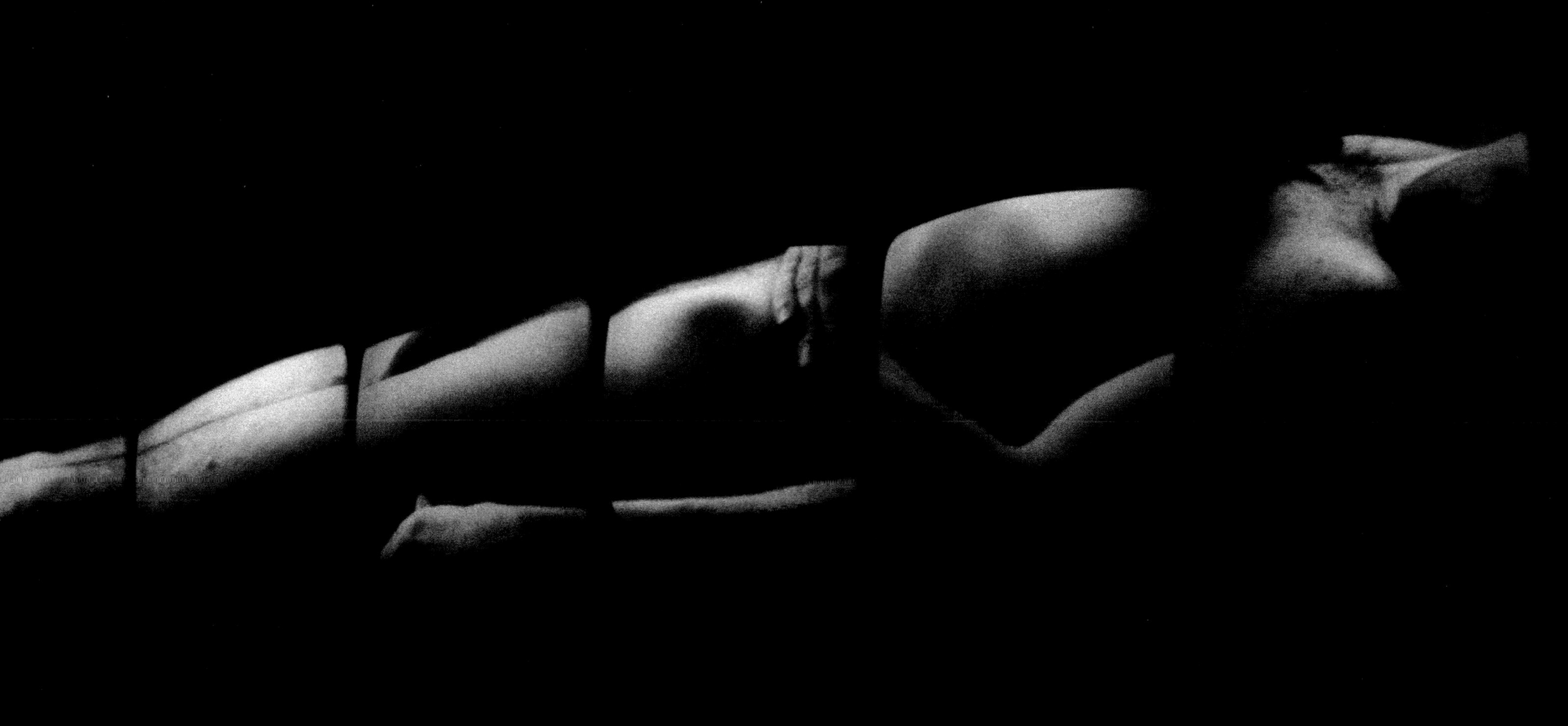

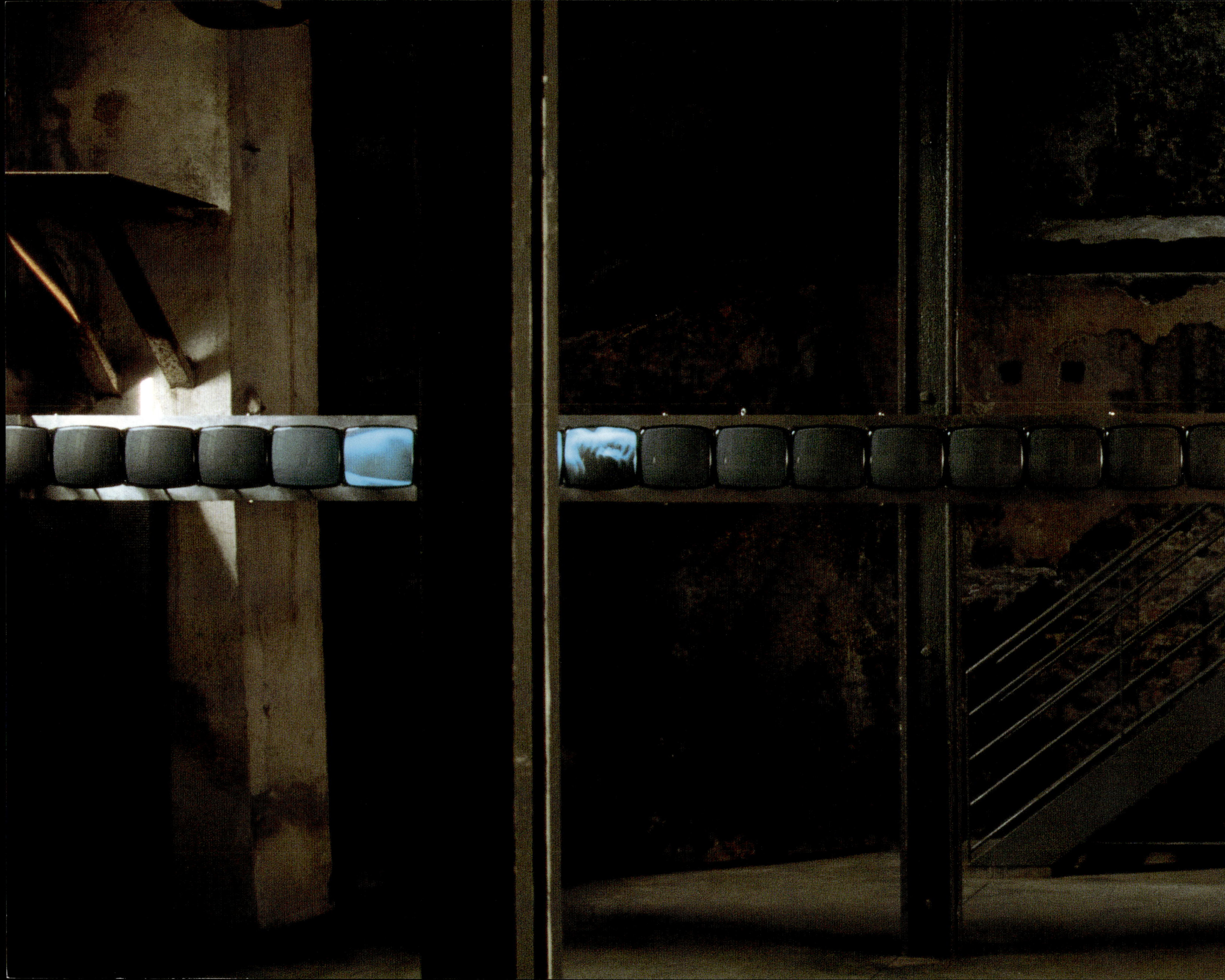

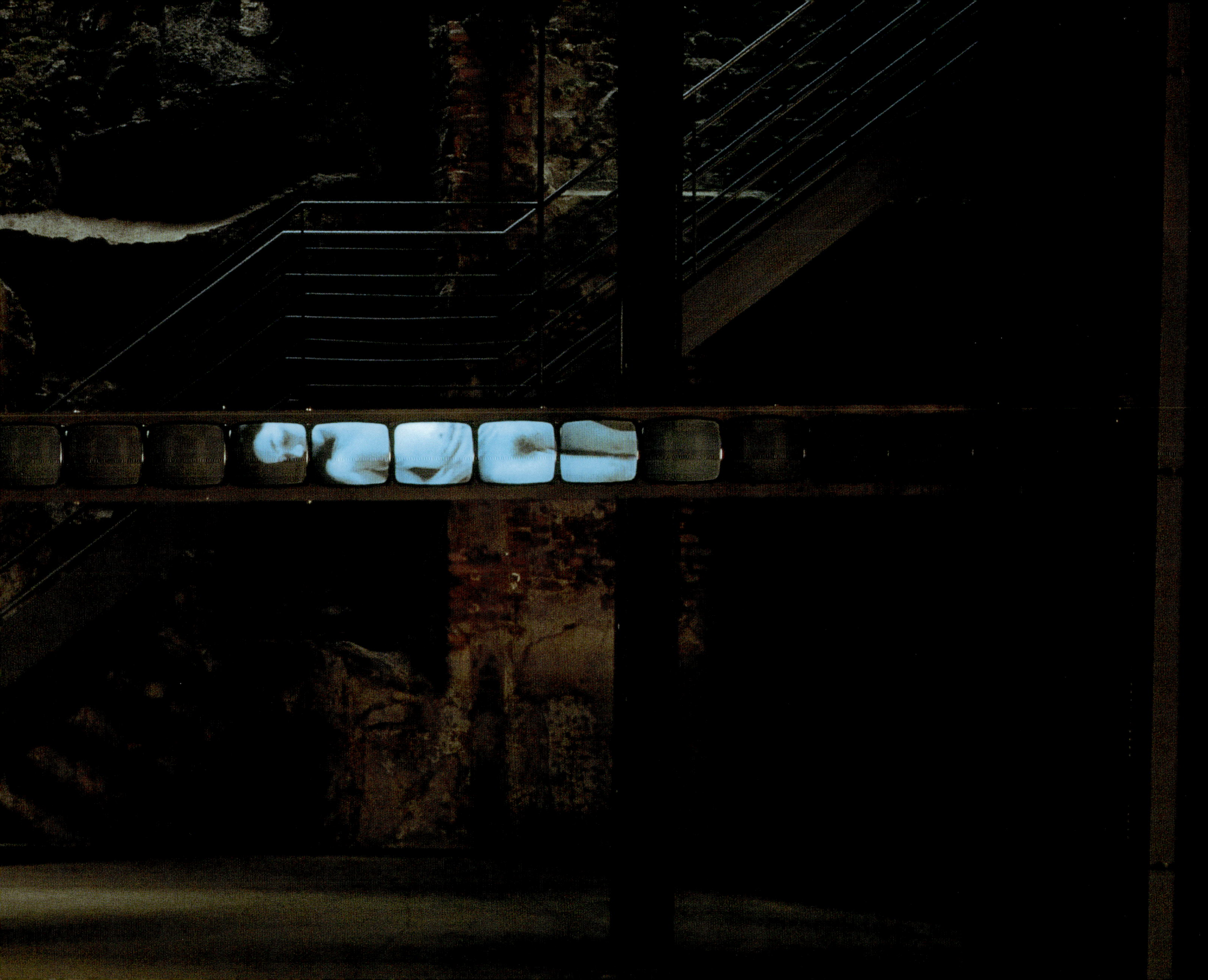

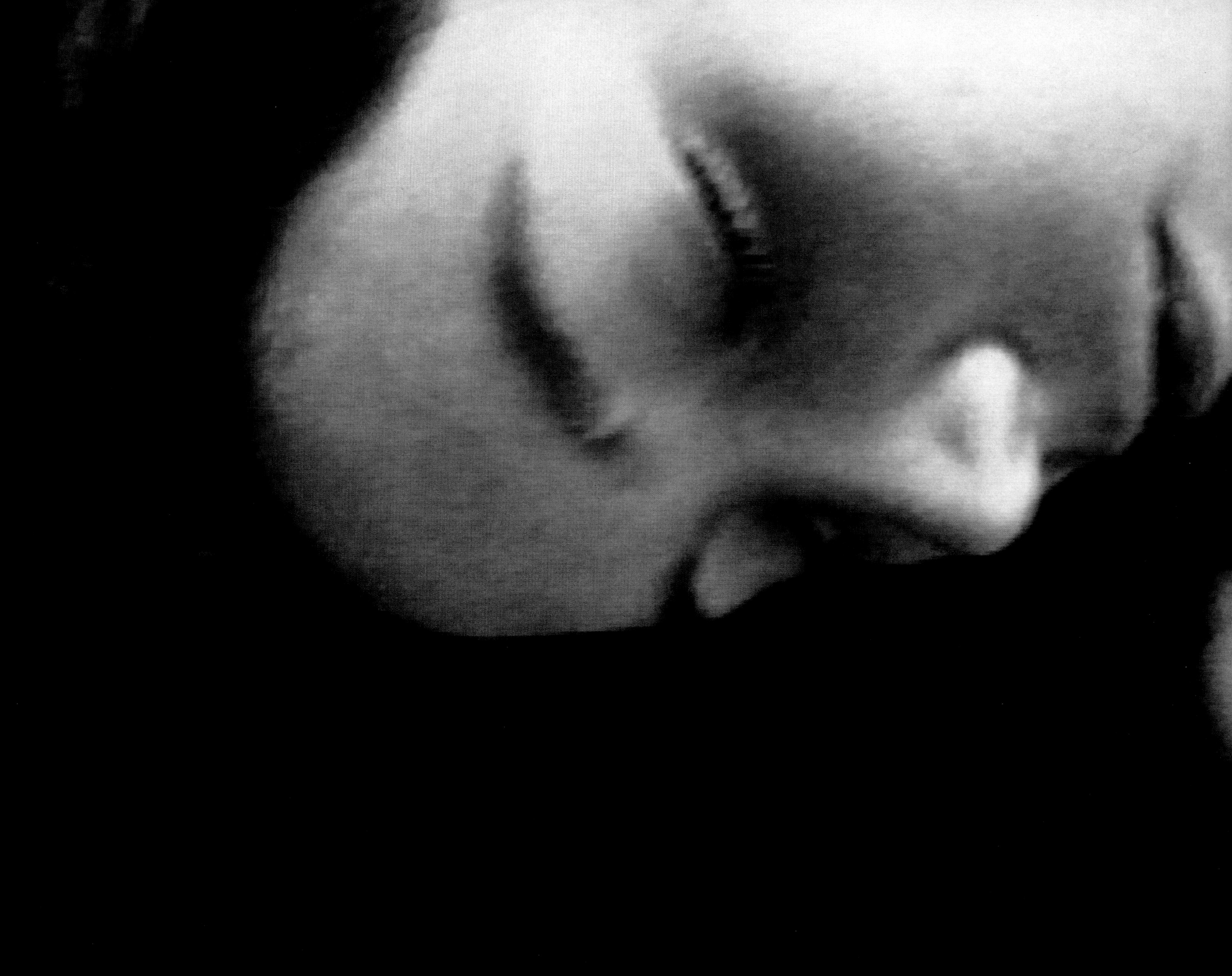

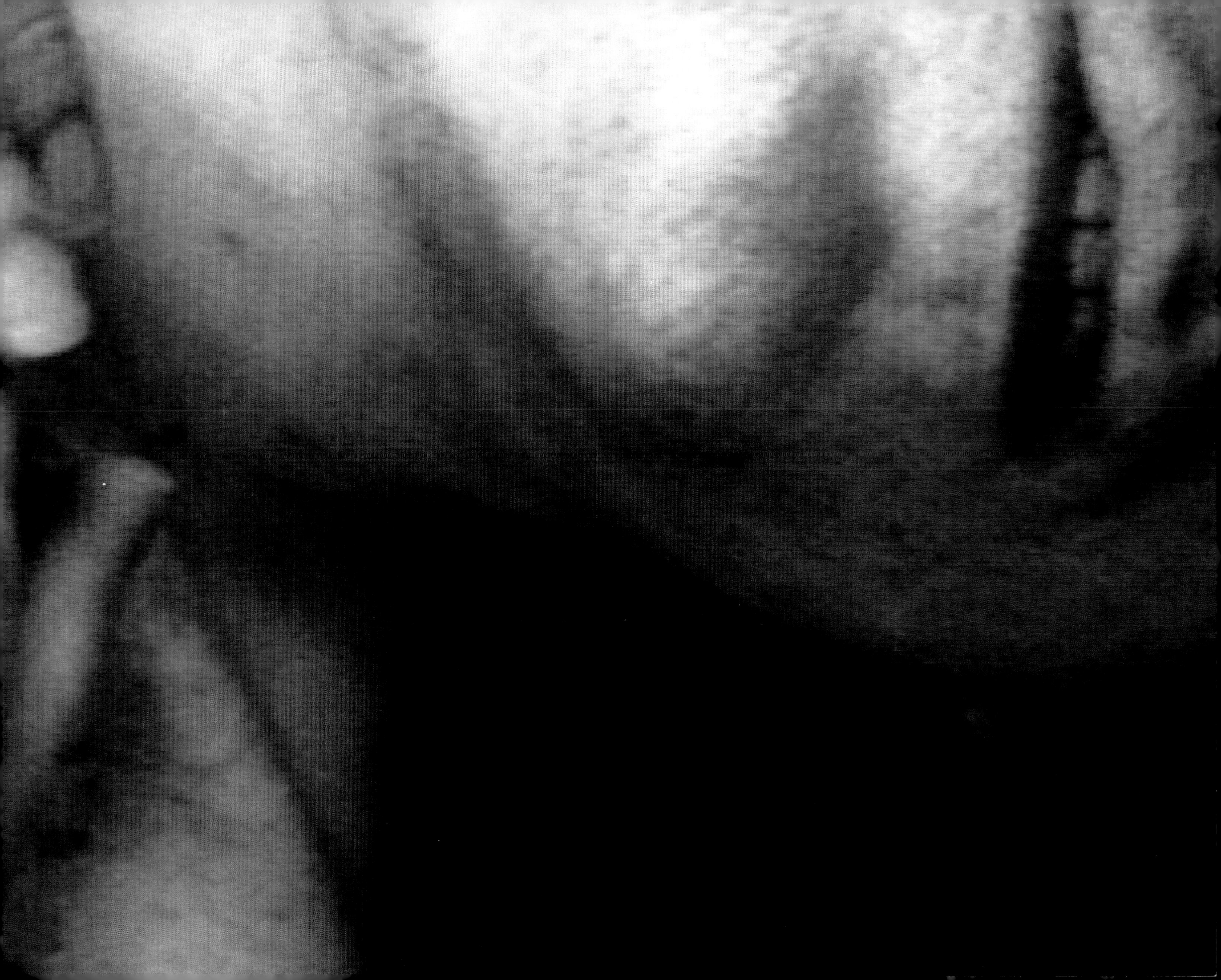

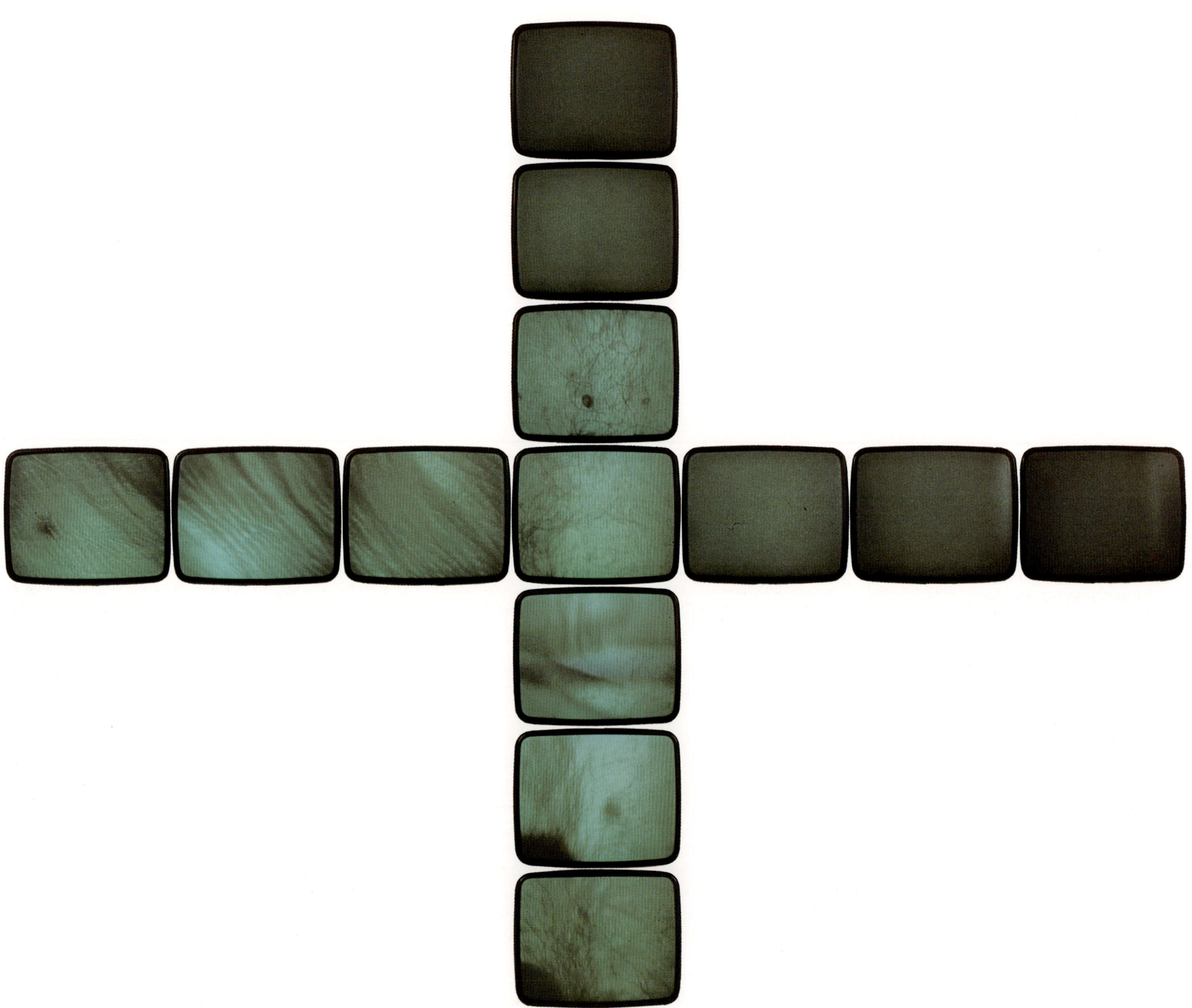

Between 1 & 0, 1993

"Anthropologists of possible selves, we are technicians of realizable futures."
Donna Haraway

Postscript: re-embodiments in alter-space

Lynne Cooke

"Images are the dominant currency of communication," Margot Lovejoy argues in her book on electronic media and postmodern culture. This has resulted, she contends, in a crisis of knowledge that is in fact a crisis of vision: "We can only see the world by forming a picture through various specialized mediations."[1] Lack of a vision adequate to the electronic datasphere has led, in turn, Scott Bukatman concludes, "to a set of allusive attempts to reconstitute the space of the computer in human—biological or physical—terms; in other words, *to permit terminal space to become phenomenal.*"[2] Among those contributing to these attempts the work of artists is seminal, he believes, quoting in support J. G. Ballard's belief that the (science fiction) writer's role is to parallel the ontological redefinitions of the electronic era: "I feel that the balance between fiction and reality has changed significantly in the past decade. Increasingly their roles are reversed. We live in a world ruled by fictions of every kind.... For the writer in particular it is less and less necessary for him to invent the fictional content of his novel. The fiction is already there. The writer's task is to invent the reality."[3]

While granting the reality of the objective world, Maurice Merleau-Ponty nonetheless stressed that it is in the interactivity that occurs between the perceptible physical object and the perceiving motile subject that consciousness is instantiated. Phenomenology thus proposes that the status of being is not an absolute condition but one that changes relative to changes in the experience of the real. Irrespective of whether electronic "presences" can be said to exist in real spaces, experience of those spaces remains a "real" experience. Thus an examination of the cognitive processes of consciousness may be accorded priority over consideration of the veracity of any given external conditions. By focusing on the activity of a guided consciousness rather than on the absolute reality of the world "in itself," it may become possible to construct a phenomenology of those abstract and nonphysical spaces peculiar to electronic technologies. From this, definitions of both the modes of communication and the forms of social interaction they make possible may be constructed.

In *Suspension of Disbelief (for Marine),* by suppressing the "willing" normally integral to this familiar phrase when titling a recent installation, Gary Hill suggests that conscious acquiescence will not be necessary: whether it is fictive or not, what is presented as real will be automatically, inevitably, even unavoidably, embraced as such. What was a goal for Ballard is for Hill, given his medium, virtually preordained. For, unlike current literature, reproductive technologies are among the principal conditioners of contemporary values and beliefs: their representations not only record objective reality but shape it to the point where they are frequently experienced as more potent than those provided by the everyday phenomenal world. As Vilèm Flusser argues, "The imagination functioning in technical images is so powerful that we not only regard these images as reality, but also live within their functions."[4]

Images of two bodies, the dominant one female, the other male, move across the screens of some thirty monitors which, stripped of their casings and attached edge to edge along a steel beam, create a potential linear continuum of electronic space. The camera has lingered lovingly on these nudes: it almost nuzzles the skin in probing their surfaces, delivering the body to the gaze with a heightened immediacy. Seldom, however, do the forms glide along the chain of monitors in a smooth, continuous flow: their passage is constantly interrupted, spliced, cut, relayed, and replayed by means of a switching mechanism. Further complicating the spectator's perception of the "lovers" is the speed at which the images travel. So rapid is their passage that it becomes impossible to focus clearly on even a single frame, to fix it and hence appropriate it. Attempts to fuse the pair as a couple are equally problematic, for the overlapping, splicing, and intercutting of their individual anatomies postulates a connection very different from the conventional one melding discrete entities into a singular whole.

The bodies never blend, join, or fuse. The skin remains an impermeable boundary even when the body is fractured, its parts overlaid and intersecting. What seems to galvanize these rapidly sequencing images is, nonetheless, a desire for proximity, a wish to suppress separation. Vividly present yet frustratingly elusive, this seductive montage of swiftly shifting shapes at once conjures notions of togetherness and simultaneously redefines them. The accelerations, reversals, slowdowns, ellipses, and fragmentary arrests within the incessant flow conjure a stream of desire—the quintessence of eroticism. While seduction plays only on the surface, and coupling remains only tenuously proximate, this nevertheless does not signify the endlessly deferred merger that characterizes frustration. A dizzying, capricious, voluptuous, and ultimately delirious swirl, *Suspension...* offers a sensuous paradigm for an ecstatic transcendence of the physicality of direct sexuality.

The intimacy which results from the camera's proximity to the bodies would seem to promise an eroticism of the kind conventionally linked to notions of voyeurism. What could have

1. Margot Lovejoy, *Postmodern Currents: Art and Artists in the Age of Electronic Media* (Ann Arbor: UMI Research Press, 1989); quoted in Scott Bukatman, *Terminal Identity: The Virtual Subject in Postmodern Science Fiction* (Durham: Duke University Press, 1993), p. 109. I am indebted to Bukatman's theses in more ways than this and the following citations indicate.

2. Ibid.

3. This statement, made in 1974 in a new preface to Ballard's 1973 novel, *Crash,* is quoted in Bukatman, op. cit., pp. 116-117.

4. Vilèm Flusser, "The Status of Images," in *Metropolis* (Berlin: Martin Gropius Bau/New York: Rizzoli, 1991), p. 53.

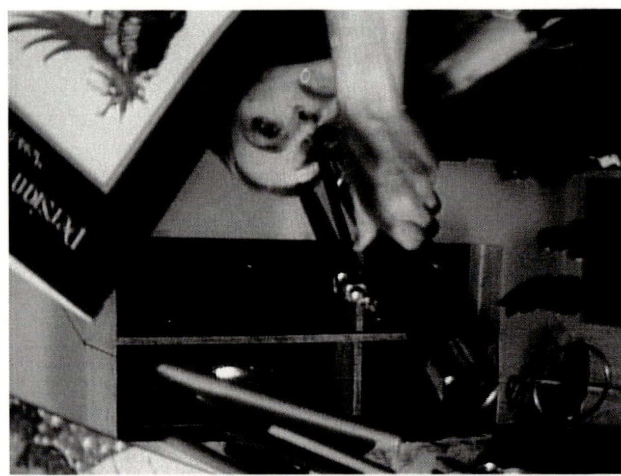

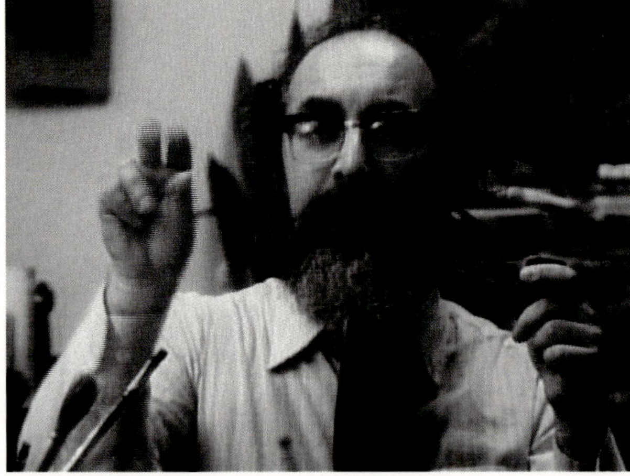

From **_Why Do Things Get in a Muddle? (Come on Petunia)_**, 1984

been private disclosures in the form of transgressive glimpses are, however, rendered spectacular by the overtly exhibitionistic presentation of the work. Far from surreptitiously revealing the clandestine, this installation has the grandeur and sweep of something deliberately devised to be seen. It offers a spectacle, in the sense that Guy Debord and others defined it: a surrogate self-contained form of reality.

The elevation of the monitors to over head height, together with the vast length of the beam, keeps the viewer back in the cavernous space of the otherwise empty room, prohibiting any physical proximity to that which is viewed. The images hover luminously in the half-light, the darkened context further enhancing their intangibility and ephemerality. Unlike previous iconic depictions of lovers suspended in a timeless optical etheria, seen, say, in paintings of Paolo and Francesca by G.F. Watts, among others, this electronically manifest duo inhabits no coherent temporal entity. Their time and space (the space of kinesis) pertain to a nonphysical realm, that of electronic technology; these are the phantasmic spaces enabled by, and constituted through, communicative technologies. "[T]ime and metaphorical spaces for texts [and subjects] to unfold are the parameters I begin with....," Gary Hill wrote recently. "It's a kind of telescopic time that makes the viewer aware of the process of seeing—of beholding the world through sight that exists in the folds of time."[5] Perception, and hence apprehension, remains rooted in bodily being, as Merleau-Ponty argued, yet that which is perceived belongs now to another reality. Vision is at once imbricated in the world and disembodied, embedded yet suspended, precluded from grasping what it surveys.

In its exclusive focus on the naked body viewed in close proximity *Suspension of Disbelief (for Marine)* (1991-92) bears comparison with *Inasmuch As It Is Always Already Taking Place* which Hill made some two years earlier. Comprised of sixteen monitors varying in size from one-half inch to twenty-one inches, installed like a reliquary in a niche in the wall, this work transmits images of different parts of the human body life-size on each of its screens. By stretching the skin across the screens like a taut membrane, and by ensuring that the limbs disclose only abstract dark spaces in their interstices, Hill makes the forms vividly present to the viewer. Juxtaposed with these details of torso, organs, and limbs is an image of a finger laid on a page of text. A barely audible soundtrack draws the spectator forward in order to hear better the murmur of a voice almost obliterated by the rustle of turning pages

5. Gary Hill, "Interviewed Interview," *Gary Hill* (Valencia: IVAM Centre del Carme, 1993), p. 152.

6. The impression it gives of hovering on the borders of intelligibility recalls Maurice Blanchot's evocative characterization: "Not speech, barely a murmur, barely a tremor, less than silence, less than the abyss of the void; the fullness of the void, something one cannot silence, occupying all of space, the uninterrupted, the incessant, a tremor and already a murmur, not a murmur but speech, and not just any speech, distinct speech, precise speech, within my reach." *Celui qui ne m'accompagnait pas* (Paris: Gallimard, 1953), quoted in *Foucault—Blanchot,* Michel Foucault, "Maurice Blanchot: The Thought from Outside" (New York: Zone, 1990), pp. 22-23.

7. *Primarily Speaking* (1981-83). In this tape, images were linked to speech in such a way that as each syllable was enunciated the picture changed. Impetus to explore this and related aspects of the technology grew out of a concern, emerging in the '70s, with investigating the specifics of the medium, a concern shared at that time by many pioneers working in this rapidly changing field of electronics. In Hill's video work from the late '70s, sound was a key element; in the early '80s it took on the guise of language and text, as well as speech.

and other ambient sounds.[6] This incessant but nearly inaudible speech finds its visual counterpart in the almost imperceptible motion of the anatomy. Such slight movement can be read as evidence simultaneously that the body is alive and that it is being observed. The act of visual interpretion can be understood as isomorphic to the reading of a text: just as reading creates the text, so seeing conjures meaning. In one of his most prophetic early works, Hill had asked "who am I but a figure of speech?"[7] This was in fact a rhetorical question, for much of the artist's work at that time was expressly focused on the generation of reality by language.[8] Subsequently, however, Hill affirmed on a number of occasions that the products of this verbal encoding may not be revelation, enlightenment or clarification, but their very obverse. As seen in *Why Do Things Get in a Muddle? (Come on Petunia), URA ARU (the backside exists), Incidence of Catastrophe* and, above all, *DISTURBANCE (among the jars)*, language only too easily unravels, dissolves, implodes, or shatters into multiple contrary pronouncements. As speech disintegrates, infantile babbling, nonsense, and glossolalia ensue, freeing the body from the restrictions of the conceptual into the sensual embrace of anatomically generated sound. Given that speech has been pulverized in *Inasmuch...* to what Hill calls "the debris of utterance," rather than incorporating the listener/viewer as it normally does, it serves now to emphasize a cleavage in communication: the body wrapped in its own "hum."[9]

Video has often been described as a medium of surface effects. The delimited scale of the monitor, together with the relatively poor resolution of the image and the constant motion of light particles all, as Jean Fisher argues, mitigate against viewers "entering" the image in ways akin to those by which they imaginatively inscribe themselves into filmic space.[10] Moreover, since deep focus translates poorly onto the screen, video operates optimally with a quite shallow depth of field. Thus instead of the viewer entering the illusory space of the recorded world, the motion and fluorescence of the photons propel the image forward so that it "invades" the observer's ambience. For most of its early avatars, Hill included, video was a medium that privileged time-based experience, with real time normally replacing the reality of actual space. Yet in his recent work Hill has steadily relinquished conventional usages and forms of time in order to explore more complex spatio-temporalities. In *Inasmuch...* he capitalizes on these potentialities to great effect. Because the hand-held camera does not alter either its focus or its position, and because the

8. Heidegger's notion, "Language is the house of being in which man dwells," has been central to much of Hill's thought, though he arrived at it via Blanchot, Ludwig Wittgenstein and other writers rather than directly through the texts of the German philosopher. For a fuller discussion see Lynne Cooke, "Gary Hill: Beyond Babel," *Gary Hill* (Valencia: IVAM Centre del Carme, 1993), pp. 163-171. That this notion has continued to be important to Hill's thinking is evident from two pieces he has made recently: the four-minute tape *Site Recite (a prologue)* (1989) and *I Believe It Is an Image in Light of the Other* (1991-92). In *Site Recite...*, language not only generates and shapes all, it threatens to consume all. For most of this tape the camera moves in a circular tracking shot that evokes an omniscient vision, or a model of a mind generating a world. During its final few seconds, however, an image of a mouth speaking, recorded from a point near the back of the tongue, is suddenly substituted for the displaced, and hence placeless, still life which had up to that moment been the sole subject under review. Its highly charged concluding statement—"imagining the brain closer than the eyes"—gives weight to Raymond Bellour's claim that "there is no visual image that is not more and more tightly gripped, even in its essential, radical withdrawal, inside an audiovisual or scriptovisual...image that envelops it." (Raymond Bellour, "The Double Helix," *Passages de l'Image* (Barcelona: Centre Cultural de la Fundacio Caixa de Pensions, 1991), p. 72. In *I Believe...* seven canisters containing monitors and lenses are suspended over open books strewn on the floor in a darkened space. Images of the body and of writing are literally overlaid so that text becomes embodied and anatomy encoded in the printed script.

9. Gary Hill, "Inasmuch As It Is Always Already Taking Place," in *OTHERWORDSANDIMAGES* (Copenhagen: Video Gallerie/Ny Carlberg Glyptotek, 1990), p. 27.

10. Jean Fisher, "V-I-D-E-O-Z-O-N-E," in *Topographie II: Untergrund* (Vienna: 1991), pp. 26-50.

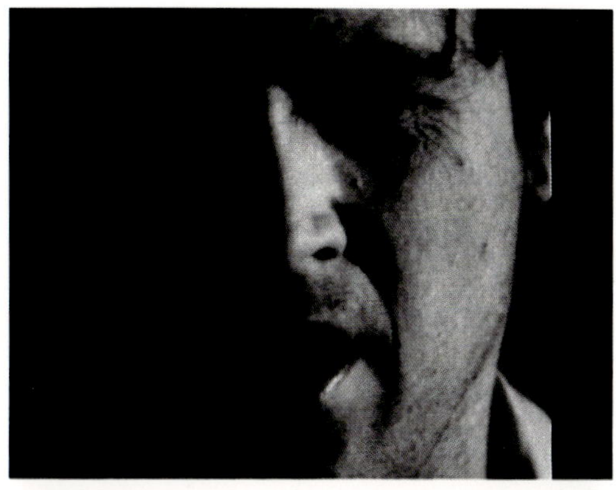

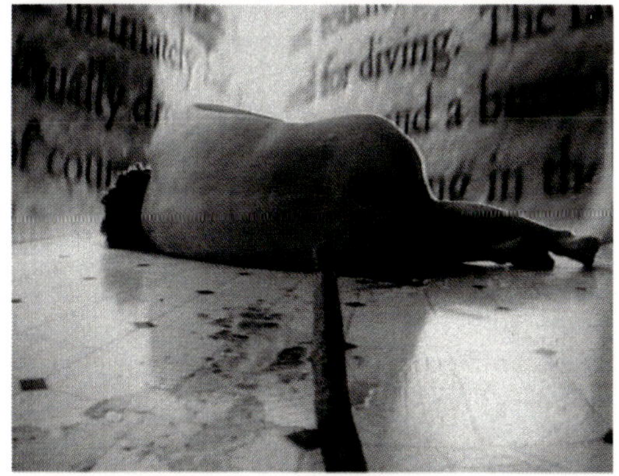

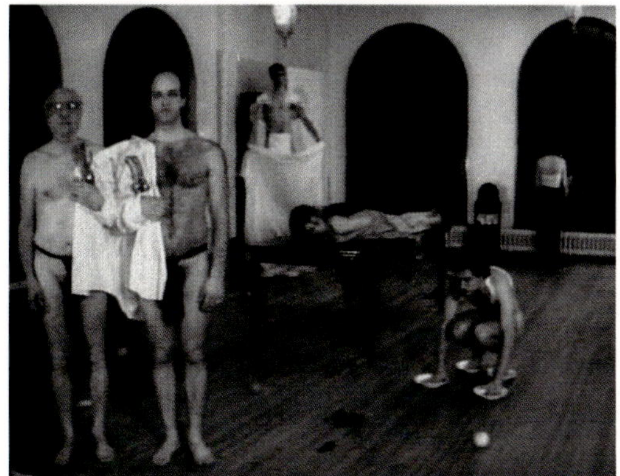

From ***Incidence of Catastrophe***, 1987-88

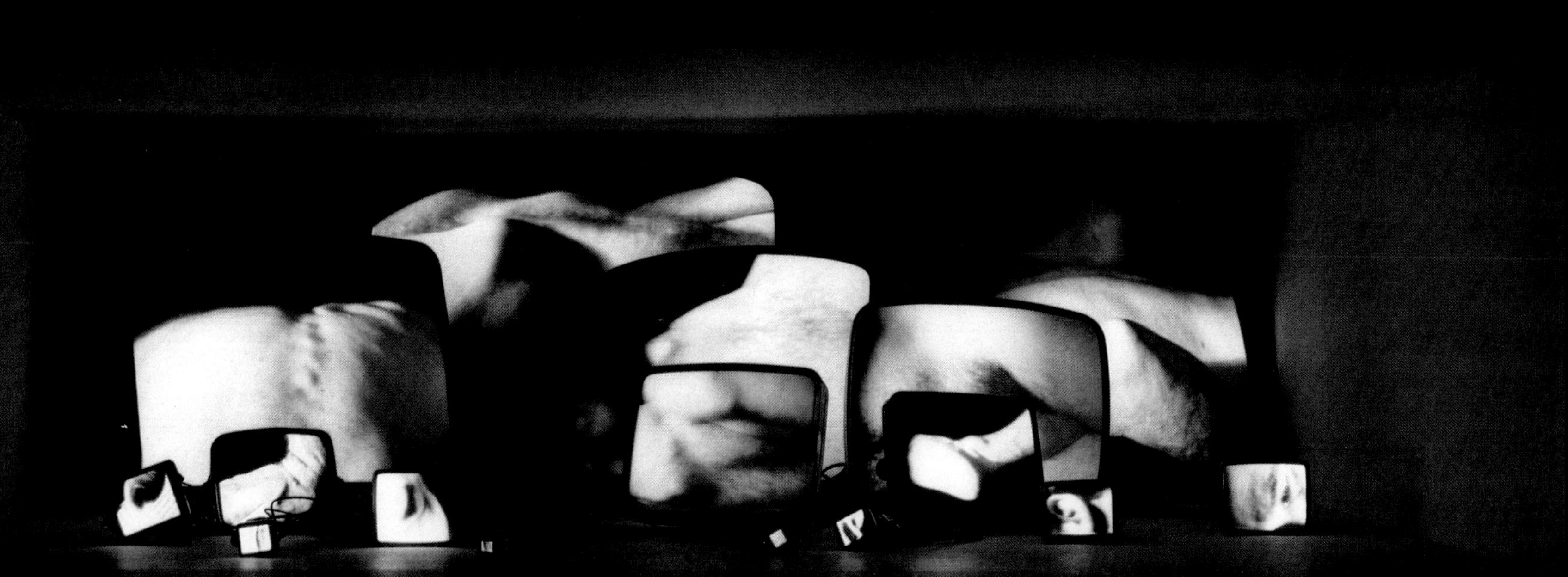

11. Gary Hill, *OTHERWORDSANDIMAGES,* op. cit., p. 27.

12. By contrast, *Site Recite,* subtitled *(a prologue),* was originally meant to be an interactive video, that is, to provide a context in which viewers could enter and move around according to their own impulses. Through a kind of phenomenological insistence, it would have been able, Hill hoped, to "make participants aware of their own mediation process." Quoted in Christine van Assche, "Interview with Gary Hill," *Galeries Magazine,* December 1990/ January 1991, p. 141.

13. Gary Hill, "Between Cinema and a Hard Place," unpublished text, 1991, unpaginated.

14. Ibid.

Inasmuch As It Is Always Already Taking Place, 1990 Museum of Modern Art, New York, 1990

recordings are continuously replayed, the flux of real time seems disconnected from the norms of daily temporality, collapsed into an eternal present. Each monitor is thus the site of the body which appears on the screens as immutably present and yet outside actual time. Its impregnable solitude reduces the viewer's role to that of mute witness at what Hill describes, disquieteningly, as "the incessant, however fragmentary, anatomical site."[11] Presence is brought to betray a haunting absence.

Hill's most recent works reveal a growing preoccupation with place, space, and time, and in particular with the kinds of spaces inhabited by or made available through the new electronic technologies. *Inasmuch*...has the proximity of a still life, but the site is not available to the body as a fully embodied agent. In *Between Cinema and a Hard Place* (1991) and, subsequently, *Suspension...* and *Tall Ships* (1992), a more fully developed interplay linking actual and visualized spaces occurs as Hill capitalizes on the spatio-temporal malleability of the electronic signal. Like *Suspension...*, *Tall Ships* has no verbal component, and so provides no possibility of overcoming estrangement via language. Projected directly onto the walls of the installation, the images have been freed into the materiality of real time and space. Walking the ninety-foot-long corridor-like space of *Tall Ships,* the spectator is confronted with life-size figures who approach (and recede) apparently to intercept the viewer's passage. But proximity fails to ensure connectedness. These sixteen figures of varying ages and sexes are first viewed from a multiplicity of vanishing points. Initially glimpsed small, as if seen at a distance, they rapidly draw near as if to effect what is the simplest of encounters, a one-to-one confrontation. As in many of Hill's previous works, relationships with the other are found necessarily to involve, if indeed they are not strictly confined to, forms of representation. On one level, such relationships might be described as projections. Here, exceptionally to date in Hill's oeuvre, the interface between the image and the actual becomes the site of potential interaction.[12]

In *Inasmuch...*, the relation between self and other is defined by the impregnable frontiers of the physical and illusory, which in this work lie at the interface between body and screen, skin and electronic surface. *Tall Ships* posits other relations by divesting the frameless continuum that is the hallmark of the video signal of its conventional physical constraint, the monitor. Whereas this might normally imperil the proximity of the image as it became absorbed into a continuous linear matrix, the fact that in this installation the projections are the sole source of light imbues them with an unexpected effect of embodiment in real space. Nonetheless, interaction cannot transgress the essential separateness of each protagonist: proximity does not vouchsafe connectedness. By contrast, *Between Cinema and a Hard Place* focuses directly on themes of division—more specifically, on frontiers in space—by setting up rapid and unpredictable movements from one kind of space to another at the same time as moving images from monitor to monitor. "Heidegger's use of nature as a metaphorical place of thought is intervened upon, with images of landscapes and pastoral scenes being interrupted by variable fencing, posted signs and other interventions of spatial temporal limits," Hill recently wrote of this work.[13] In this way various—and sometimes contradictory—levels of time are conjured.

The text and pretext for this critique of "neighboring nearness" is a passage from Heidegger's "The Nature of Language," which Hill adapted for his soundtrack. The installation comprises twenty-three monitors of varying sizes laid out irregularly on the ground. In physically occupying an indeterminate space, the piece provides an apt metaphor for an extract which the artist describes as "question[ing]a strictly parametrical view of space and time, posing the possibility of a "neighboring nearness" that does not depend on a spatial-temporal relationship."[14]

Tall Ships operates in real time and space, but with the aid of a complex technology manifests the other as an ineluctably but teasingly unreachable image in projected spaces which are nonetheless extensions of the viewer's own world. *Suspension...* and *Between 1 & 0,* by contrast, postulate very different versions of subjects imbricated in electronic technologies, and hence of the relationships—the "proximity"—they permit. For common to both *Suspension...* and *Between 1 & 0* is a form of computer switching which renders their bodily subject(s) radically unlike anything Hill had devised before. Eschewing identifications based in bodily-kinetic knowledge, Hill presents a relationship between the self and the other that is irremediably based in exteriority. In his early works this self is rendered locked in an essential solitude, to borrow a phrase from Maurice Blanchot who has been an important influence. Recently the impenetrable solitude which, for him as for Blanchot, lies at the heart of consciousness has begun to be re-examined as the body is inserted into the different kinds of non-Cartesian space facilitated by electronic technology. Precluded from inscribing him or her self into the novel spatio-temporal geographies which Hill devises (unlike many others working with virtual space who simulate actual space), the spectator is brought

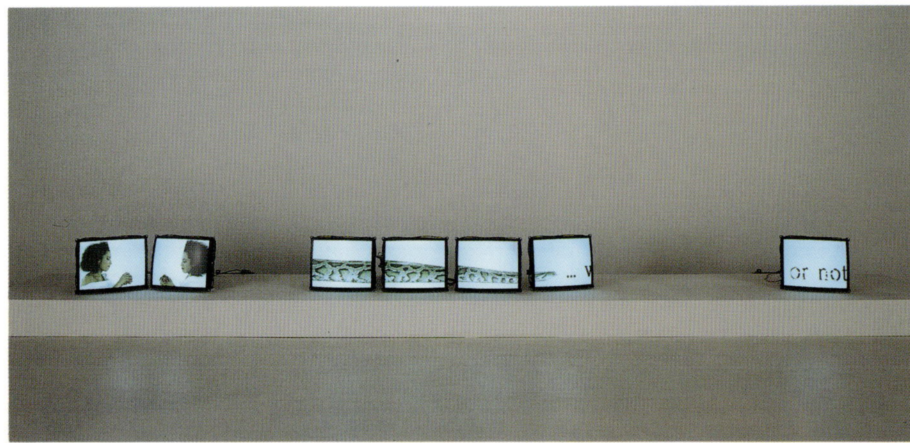

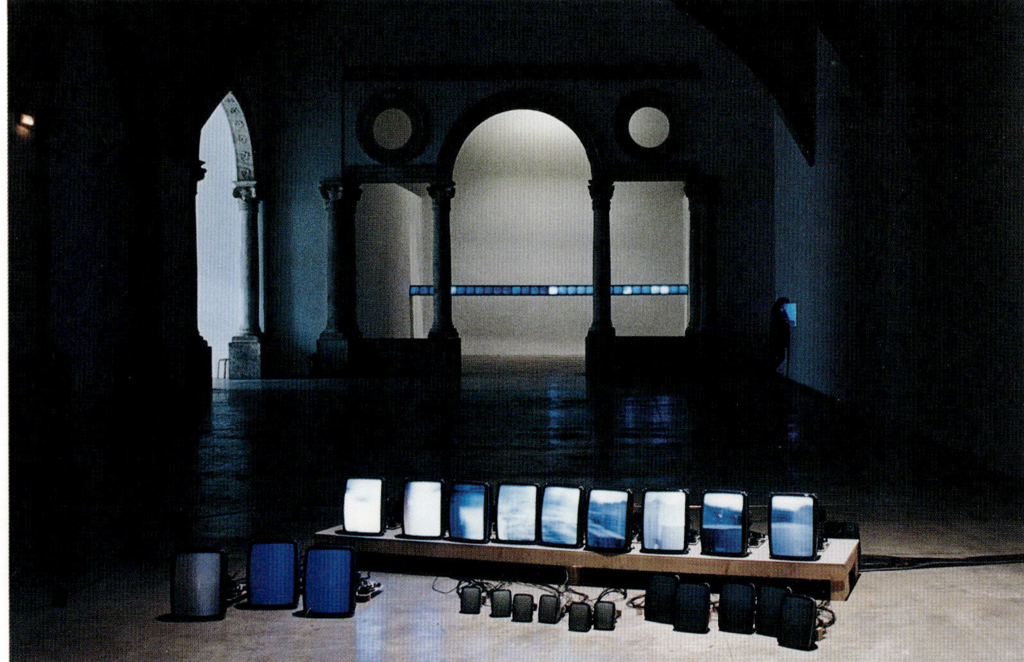

DISTURBANCE (among the jars), 1988 Centre Georges Pompidou, Paris, 1992

Between Cinema and a Hard Place, IVAM Centre del Carme, Valencia, Spain, 1993, in background *Suspension of Disbelief (for Marine)*

into an unfamiliar and uncertain proximity with the subject. Relaying images across banks of monitors in rapid but not necessarily linear succession, the switching mechanism creates a mode of temporality that has little to do with actual time, that is, with time lived (or recorded as in live relay). Likewise, the spaces opened in these works, if and when continuous, do not have the coordinates of Cartesian space. In this way Hill's fragmentation and multiplication of bodily imagery in phantasmic spaces may be read as conforming to current notions of social identity in the technological era. In adopting such strategies of visualization, these works open to scrutiny the "spatio-temporal" zones of electronic sociality.

Vivian Sobchack's perceptive article, "The Scene of the Screen: Towards a Phenomenology of Cinematic and Electronic Presence," provides an invaluable discussion of the ontology of this kind of visual space.[15] In exploring the phenomenological distinctions that separate photographic, cinematic, and electronic "presences," she argues that only the space of the last is discrete, ahistoric, and disembodied. A record of human vision and presence, the photograph depicts a frozen moment from the past. In its immutability it, as Merleau-Ponty notes, "keeps open the instants which the onrush of time closes up forthwith; it destroys the overtaking, the overlapping, the 'metamorphosis'... of time."[16] Cinema enacts a present-time experience of physical, bodily spatial reality. Very different again is digital electronic technology which "atomizes and *abstractly schematizes* the analogic quality of the photographic and cinematic into discrete *pixels* and *bits* of information that are transmitted *serially,* each bit discontinuous, discontiguous, and absolute—each bit 'being-in-itself' even as it is part of a system."[17] In *Suspension...* the scale of the electronic band is that of a cinema screen. Through the close alignment of the frames an almost filmic sense of connectedness in space/time is hypothetically established. Moreover, on at least one occasion in the cycle, a single shot moves continuously from monitor to monitor, creating a spatial analogue for the cinematic flow of frame after frame. Yet, ultimately, these allusions serve only to make more apparent the distinctiveness of the spatio-temporal matrices of electronic technology.

In *Between 1 & 0,* thirteen monitors are grouped on a wall in a configuration that resembles a plus sign. The viewer is confronted with a subject which is locked in what seems to be an unfinishable process of writing itself—literally *and* figuratively writing itself. Literally in the sense of employing codes integral to that system, and metaphorically in several ways. Although not easily identified precisely, the soundtrack (made by graphite scratching a sheet of paper) is obviously of something scraping itself along a surface, etching itself into existence. And the backwards and forwards movement of the frames on the sign may be likened to the process of beginning a sketch: the pen hovers, wavering, over the ground, searching for the proper point at which to begin the process of definition.

"[E]lectronic space," Sobchack writes, "constructs objective and superficial equivalents to depth, texture and invested bodily movement.... [C]onstant action and 'busyness' replace the gravity which grounds and orients the movement of the lived-body with a purely spectacular, kinetically exciting, and often dizzying, sense of bodily freedom (and freedom from the body)."[18] Devoid of center and ground, these phantasmic spaces have at best only a vector graphic simulation of perspective to guide a human eye that has become distinct from its corporeality, its spatiality, its temporality, and its subjectivity. In *Between 1 & 0,* as in *Suspension...*, Hill constructs a disembodied space in place of a Cartesian one: "machinic" images spin across a field voided of spatio-temporal metrics in a vertiginous display of their very depthlessness.

No rapport connecting viewer and projection of the kind initially proposed in *Tall Ships* is possible in *Between 1 & 0.* But neither is there that divorce of the spectator inherent in the spectacle found in *Suspension....* In fact, this is not an installation, properly speaking: the work is best seen as a transmission *tout court.* Phenomenologically, the electronic is experienced as a discrete and simultaneous transmission, Sobchack argues, for "The materiality of the electronic digitalizes *durée* and situation so that narrative, history, and a centered (and central) investment in the lived body become atomized and dispersed across a system that constitutes temporality not as a *flow of conscious experience,* but as the *transmission of random information.*" The primary value of electronic temporality is thus the instant, she concludes: "Temporality becomes paradoxically constituted as a *homogeneous* experience of *discontinuity* in which the temporal distinctions between objective and subjective experience... disappear, and time seems to turn back on itself in a structure of equivalence and reversibility." Similarly, the nature of the space experienced is redefined, disembodied: "Without the temporal emphases of historical consciousness and personal history, space also becomes abstract, ungrounded and flat—a site for *play* and *display* rather than an invested situation in which action 'counts.'"[19]

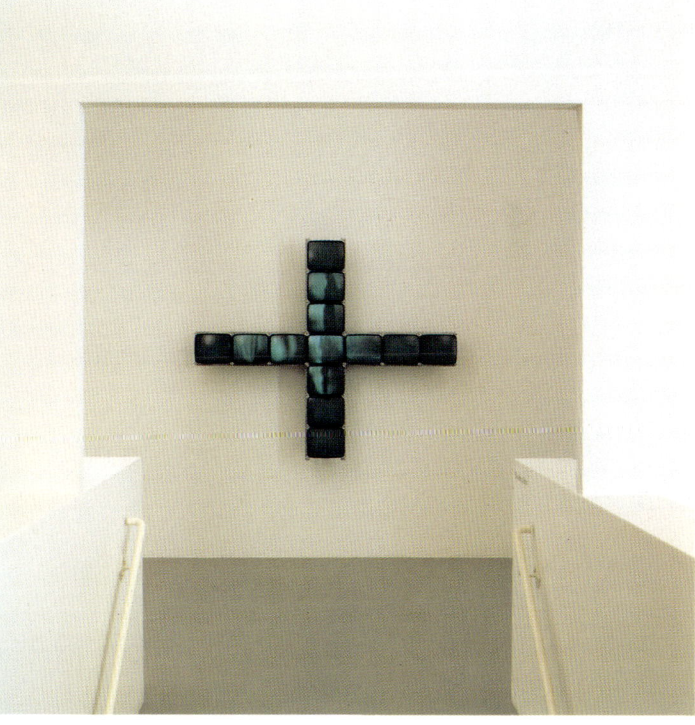

Between 1 & 0, 1993

15. Vivian Sobchack, "The Scene of the Screen: Towards a Phenomenology of Cinematic and Electronic Presence," *Post-Script,* 10, 1990, pp. 50-59.

16. Maurice Merleau-Ponty, "Eye and Mind," in *The Primacy of Perception*, ed. James M. Edie (Evanston: Northwestern University Press, 1964), p. 186.

17. Sobchack, op. cit., p. 56.

18. Sobchack, op. cit., pp. 57-58.

19. Sobchack, op. cit., p. 57.

In *Between 1 & 0,* as befits a relationship with a sign, or matrix, the physical relation inherent in the phenomenology of perception has been abstracted, and temporality destabilized. Yet as in *Suspension...*, seeing remains a highly participatory activity as the spectator relentlessly scans this configuration trying vainly to compress the whirling shards of information into a whole.

If in *Inasmuch...* Hill disembodied the self, and in *CRUX* (1983-87) decentered it, in *Between 1 & 0* he might be said to have dismantled it. So rapidly do the microcosmic fragments of the body seen in closeup course across, and up and down, the surfaces of the monitors that it is difficult to identify them—with the notable exception of the teeth, whose intermittent yet recurrent presence reveals the program to be a circular one, one seemingly without beginning or end, origin or conclusion. Given the title as well as the interplay between absence and presence on the screens, several of which receive only a single frame lasting one-thirtieth of a second, this subject might be said to have been written literally in the coding of electronic technologies. Yet in being resolutely "between," the fragments could be said to refuse a unitary identity. *"Between* things does not designate a localizable relation going from one thing to another and back again, but a perpendicular direction, a transversal movement that sweeps one *and* the other away, a stream without beginning or end that undermines its banks and picks up speed in the middle," write Gilles Deleuze and Felix Guattari in their chapter in *A Thousand Plateaus: Capitalism and Schizophrenia* devoted to the "Body without Organs" (BwO).[20] Their discussion has great pertinence for Hill's piece, whose subject too is always in the process of becoming, and so precludes any straightforward way of conceptualizing it. For them the BwO is unattainable: it is a limit that is never reached, with no point of origin and no fundaments. Instead, "it proceeds from the middle, through the middle, coming and going rather than starting and finishing."[21] To establish a "logic of the AND" it overthrows ontology, and so it "is not at all a notion or a concept but a practice, [a] set of practices." They contend: "The modes are everything that comes to pass: waves and vibrations, migrations, thresholds and gradients, intensities produced in a given type of substance starting from a given matrix."[22] The better to illustrate this, they cite a passage from William Burroughs' *Naked Lunch* which (coincidentally) parallels the imagery seen on Hill's screen in striking fashion: "No organ is constant as regards either function or position,... sex organs sprout anywhere,... the entire organism changes color and consistency in split-second adjustments."[23] But equally apposite is their contention that: "There are not organs in the sense of fragments in relation to a lost unity, nor is there a return to the undifferentiated in relation to a differentiated totality. There is a distribution of intensive principles of organs, with their positive indefinite articles, within a collectivity or multiplicity, inside an assemblage, and according to machinic connections operating on a BwO."[24] Thus, in the BwO "flows of intensity, their fluids, their fibers, their continuums and conjunctions of affects" replace the world of the unitary, centered subject.[25]

The body has traditionally been construed in manifold ways: as self, as historical object, as organic substrate. It is in terms of the third of these constructs that it has been most extensively examined in recent theory—tellingly, theory which situates it in relation to technology. Yet assessments of the value, implications, and consequences of the new electronic technologies remain in contention. For all their great differences, two of the most influential theorists of this discourse, Jean Baudrillard and Donna Haraway, are united in their recognition of the enveloping and determining parameters of a fully technologized existence that has forced a crisis around untenable definitions of the human, rendering technology and the human no longer dichotomized. Through the interface between technology and the human subject, new technological modes of being in the world are emerging, along with reconceptions of the subject as one in whom human and technology are coextensive, codependent, and mutually defining. In *Between 1 & 0,* Hill's body/subject/self may be said to have become a cyborg.[26]

In her suggestive article, titled "Virtual Systems," Allucquère Roseanne Stone charts the transforming effects of the new technologies on the character and locus of the social arenas of Western industrialized societies. In character, this has meant, she argues, "a change from individual or group interaction, which implied physical presence, to decentered and fragmented communication whose nature and quality took on rapidly shifting and fundamentally novel forms. In locus, it meant a shift from a physical space [to one] whose geographical coordinates resist traditional modes of representation."[27] "The kind and quality of human interactions created by these shifts—interactions of a character quite unrecognizable from the standpoint of geographically located agoras—have been described [and explored] in many different ways," she contends.[28] When manifest as interactive computer systems, they offer possibilities for a novel sociality that has been eagerly appropriated by a broad spectrum

20. Gilles Deleuze and Felix Guattari, *A Thousand Plateaus: Capitalism and Schizophrenia* (Minneapolis: University of Minneapolis Press, 1987), p. 25.

21. Ibid.

22. Ibid, p. 153.

23. Ibid.

24. Ibid, pp. 164-165.

25. Ibid, p. 162.

26. In her now celebrated text, "A Cyborg Manifesto: Science, Technology and Socialist-Feminism in the Late Twentieth Century," Haraway starts from the premise that the cyborg (a term she analyzes at length) literalizes the inseparability of the human and machine in a symbiosis of body and technology from which she formulates a potential utopian future for this mythic state of being, one which will elude those racial, gendered, and class-based dichotomies that have lain at the very heart of western culture. Donna J. Haraway, "A Cyborg Manifesto: Science, Technology, and Socialist-Feminism in the Late Twentieth Century," reprinted in *Simians, Cyborgs, and Women: The Reinvention of Nature* (New York: Routledge, Chapman and Hall, Inc., 1991), pp. 149-182.

27. Allucquère Roseanne Stone, "Virtual Systems," in *Incorporations,* eds. Jonathan Crary and Sanford Kwinter (New York: Zone, 1992), p. 609.

28. Ibid.

of interests ranging from the military, to institutions of psychology and education, and business. Among notable explorations in the fictive realm are those by the inventors of computer games, writers of science fiction film and literature, and visual artists working with multimedia.

Whether or not they dwell in "real" or "fictional" systems, the inhabitants of these technosocial spaces are new kinds of beings with whom interaction may be not only novel but, perhaps, transformative. For, as Stone argues, such exchange contains "the potential for emergent behavior, for new social forms that arise in a circumstance in which 'body,' 'meeting,' 'place,' and even 'space' mean things quite different from our accustomed understanding."[29] The binaries—1/0, plus/minus, etc.—which rewrite the body in computer code simultaneously redefine it, offering potent alternatives to the bounded individual as the standard social unit and validated social actant. For the subject in virtual systems may become uncoupled (from the living body), ungrounded, constituted solely through communication technologies. The history of such technologies is therefore one of tensions between selves and bodies, as the play of their interactions, separations, and fusions constantly broadens. Once the authorizing body can be manifested through technological prosthetics, agency in these spaces becomes proximate. This, in turn, entails, Stone contends, "that as these prosthetics become more complex, the relationship between agency and authorizing body becomes more discursive."[30]

For optimistic theorists like Haraway and Stone, "virtual systems and the social worlds they imply are examples of the flexible and lively adaptations that persons seeking community are beginning to explore."[31] They discern a potential range of innovative solutions to prevailing constraints in social interaction, whereas Hill's vision of these communicative capacities seems at present more ambivalent. His version of their erotic capability, adumbrated in *Suspension...* may be lyrical, just as his refiguring of the subject in *Between 1 & 0* apparently offers the cyborg a liberating "schizo" mode (in the sense outlined by Deleuze and Guattari), yet his embrace of the simulated remains qualified. At the heart of his doubt lies an ongoing struggle with the question of what the differences in our relationships with the simulated and the actual amount to. His refusal of any prescriptive answer suggests that these recent works are likely to prove but prologues to further reworkings of the structure of sociality and more detailed mappings of the geography of elsewheres.

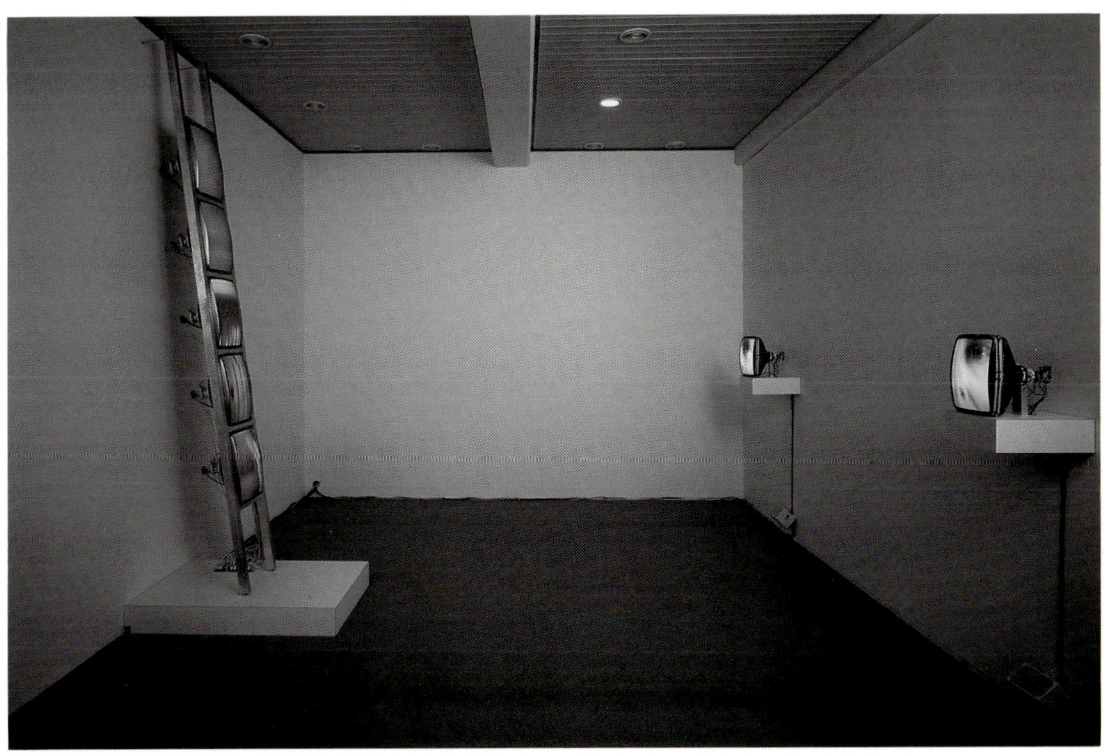

House of Cards, 1993

29. Ibid, p. 610.

30. Ibid, p. 616.

31. Ibid, p. 620.

Lynne Cooke is curator at the Dia Center for the Arts in New York. She was cocurator of the 1991 Carnegie International and cocurator of *Double Take: Collective Memory and Current Art* (London and Vienna). She writes frequently on contemporary art.

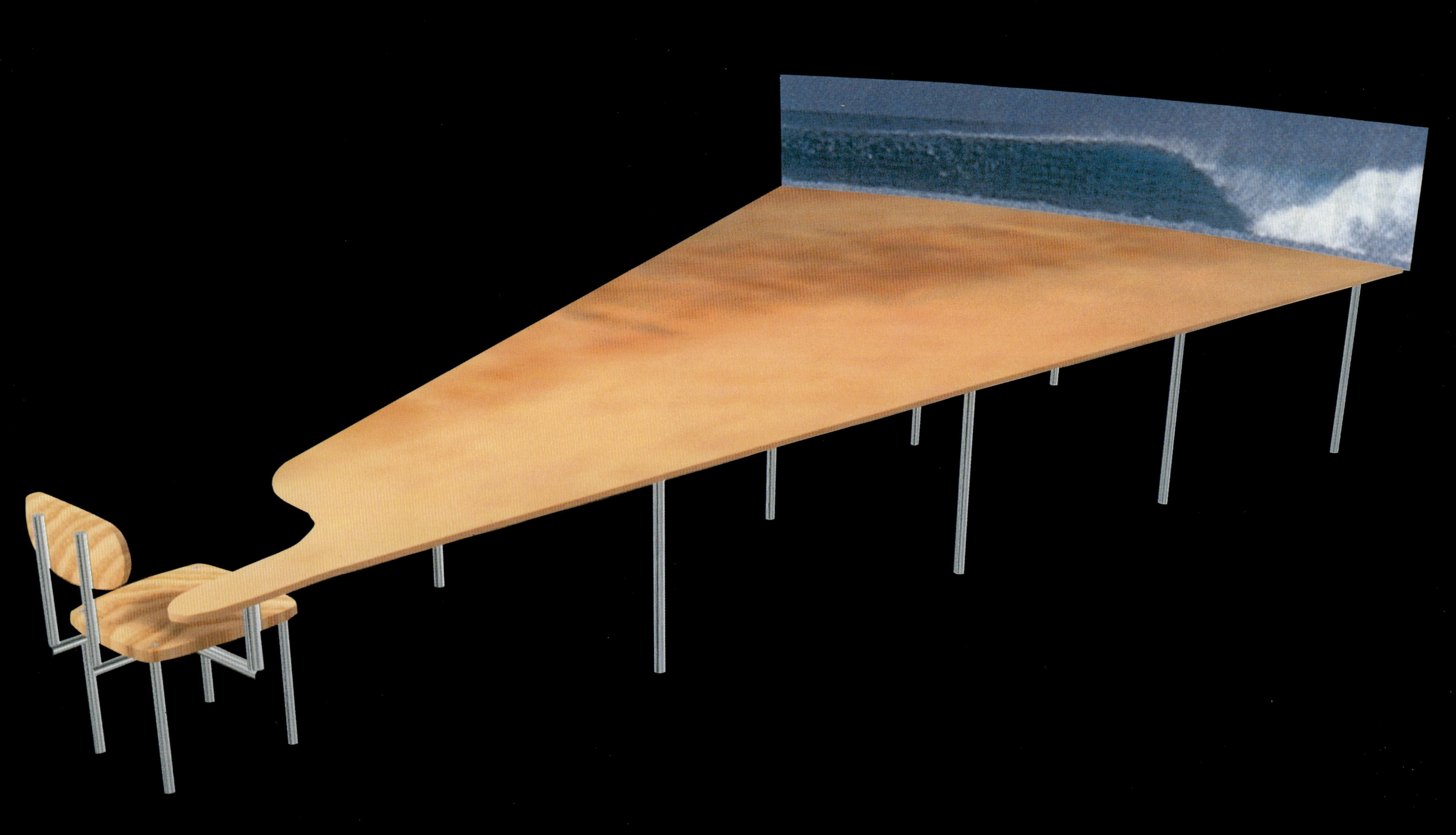

Standing Still on the Lip of Being: Gary Hill's *Learning Curve*

Robert Mittenthal

In his preface to the monograph titled *Surfing The Medium,* Gary Hill reveals his surfing roots and acknowledges the presence of "the surfing mind" in many of his works. A *surfing mind* may sound a bit "kooky" to the uninitiated, but it does make sense in relation to the way Hill describes surfing's "green room": It is the moment of ecstasy—being inside the question that asks of itself while revealing itself. This process of immanent revealing is what drives Hill. From the chaos of ocean, waves are revealed. This is as religious as Hill gets. He has educated himself in the reading of these revelations.

When the surfer stands and looks down the face of the wave he knows he is on the way to being there. He is lifted in the process of entering the extant question of Being. It is not about whether he makes it to the green room or not, for it is all grounded in the process of becoming with the wave. Is not the television display with its spray of information another green room of sorts that we've lost control of, that has "closed out"? (The surfing term for waves that are too big for a particular location and collapse without any form.)[1]

Hill's description of the green room is linked to Heidegger's notion of clearing, that moment when the "obscuring curtain of things" is lifted. Indeed, Hill opens the preface with a quote that foregrounds his involvement with Heidegger. These first few words from Marshall McLuhan would make a fitting tabloid headline: "Heidegger surfboards along on the electronic wave as triumphantly as Descartes rode the mechanical wave." In "becoming with the wave," Hill tucks Heidegger under arm and heads out into the electronic surf.

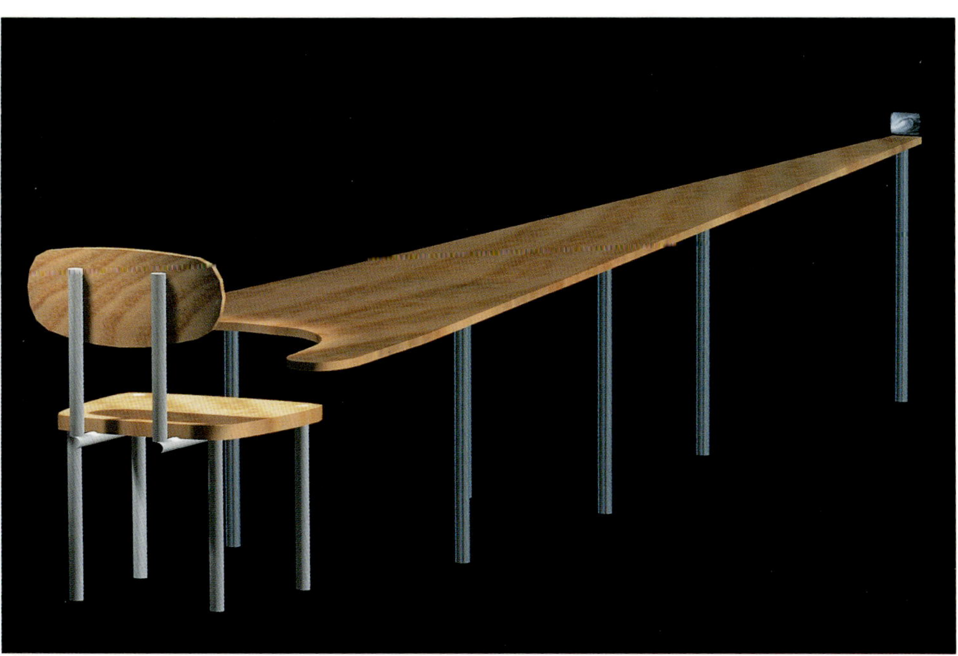

Learning Curve (Still Point), 1993
computer generated model

With *Learning Curve,* Hill is trying virtually to enact that perfect wave that "appears to stand frozen in its own becoming as if it were requesting existence from the world." Hill has designed an industrial-strength school chair to support a huge desktop that resembles a desert or beach, rising up and out till it reaches a curved wall that forms the horizon-line for a looped projection of a seemingly endless breaking wave. The expanse of whitish stained wood emphasizes the separation between viewer and image, between the material (chair) and the immaterial (wave image).

Besides the obvious reference to surfing, *Learning Curve* puns on the slide-in functionality of the school chair, which wraps around the student in a suggestive curve and, if viewed from above, resembles a cross-section of a wave. While a *learning curve* is a projection or quantification of how quickly someone will be able to acquire a particular skill or ability, video feedback resembles

1. Gary Hill, preface to Stephen Sarrazin's *Surfing The Medium* (Montbéliard: Chimaera Monograph No. 10, Edition du Centre International de Création Vidéo Montbéliard, Belfort, 1992), p. 9. All unfootnoted citations are from pages 8 and 9.

Opposite page
Learning Curve, 1993
computer generated model

a kind of *learning* in that it involves a dialogue between being and becoming. Hill describes this nearly instantaneous feedback loop as a "near future" that simultaneously absents and makes present the camera's subject.

Learning Curve has an imposing presence which calls up particular narrative associations. To students forced to sit through hour after hour in room after room, the school classroom can become a kind of dystopia, whose artificial, imposed structure can only be overcome by the mind. Faced with *Learning Curve,* one might think of an interactive video game, but here, instead of losing oneself in the thrill of trying to survive in a rigidly rule-governed visual space, we are faced with an image of relentless steadiness. There is no game and no diversion, only a kind of confrontation between chair and wave. One may well wonder: something is there, but is anything happening?

To sit in *Learning Curve* is to become part of the piece; one is physically supported by the same object that focuses one's attention on the pure visual space of the projected wave. The chair forces the viewer into a single-point perspective, where time seems slowed down. Conversely, speed is exactly what television relies upon to eliminate the time to think. In *Learning Curve,* sensory diversions are minimized, so that one's perception of the wave easily becomes abstracted or estranged. Heidegger suggests that in order to see the truth in mere things, just such an abstraction is necessary.

Much closer to us than all sensations are the things themselves. We hear the door shut in the house and never hear acoustical sensations or even mere sounds. In order to hear a bare sound we have to listen away from things, divert our ear from them, i.e., listen abstractly.[2]

This renewal of perception is at the heart of Heidegger's claims about art. However, Hill is not interested in renewing the viewer's perception of a wave, nor in helping us see what makes the wave *wavy.* Rather, Hill wants the viewer to see something else, to find a mental path, any mental path, but not one that he would want to predict or dictate.

If we are able to see the wave abstractly, we may be, after Heidegger, *on the way to thinking.* The desktop physically connects the viewer to the projection of the wave at the same time as it separates him or her from it. Sitting in the frame of this chair, another perceptual frame opens; one enters the ground of the piece, where seeing can become "a sort of touch...a *contact* at a distance."[3] If *Learning Curve* is about anything, perhaps it is about

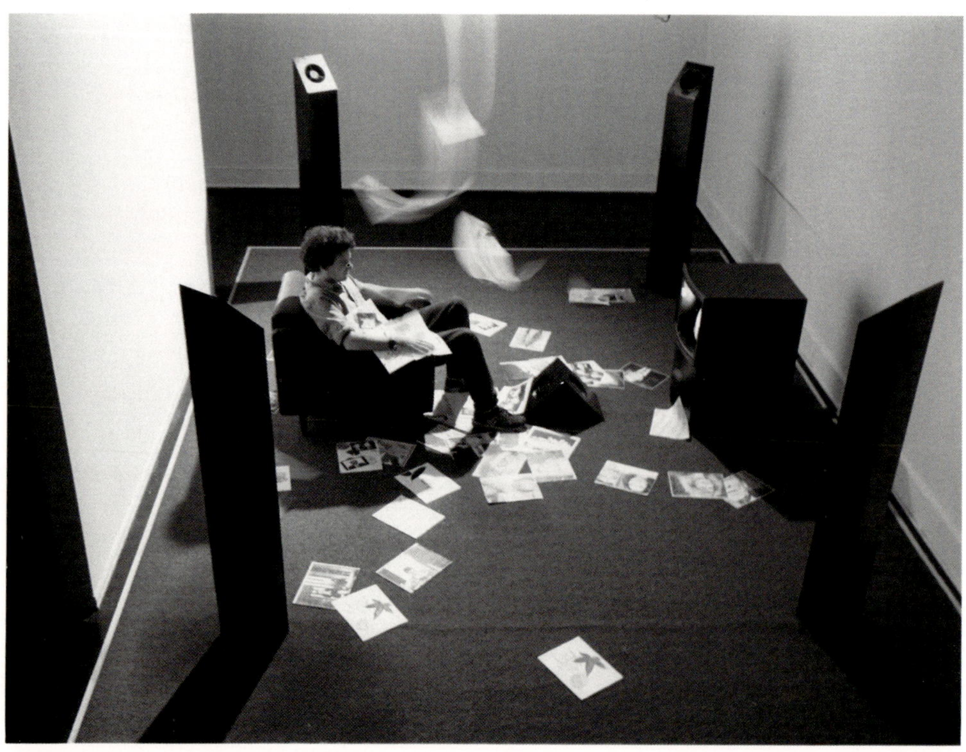

In Situ, 1986
Cornish College of the Arts, Seattle

2. Martin Heidegger, "The Origin of the Work of Art," in *Basic Writings* (New York: Harper & Row, 1977), p. 156.

3. Maurice Blanchot, *The Gaze of Orpheus* (Barrytown, N.Y.: Station Hill Press, 1981), p. 75.

one's ability to read and write one's self. Those who insist only on *looking* will likely be baffled and disappointed.

The second piece of the series, *Learning Curve (Still Point),* uses the same school chair design, this time with an extended desktop that narrows to a point, resembling an old fashioned surfing long-board. In what from some perspectives seems an optical illusion, a disproportionately small monitor sits precariously out on the toe of the board, spitting light out at us from an image of the green room. One imagines a California schoolboy daydreaming of surfing, suddenly called upon to answer one of his teacher's queries. *Still Point* suggests the physical motion of standing to answer. If the secret of poetry is, to paraphrase poet Charles Olson, learning to dance sitting down, one can say that *Still Point* invites us to leap upon the desktop and ride our minds wherever they might take us.

The third piece in this series, *Learning Curves,* is a proposed installation at the École Nationale Supérieur de Mécanique et Aérotechnique in Poitiers, France. Hill has designed an extended desktop that will connect four or five chairs similar to those used in the first two pieces. However, unlike the flat surfaces of these desktops, here the desktop will be shaped by the interactions of the various chair-sites. Hill proposes to make an analogue for the complexity of wave currents. There will be one monitor for each chair to serve as a mirror for the viewer to contemplate. According to Hill, the perspective each chair provides is to be isolated from the other chairs' perspectives. This echoes Maurice Blanchot's fascination with the solitary gaze. Hill wants to elicit an interminable gaze, "when what is seen imposes itself on your gaze, as though the gaze has been seized, touched, put in contact with appearance. . . ."[4]

This is not the first time Hill has used a single-point perspective in an installation. In *In Situ* (1986), he positioned a monitor, speakers, four fans and a spotlight so that they focused on a single armchair. The chair invites the viewer with a curious "too-small" seat cushion, as if this cushion were a frame within the larger frame of another armchair. Photocopies of images from the video float down to an area rug, which is cut to match the dimensions of a television monitor. The videotape begins with images of Hill's eye blinking, as if something horrible had entered it. Images of Hill reading, trying to eat, are interrupted by a loss of equilibrium. As if tumbling off a wave, Hill falls, pulling a tablecloth with everything on it down with him. Voices from the then-current Iran-Contra hearings are slowed down so that they seem disembodied. When the monitor switches off unexpectedly, we are left in silence, looking at ourselves in the reflection of the empty tube, the remnants of the "news" on the floor around us. When the video suddenly returns, it is each time in a smaller frame.

In Situ goes to great lengths to physically confront the viewer with various events, from the shrinking start/stop news images on the monitor, to the paper erratically jettisoned and blown around the room by the fans, to a sound source hidden beneath the seat cushion. Forcing the viewer to see where she sits, *In Situ* literally jars her out of the seat. In contrast to this framing frenzy, *Learning Curve* employs far less aggressive means to alienate the viewer. Creating an immobility that he hopes will fascinate and/or disturb us, Hill pursues what Blanchot calls the "ultimate form of communitarian experience, after which there will be nothing left to say, because it has to know itself by ignoring itself."[5] Mirroring the viewer's position, *Learning Curve* and *Still Point* provide sites for thinking, inviting us to lose ourselves in our own gaze.

In Michael Snow's film *Wavelength,* the camera takes a real-time plunge into a photograph of waves. This sudden climax occurs when, after more than one-half hour, the picture frame finally reaches the water, leaving the viewer gasping for air. Conversely, *Learning Curve* resists any sudden climax, presenting a wave ceaselessly curling toward us. Hill's *Learning Curve* series invokes a steady state, all middle ground, where there is no beginning or end, where there is no climax (or all climax).

Hill's suspicion of visuality is an undercurrent in many of his works: "If I have a position, it's to question the privileged place that image, and for that matter sight, hold in our consciousness."[6] Like the Greeks, we tend to think of understanding as a kind of seeing. While most video disembodies sight, relying on the image to titillate the viewer, Hill foregrounds the physical *seeing* of the image. He would remind us that the eye is flesh and that the body is both perceiver and perceived, both subject and object. This separates him from those who, after Blake, enamored of the image, pursue a kind of *received* or visionary experience. Against Blake's infinite Vision, Hill proposes that we imagine "the brain closer than the eyes."[7]

Robert Mittenthal is a poet and critic living in Seattle. His most recent book of poems, *Martyr Economy,* was published by Sprang Texts in Vancouver, B.C.

4. Ibid, p. 75.

5. Maurice Blanchot, *The Unavowable Community* (Barrytown, N.Y.: Station Hill Press, 1988), p. 25.

6. Interview with Stephen Sarrazin, in *Surfing The Medium,* op. cit., p. 84.

7. Gary Hill, *Site Recite* script, quoted in *Gary Hill* (Paris: Editions du Centre Pompidou, 1992), p. 32. Hill's reference to "dormitories of perception" in this text plays off of Blake's "doors of perception."

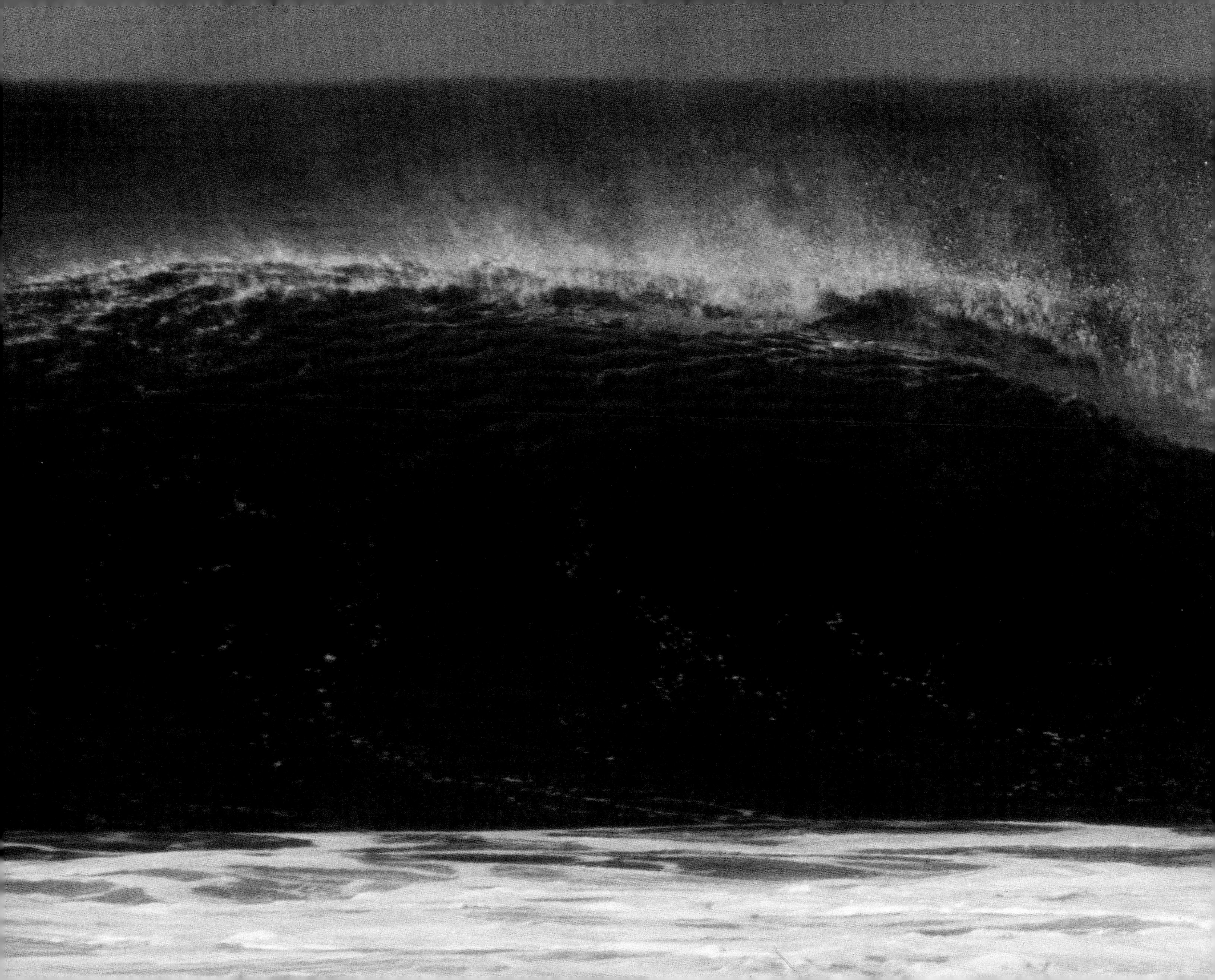

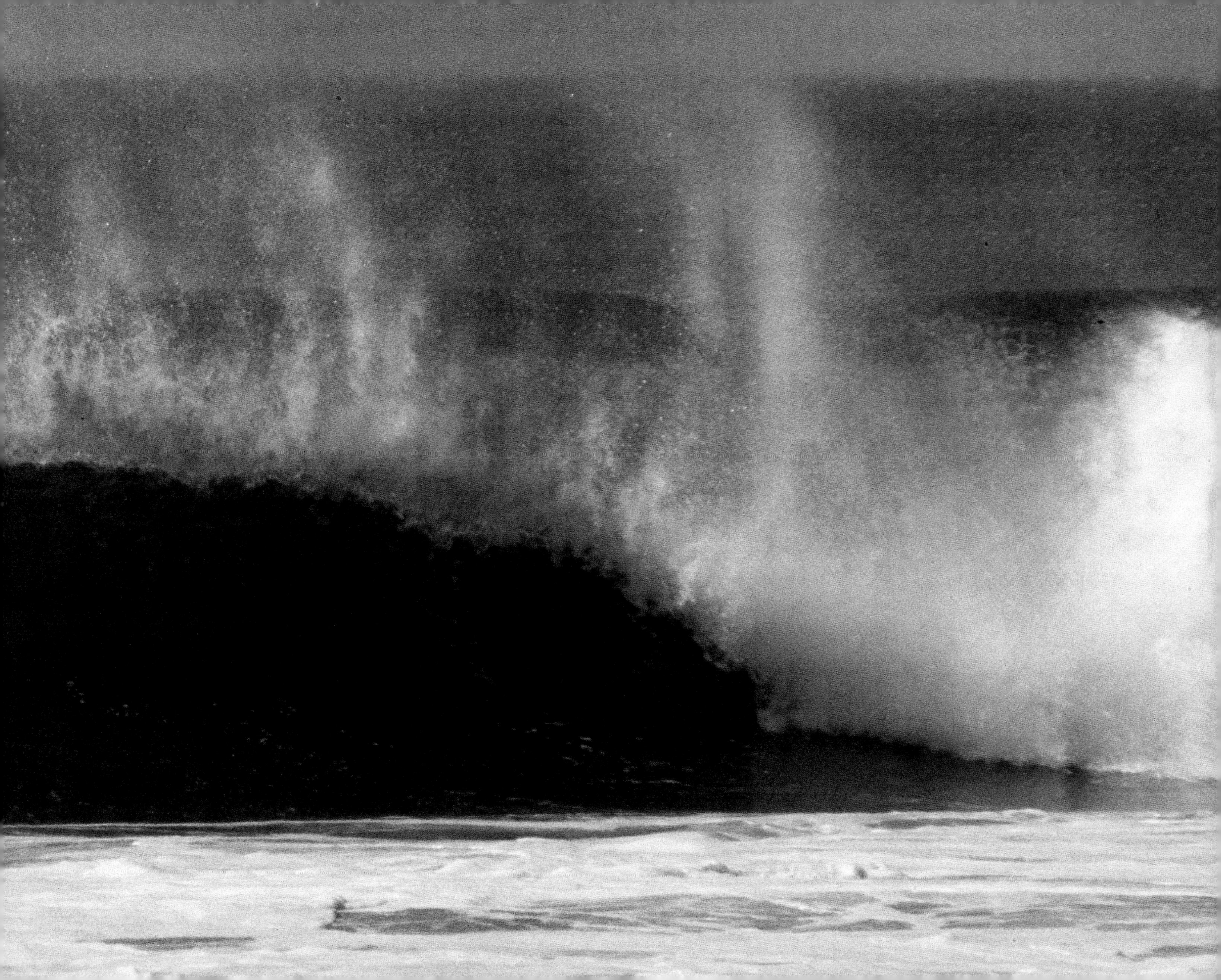

Biography

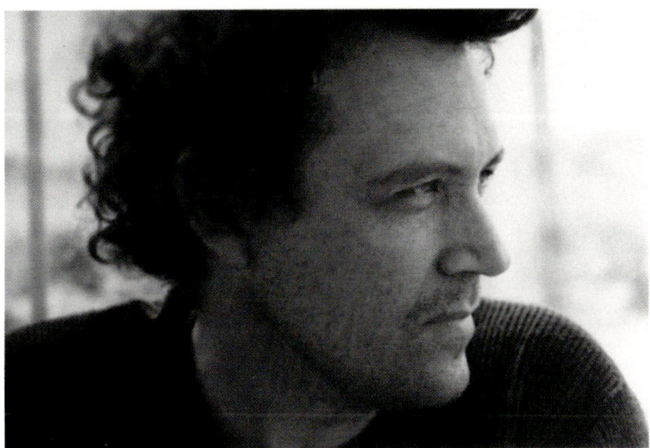

Gary Hill, 1993

Gary Hill was born in Santa Monica, California on April 4, 1951. He spent his youth in southern California surfing and skateboarding. At age fifteen while still in high school he began making welded sculpture. In 1969 he moved to the East Coast and briefly attended the Art Student's League in Woodstock, New York, and a small workshop class with the painter Bruce Dorfman. In 1973 Hill borrowed a camera from Woodstock Community Video and experimented with video's inherent characteristic of feedback by turning the camera on himself and recording layers of multiple selves in conversation. This brief encounter with the electronic medium was a decidedly pivotal one.

From 1974 to 1976 Hill was employed as a TV-lab coordinator for Woodstock Community Video, enabling him to continue exploring his new medium. His earliest videos, *The Fall* and *Air Raid* used sound/ image montage with a decidedly ecological subtext. His first video installation, *Hole in the Wall* (1974) was a kind of post-minimal political statement where he literally cut a hole through the wall of the Woodstock Artists Association, which at the time did not consider video a legitimate art form, and placed a monitor in the space playing back the action. From 1975 to 1977 Hill immersed himself in the electronic possibilities of video while artist-in-residence at the Experimental Television Center in Binghamton, New York. There he worked with electronic designer Dave Jones who has designed a number of special electronic tools, enabling Hill to pursue some of his more complex work.

In 1976 Hill met poet George Quasha who, along with Charles Stein, was inspirational in Hill's initial experiments with language. His first works dealing with the intertextuality of image, sound, speech, and language emerged in the late 1970s and early 1980s. Throughout the '80s Hill received multiple fellowships from the Rockefeller and Guggenheim Foundations as well as the National Endowment for the Arts, enabling him to concentrate exclusively on his work. From 1984 to 1985 he lived in Japan supported by a Japan/ United States Cultural Exchange Fellowship, during which time he produced *URA ARU (the backside exists).* For a short period of time during his fellowship he returned to New York to make *Why Do Things Get in a Muddle? (Come on Petunia),* his first work to incorporate the mise-en-scène. Hill has lived in Seattle since 1985 where he established a video program at Cornish College of the Arts.

In 1988 Hill completed *Incidence of Catastrophe,* one of several works he has made inspired by the writing of Maurice Blanchot. During the same year he was artist-in-residence at the Centre Georges Pompidou in Paris, which culminated in the making of *DISTURBANCE (among the jars).* Hill had his first gallery solo exhibition of video installations in 1990 at Galerie des Archives, for which he produced the series *And Sat Down Beside Her.* His *BEACON (Two Versions of the Imaginary)* was part of the Energieen exhibition at the Stedelijk Museum in Amsterdam, a notable group exhibition for Hill in that it was the first time his work was seen within an overall contemporary art context. Since then, Hill has continued to work almost exclusively with installations and has been included in several major international exhibitions, including Metropolis, Doubletake, and every Whitney Biennial since 1981. At Documenta 9 he premiered his most ambitious work to date, *Tall Ships.* Hill is currently working on two large-scale public commissions. His work is represented by the Donald Young Gallery in Seattle.

Selected Video Works 1973-1994

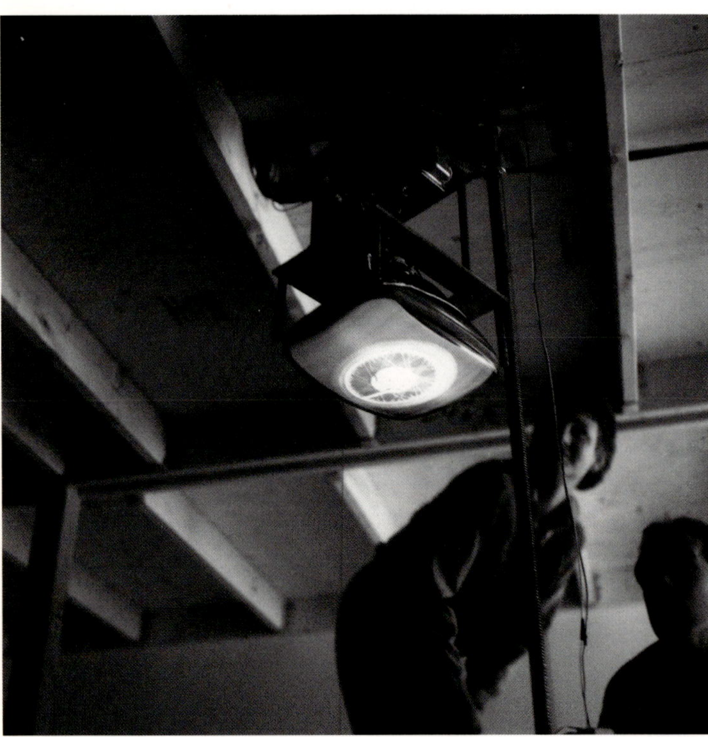

Mediarite, Seattle, 1987

Videotapes

The Fall, 1973.
Black and white; 11:00

Air Raid, 1974.
Black and white; 6:00

Rock City Road, 1974-75.
Color, silent; 12:00

Earth Pulse, 1975.
Color; 6:00

Improvisations with Bluestone, 1976.
Color; 6:00

Mirror Road, 1976.
Color, silent; 6:00

Bits, 1977.
Color; 4:25

Bathing, 1977.
Color, silent; 4:25

Windows, 1978.
Color, silent; 8:00

Electronic Linguistics, 1978.
Black and white; 3:45

Sums & Differences, 1978.
Black and white; 8:00

Mouth Piece, 1978.
Color; 1:00

Full Circle, 1978.
Color; 3:25

Primary, 1978.
Color; 1:40

Elements, 1978.
Black and white; 2:00

Objects with Destinations, 1979.
Color, silent; 3:40

Equal Time, 1979.
Color, stereo sound; 4:00

Picture Story, 1979.
Color; 7:00

Soundings, 1979.
Color; 17:00

Processual Video, 1980.
Black and white; 11:30

Black/White/ Text, 1980.
Black and white, stereo sound; 7:00

Commentary, 1980.
Color; 0:40

Around & About, 1980.
Color; 4:45

Videograms, 1980-81.
Black and white; 13:25

Primarily Speaking, 1981-83.
Color, stereo sound; 18:40

Happenstance (part one of many parts), 1982-83.
Black and white, stereo sound; 6:30

Why Do Things Get in a Muddle? (Come on Petunia), 1984.
Color; 32:00

Tale Enclosure, 1985.
Color, stereo sound; 5:30

URA ARU (the backside exists), 1985-86.
Color; 28:00

Mediations (towards a remake of Soundings), 1979-86.
Color, stereo sound; 4:45

Incidence of Catastrophe, 1987-88.
Color, stereo sound; 43:51

Site Recite (a prologue), 1989.
Color, stereo sound; 4:00

Solstice d'Hiver, 1990.
Color, sound; 60:00

Installations

Hole in the Wall. 1974
Site-specific, single-channel video/sound installation
Two monitors

Mesh. 1979
Mixed media installation
Three live cameras, four black and white monitors, wire mesh, electronics and speakers

War Zone. 1980
Mixed media installation
Live stereo camera/viewfinder, two videotapes, sixteen loudspeakers, objects, motor-controlled lights and live rabbit

Around & About. 1980 (destroyed)
Video/sound installation
Two versions:
1. Two monitors (black and white and color) and videotape;
2. Eight monitors (four black and white and four color), videotape and controlling electronics

Glass Onion. 1981
Two-channel video/sound installation
Live camera with remote-controlled zoom lens, two videotapes, five monitors, eight speakers and controlling electronics

Primarily Speaking. 1981-83
Two-channel video/sound installation
Two versions:
1. Eight monitors, four speakers and controlling electronics;
2. Two monitors, chairs and mirrors

Equal Time. 1982
Three-channel video/sound installation
Four monitors and two speakers

● *CRUX.* 1983-87
Five-channel video/sound installation
Five color monitors and five speakers

In Situ. 1986
Mixed media installation
Modified easy chair, modified monitor, six electric fans, sculptural elements, motorized paper feeder, controlling electronics and speakers

Mediarite. 1987
Site-specific mixed media installation
Three videotapes/VTRs, six monitors, four electric motors, lenses, mineral oil, sculptural elements, controlling electronics and speakers

DIG. 1987-92
(based on *Mediarite)*
Mixed media installation
Three-channel video, six monitors, four electric motors, lenses, mineral oil, sculptural elements, computer-controlled electronics and speakers

DISTURBANCE (among the jars). 1988
Seven-channel video/sound installation

● *And Sat Down Beside Her.* 1990
Mixed media installation consisting of three works:
1. Single-channel video and hanging TV tube with table, chair, lens, book and speaker;
2. Single-channel video and glass tube enclosing one-inch TV tube, text applied on floor and speaker;
3. Two-channel video and two one-inch TV tubes with four lenses

● *BEACON (Two Versions of the Imaginary).* 1990
Two-channel video/sound installation
Two TV tubes mounted in aluminum cylinder, projection lenses, four speakers, motor and controlling electronics

Inasmuch As It Is Always Already Taking Place. 1990
Sixteen-channel video/sound installation
Sixteen one-half-inch to twenty-one-inch black and white TV tubes positioned in horizontal inset in wall

Between Cinema and a Hard Place. 1991
Three-channel video/sound installation
Twenty-three modified monitors and computer-controlled switching matrix

CORE SERIES (two works: *"Glasses"* and *"Leaves").* 1991
Single-channel video/sound installations
Each work: two modified monitors and electronic switch with tone decoder

I Believe It Is an Image in Light of the Other. 1991-92
Mixed media installation
Seven-channel video, modified TV tubes for projection, books and speaker

● *Suspension of Disbelief (for Marine).* 1991-92
Four-channel video installation
Thirty twelve-inch TV tubes mounted on aluminum beam and computer-controlled switching matrix

CORE SERIES ("No Evil"). 1992
Single-channel video/sound installation
Three modified monitors and electronic switch with tone decoder

Tall Ships. 1992
Sixteen-channel video installation
Sixteen black and white monitors, sixteen projection units, sixteen laserdisc players and computer-controlled interactive system

● *Cut Pipe.* 1992
Single-channel video/sound installation
Black and white video monitor, projection lens, two aluminum cylinders and three loudspeakers

Some Times Things. 1992
Nine-channel video/sound installation
Nine modified monitors, nine projection lenses, nine loudspeakers, and nine aluminum tubes

If Two People. 1993 (destroyed)
Two-channel video/sound installation
Ten black and white monitors mounted on two aluminum ladders, two speakers, and spoken text

Between 1 & 0. 1993
Two-channel video/sound installation
Thirteen black and white monitors mounted on aluminum cross, computer-controlled video switcher and audio

● *House of Cards.* 1993
Seven-channel video/sound installation
Five black and white monitors vertically mounted on an aluminum ladder-like structure, two color monitors vertically mounted on wall shelves, two speakers.

● *Dervish.* 1993-94 (working title)
In progress

● *Learning Curve.* 1993
Single-channel video installation
Video projector, custom-made screen and plywood chair/table construction, silent

● *Learning Curve (Still Point),* 1993
Single-channel video installation, silent
One five-inch monitor, plywood chair/table construction

● *indicates work in the exhibition.*

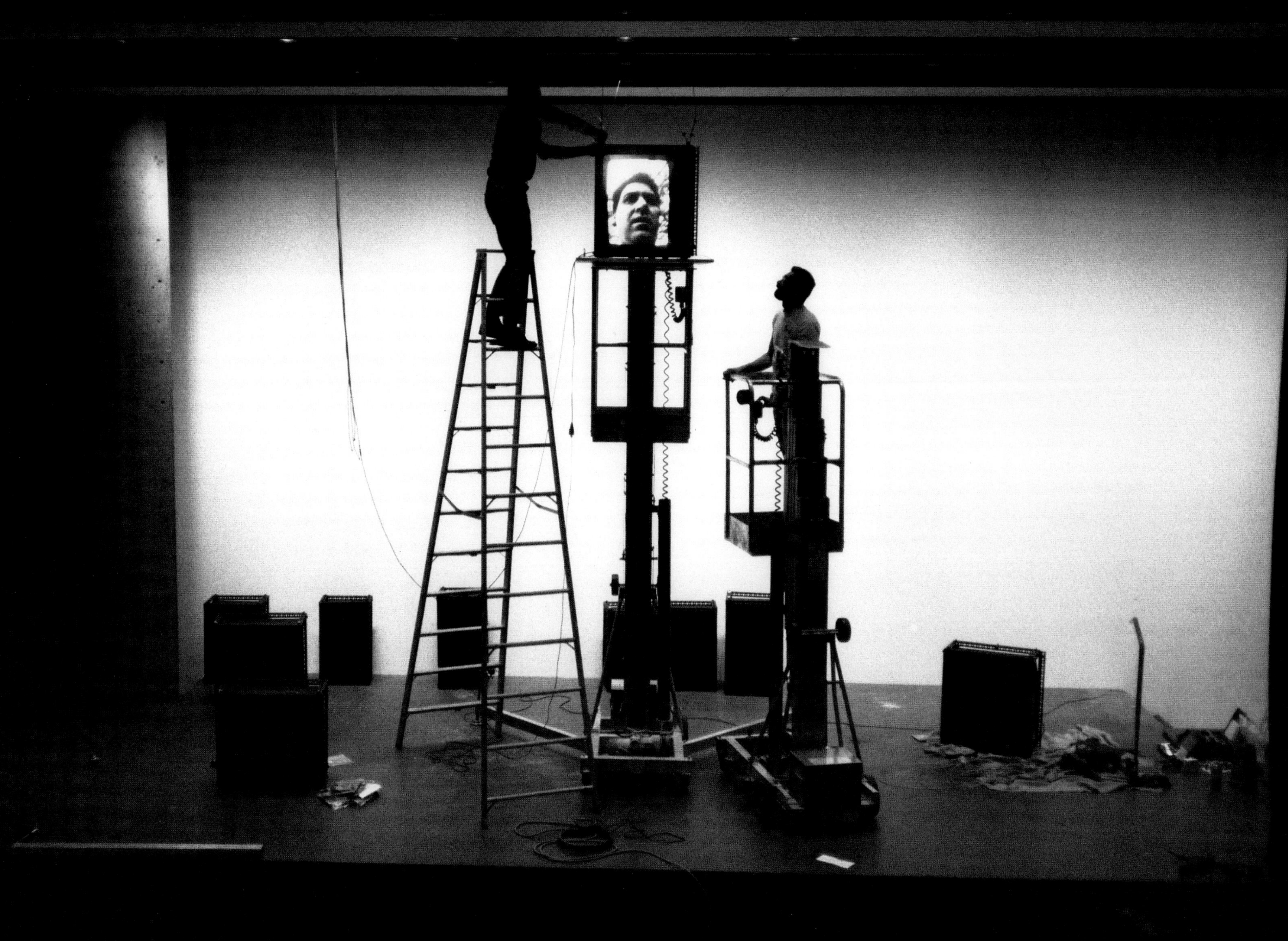

Profile

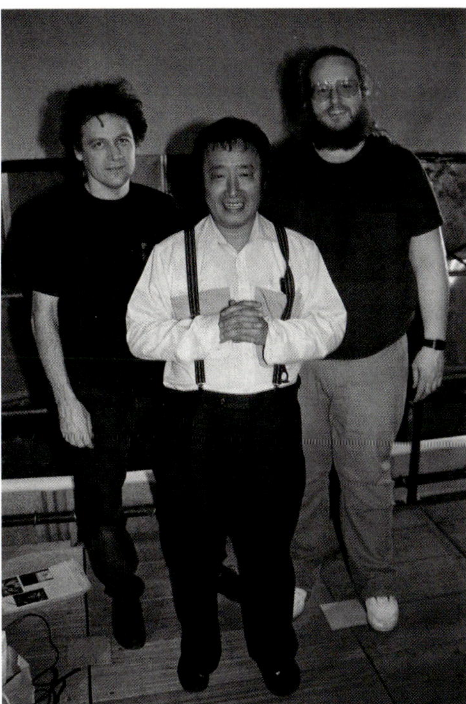

Gary Hill, Nam June Paik and Dave Jones, Tokyo, 1992

1991
Artist-in-residence, Hôpital Éphémère, Paris
1985-92
Art faculty, Cornish College of the Arts, Seattle, Washington
1988
National Endowment for the Arts, France/U.S. Exchange Fellow
Commissioned by the Musée National d'Art Moderne, Centre Georges Pompidou, Paris (to produce a new video installation)
1987
Artist-in-residence, California Institute for the Arts, Valencia, California
1986
Artist-in-residence, Chicago Art Institute, Chicago
1985
Artist-in-residence, Sony Corporation, Hon Atsugi, Japan
Established Video Program, Cornish College of the Arts, Seattle, Washington
1984-85
Lived in Japan under a Japan/U.S. Exchange Fellowship
1983
Visiting Professor of Art, Bard College, Annandale-on-Hudson, New York
Participant, "Intersection of the Word and Image," Women's Interart Center, New York
1982
Media Panelist, New York State Council on the Arts, Ithaca Video Festival, Ithaca, New York
Visiting Artist, American Center, Paris
1981-82
Member, Board of Directors, Media Alliance, New York
1981
Video Panelist, Creative Artist Public Service Program, New York
1979-80
Visiting Associate Professor, Center for Media, State University of New York, Buffalo, New York
1978
Artist-in-residence, Portable Channel, Rochester, New York
1977-79
Founder and Director, Open Studio Video Project, Barrytown, New York
1975-77
Artist-in-residence, Experimental Television Center, Binghamton, New York
1975-76
Conceived and directed *Synergism,* a series of intermedia performances for dance, music and video, Woodstock, New York
1974-76
Artist-in-residence and Artists' TV Lab Coordinator, Woodstock Community Video, Woodstock and Rhinebeck, New York

Grants and Fellowships

1990
Guggenheim Fellowship
Rockefeller Intercultural Media Arts Fellowship (stage two)
1989
Rockefeller Intercultural Media Arts Fellowship
1988
"Seattle Artists 1988" (selected for City Lights portable works), Seattle, Washington
1987
National Endowment for the Arts Fellowship
Artist Trust Fellowship
1986
American Film Institute Fellowship
Guggenheim Fellowship
National Endowment for the Arts Production Grant
1985-86
New York State Council on the Arts Production Grant
New York State Foundation on the Arts Fellowship
1985
National Endowment for the Arts Fellowship
1984
New Works Grant, Massachusetts Council on the Arts
1983-84
New York State Council on the Arts Production Grant
1982
Channel Thirteen/WNET Artist-in-Residence Production Grant
Japan/U.S. Exchange Fellowship sponsored by the National Endowment for the Arts and the Japan/U.S. Friendship Commission
1981-82
Rockefeller Video Artist Fellowship
National Endowment for the Arts Media Production Grant
New York State Council on the Arts Production Grant
1980-81
New York State Council on the Arts Production Grant
1979
Channel Thirteen/WNET Artist-in-Residence Production Grant
National Endowment for the Arts Fellowship
1978-79
Creative Artist Public Service Fellowship
New York State Council on the Arts Production Grant

Awards

1991
Prize Winner, "ARTEC 91" International Biennale, Nagoya, Japan
1989
Prize Winner (Performance Video), 13th Atlanta Film/Video Festival, Atlanta, Georgia
1988
Grand Prix, World Wide Video Festival, The Hague, The Netherlands
Honorable Mention, 3rd Bonn Video Art Festival, Bonn, Germany
Prix Alcan (video), 18th Annual Montreal Film and Video Festival, Montreal, Quebec, Canada
1987
1st Prize, Structuralist Video, Athens International Video Festival, Athens, Ohio
Grand Prize, 6th Annual Daniel Wadsworth Video Festival, Real Art Ways, Hartford, Connecticut
1986
1st Prize (shared), Narrative Video, Athens International Video Festival, Athens, Ohio
James D. Phelan Art Award, San Francisco Foundation, San Francisco
Honorable Mention (Non-Narrative Video), Video Culture International, Toronto, Ontario, Canada
1985
Grand Prix (shared), 1st Tokyo International Video Biennale, Tokyo
Sony Grand Prize, ¾ Inch Video/New Media, Video Culture International, Montreal, Quebec, Canada

Opposite page
CRUX installation, Abrahamson Auditorium, Museum of Contemporary Art, Los Angeles, 1987

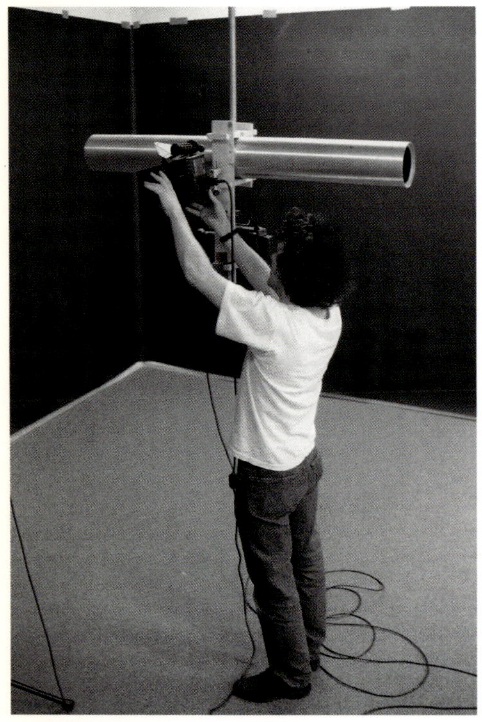

BEACON (Two Versions of the Imaginary) in production, Gary Hill Studio, Seattle, 1990

1st Prize, Art Video/New Media, Video Culture International, Montreal, Quebec, Canada
1st Prize, ¾ Inch Non-Narrative Art Video/New Media, Video Culture International, Montreal, Quebec, Canada

1983
1st Prize (shared), San Sebastian International Video Festival, San Sebastian, Spain
Merit Award, Chicago International Film/Video Festival, Chicago

1982
2nd Prize, Video Art, United States Film/Video Festival, Salt Lake City, Utah

1981
The Video Art Award, 3rd Annual Daniel Wadsworth Memorial Video Festival, Hartford, Connecticut

1978
Merit Award, Experimental Video, Athens International Video Festival, Athens, Ohio

1976
Merit Award, Experimental Video, Athens International Video Festival, Athens, Ohio

Selected Solo Exhibitions

1994
"Gary Hill," Henry Art Gallery, Seattle, Hirshhorn Museum, Washington, D.C., and Museum of Contemporary Art, L.A.
"Gary Hill," Tate Gallery, Liverpool, England

1993
"Gary Hill," Donald Young Gallery, Seattle, Washington (installations)
"Gary Hill," IVAM Centre Julio Gonzalez, Valencia, Spain (traveling exhibition organized by the Centre Georges Pompidou)
"Gary Hill," Stedelijk Museum, Amsterdam, The Netherlands (traveling exhibition organized by the Centre Georges Pompidou)
"Gary Hill," Künsthalle, Vienna, Austria (traveling exhibition organized by the Centre Georges Pompidou)
"Gary Hill: In Light of the Other," Museum of Modern Art, Oxford, England (installations)
"Gary Hill: Sites Recited," Long Beach Museum of Art, Long Beach, California

1992
Watari Museum of Contemporary Art, Tokyo (installations)
"Gary Hill," Le Creux de L'Enfer, Centre d'Art Contemporain, Thiers, France (installations)
"Gary Hill," traveling exhibition organized by the Musée National d'Art Moderne, Centre Georges Pompidou, Paris (installations, videotapes)
Stedelijk Van Abbemuseum, Eindhoven, The Netherlands (installations)

1991
Galerie des Archives, Paris (installations)
OCO Espace d'Art Contemporain, Paris (installation)
Nykytaiteen Museo: The Museum of Contemporary Art, Helsinki, Finland (retrospective of videotapes)

1990
Galerie des Archives, Paris (installations)
Galerie Huset/Ny Carlsberg Glyptotek Museum, Copenhagen, Denmark (installations)
YYZ Artist's Outlet, Toronto, Ontario, Canada (screening, installation)
Museum of Modern Art, New York (installation)

1989
Beursschouwburg, Brussels (screening)
Kijkhuis, The Hague, The Netherlands (installation)
Musée d'Art Moderne, Villeneuve d'Ascq, France (installation, screening)
Pacific Film Archives, San Francisco (screening)

1988
Western Front, Vancouver, B.C., Canada (screening)
Video Wochen, Basel, Switzerland (performance, screening)
L'Espace Lyonnais d'Art Contemporain, Lyon, France (retrospective of videotapes)

1987
Museum of Contemporary Art, Los Angeles (installation)
Los Angeles Contemporary Exhibitions, Los Angeles (screening)
Cornish College of the Arts, Seattle, Washington (installation)
2nd Seminar on International Video, St. Gervais-Genève, Geneva, Switzerland (retrospective of videotapes)

1986
Whitney Museum of American Art, New York (retrospective of videotapes)
Nexus Gallery, Philadelphia (screening)

1985
Scan Gallery, Tokyo (videotapes)

1983
International Cultural Center, Antwerp, Belgium (screening)
The American Center, Paris (retrospective of videotapes)
Whitney Museum of American Art, New York (installation)
Monte Video, Amsterdam (screening)

1982
Galerie H at ORF, Steirischer Herbst, Graz, Austria (installation)
Long Beach Museum of Art, Long Beach, California (installation)

1981
The Kitchen Center for Music, Video and Dance, New York (installation)
And/Or Gallery, Seattle, Washington (installation)
Anthology Film Archives, New York (screening)

1980
Media Study, Buffalo, New York (installation)
"Video Viewpoints," Museum of Modern Art, New York (screening)
Image Dissector Screening Series, University of California at Los Angeles, Los Angeles (screening)

1979
The Kitchen Center for Music, Video and Dance, New York (installation)
Everson Museum, Syracuse, New York (installation)
"Meet the Makers: Gary Hill," Donnell Library, New York (screening)

1978
Rochester Memorial Art Gallery, Rochester, New York (screening)

1976
Anthology Film Archives, New York (screening)

1974
South Houston Gallery, New York

1973
Woodstock Artists' Association, Woodstock, New York

1971
Polaris Gallery, Woodstock, New York

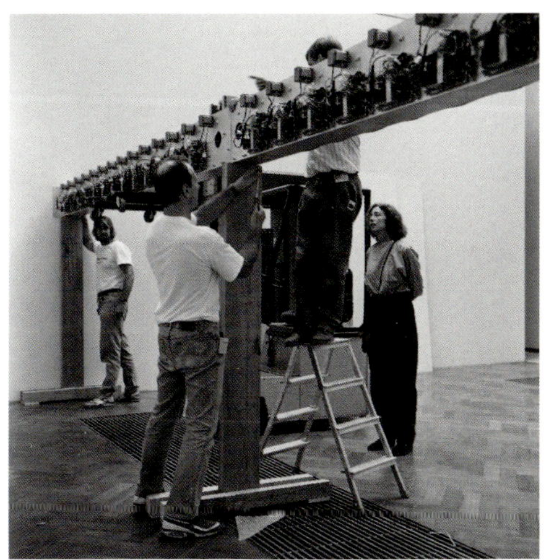

Suspension of Disbelief (for Marine) installation Amsterdam, 1993

Selected Group Exhibitions

1993

"Doubletake: Collective Memory and Current Art," Künsthalle, Vienna

"Biennial Exhibition," Whitney Museum of American Art, New York

"The Binary Era: New Interactions," Künsthalle, Vienna

"The 21st Century," Künsthalle Basel, Basel, Switzerland

"American Art in the 20th Century—Painting and Sculpture," Martin Gropius Bau, Berlin

"Passageworks," Rooseum, Malmo, Sweden

"American Art in the 20th Century," Royal Academy, London

"Eadweard Muybridge, Bill Viola, Giulio Paolini, Gary Hill, James Coleman," Ydessa Hendeles Art Foundation, Toronto, Ontario, Canada

"Fifth Fukui International Video Biennal," Fukui, Japan

"'Strange' HOTEL," Aarhus Kuntsmuseum, Aarhus, Denmark

1992

"Doubletake: Collective Memory & Current Art," Hayward Gallery, London

"Passages de l'Image," San Francisco Museum of Modern Art, San Francisco

"Japan 92 Video and Television Festival," Tokyo

Donald Young Gallery, Seattle, Washington

"Dance," California Museum of Photography, Riverside, California

"Documenta IX," Museum Fridericianum, Kassel, Germany

"Filmladen Festival," Kassel, Germany (also Botschaft Festival, Berlin and Hinterhaus, Wiesbaden)

"Japan: Outside/Inside/Inbetween," Artists Space, New York

"The Binary Era: New Interactions," Musée d'Ixelles, Brussels, Belgium

"Art at the Armory: Occupied Territory," Museum of Contemporary Art, Chicago

"Manifest," Musée National d'Art Moderne, Centre Georges Pompidou, Paris

"Performing Objects," Institute of Contemporary Art, Boston

"Metamorphose," St. Gervais-Genève, Geneva

1991

"Biennial Exhibition," Whitney Museum of American Art, New York

"Currents," Institute of Contemporary Art, Boston

"The Body (2)," The Renaissance Society at the University of Chicago, Chicago

"In Public: Seattle, 1991," Security Pacific Gallery, Seattle, Washington

"The Body," The Renaissance Society at the University of Chicago, Chicago

"Metropolis," Martin Gropius Bau, Berlin

"Topographie 2: Untergrund," Wiener Festwochen, Vienna

"ARTEC 91" International Biennale, Nagoya, Japan

"Glass: Material in the Service of Meaning," Tacoma Art Museum, Tacoma, Washington

"Passages de l'Image," Fundacio Caixa de Pensions, Barcelona

"Passages de l'Image," Wexner Art Center, Columbus, Ohio

1990

"Tendances multiples (Videos des Annees 80)," Musée National d'Art Moderne, Centre Georges Pompidou, Paris

"Energieen," Stedelijk Museum, Amsterdam

"Video Poetics," Long Beach Museum of Art, Long Beach, California

"Passages de l'Image," Musée National d'Art Moderne, Centre Georges Pompidou, Paris

"L'Amour de Berlin: Installation Video," Centre Culturel, Cavaillon, France

"A Force of Repetition," New Jersey State Museum, Newark, New Jersey

"Bienal de la Imagen en Movimento '90," Centro de Arte Reina Sofia, Madrid

1989

"Video-Skulptur Retrospektiv und Aktuell 1963-1989," Kolnischer Künstverein, Cologne, Germany (traveled to Berlin and Zürich)

"Electronic Landscapes," the National Gallery of Canada, Ottawa, Ontario, Canada

"Video and Language," Museum of Modern Art, New York

"Delicate Technology, 2nd Japan Video Television Festival," Spiral Hall, Tokyo

"Les Cent Jours d'Art Contemporain," Centre International d'Art Contemporain de Montreal, Montreal, Quebec, Canada

"Selections from the Permanent Collection: Recent Acquisitions—Video," San Francisco Museum of Modern Art, San Francisco

"Filmer à Tout Prix, No. 4," Brussels, Belgium (festival selection)

"Eye for I: Video Self-Portraits," Whitney Museum of American Art, New York

"3rd Seminar on International Video," St. Gervais-Genève, Geneva (festival selection)

"Japan 89 Video Television Festival," Tokyo

1988

"Infermental VII," Buffalo, New York

"Degrees of Reality," Long Beach Museum of Art, Long Beach, California

"Art Video American," CREDAC, Paris

"As Told To: Structures for Conversation," Walter Philips Gallery, Banff, Alberta, Canada

"4th International Manifestation of Video and TV," Montbéliard, France (festival selection)

"London Film Festival," London (festival selection)

"The World Wide Video Festival," Kijkhuis, The Hague, The Netherlands (festival selection)

"3. Videonald," Bonn, Germany (festival selection)

1987

"Documenta VIII," Museum Fridericianum, Kassel, Germany

"Video Discourse: Mediated Narratives," Institute of Contemporary Art, Boston

"Video Discourse: Mediated Narratives," La Jolla Museum of Contemporary Art, San Diego, California

"Infermental VI," Western Front, Vancouver, B.C., Canada

"Contemporary Diptychs: Divided Visions," Whitney Museum of American Art, New York

"Avenues of Thought: Cultural and Spiritual Abstractions in Video," Rutgers University, Newark, New Jersey

"The Situated Image," Mandeville Gallery, University of California at San Diego, La Jolla, California

"15th Avenue Studio #2: The Mechanics of Contemplation," Henry Art Gallery, University of Washington, Seattle, Washington

"The Arts for Television," international traveling exhibition organized by the Museum of Contemporary Art, Los Angeles and the Stedelijk Museum, Amsterdam

"Cinq Pièces Avec Vue," Centre Génevois de Gravure Contemporaine, Geneva

"Japan 87 Video Television Festival," Tokyo

"Computers and Art," Everson Museum of Art, Syracuse, New York

1986

"Video: Recent Aquisitions," Museum of Modern Art, New York

"Video and Language/Video as Language," Los Angeles Contemporary Exhibitions, Los Angeles

"National Video Festival," American Film Institute, Los Angeles

"Cryptic Languages," Washington Project for the Arts, Washington, D.C.

"Resolution: A Critique of Video Art," Los Angeles Contemporary Exhibitions, Los Angeles

"The Image of Fiction: International Videoart, Infermental 5," Con Rumore, Rotterdam, Germany

"Collections Videos—Acquisitions Depuis 1977," Musée National d'Art Moderne, Centre Georges Pompidou, Paris

"The World Wide Video Festival," Kijkhuis, The Hague, The Netherlands

"San Francisco Video Festival," San Francisco

"II National Video Festival de Madrid," Circulo de Bellas Artes, Madrid

"Poetic License," Long Beach Museum of Art, Long Beach, California

"International Festival of Video Art," Saw Gallery, Ottawa, Ontario, Canada (traveled Europe and Canada in 1986, 1987)

"Video Transformations," organized by Independent Curators Incorporated, New York (traveled U.S. and Canada)

1985

"Image/Word: The Art of Reading," New Langton Arts, San Francisco

"San Francisco Video Festival," San Francisco

"National Video Festival," American Film Institute, Los Angeles

"The World Wide Video Festival," Kijkhuis, The Hague, The Netherlands

"Video Art: Stockholm International Festival '85," Kulturhuset, Stockholm

"A Video Sampler," American Museum of the Moving Image, Astoria, New York

1984

"Biennale di Venezia," Venice

"So There, Orwell 1984," The Louisiana World Exhibition, New Orleans

"Video: A Retrospective," Long Beach Museum of Art, Long Beach, California

"Videographia," Escoia I Centre d'Activtats Video, Barcelona, Spain

"National Video Festival," American Film Institute, Los Angeles

1983

"Art Video Retrospectives et Perspectives," Palais des Beaux-Arts, Brussels, Belgium

"Video As Attitude," University Art Museum, University of New Mexico, Albuquerque, New Mexico

"Electronic Visions," Hudson River Museum, Yonkers, New York

"The Second Link: Viewpoints on Video in the Eighties," Walter Philips Gallery, Banff, Alberta, Canada

"XXXI Festival Internacional de Cine de San Sebastian," San Sebastian, Spain

"1983 Biennial Exhibition," Whitney Museum of American Art, New York

"San Francisco Video Festival," San Francisco

1982

"The Sydney Biennale," Sydney, Australia

"Gary Hill: Equal Time," Long Beach Museum of Art, Long Beach, California

1981

"Projects Video XXXV," Museum of Modern Art, New York

"National Video Festival," John F. Kennedy Center for the Performing Arts, Washington, D.C.

"New York Video," Stadtische Galerie im Lenbachhaus, Munich, Germany

"7th Annual Ithaca Video Festival," Ithaca, New York

1980

"San Francisco Video Festival," San Francisco

1979

"Projects Video XXVII," Museum of Modern Art, New York

"Video Revue," Everson Museum of Art, Syracuse, New York

"Beau Fleuve," Media Study, Buffalo, New York (traveled to: The Center for Media Art, American Center in Paris; L'Espace Lyonnais d'Action Culturelle, Lyon, France; Musée Cantini, Marseille, France)

"Political Comment in Contemporary Art," Brainerd Art Gallery, Potsdam, New York

1978

"4th Annual Ithaca Video Festival," Ithaca, New York

"Sums & Differences" (performance), Arnolfini Arts Center, Rhinebeck, New York

1977

"New Work in Abstract Video Imagery," Everson Museum of Art, Syracuse, New York

1976

"Video Expovision '76," Woodstock Community Video, Woodstock, New York

"Athens International Film Festival," Athens, Ohio

"Synergism," performance with Walter Wright and Sara Cook, Woodstock Artists' Association, Woodstock, New York

1975

"Projects Video VI," Museum of Modern Art, New York

"An Evening of Video," Walnut Street Theatre, Philadelphia

"Woodstock Video Exposition," Woodstock, New York

"Annual Avant-Garde Festival of New York," New York

1974

"Artists from Upstate New York," 55 Mercer Gallery, New York

1972

"Electronic Music: Improvisations" (performance with Jean-Yves Labat), Woodstock Artists' Association, Woodstock, New York

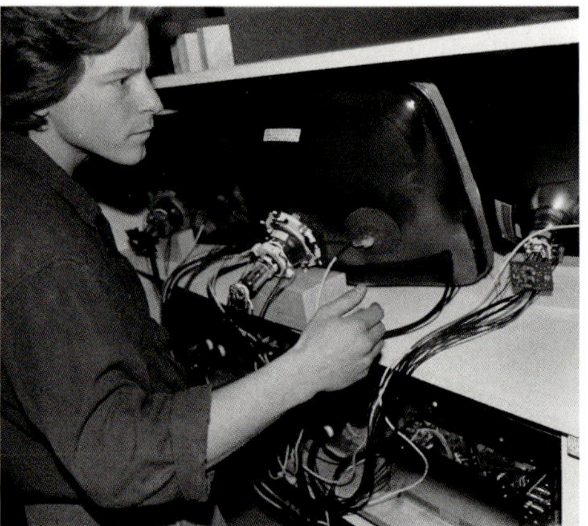

Paul Kuranko installing *Inasmuch*... at Centre Georges Pompidou, Paris, 1992

Bibliography

Writings by the Artist

Arranged chronologically.

"Processual Video." *Video Viewpoints* (New York: Museum of Modern Art, February 1980).

"War Zone." *Media Study/Buffalo* (January/ May 1980).

"Videograms." *Themes in Electronic Image Processing* (New York: The Kitchen Center for Music, Video and Dance, December 1981).

Primarily Speaking, 1981-83 (New York: Whitney Museum of American Art, 1983).

"Happenstance (explaining it to death)." *Video d'Artistes* (Geneva: Bel Vedere, 1986).

"URA ARU: The Acoustic Palindrome." *Video Guide* 7 (No. 4, 1986).

"Processual Video" (videotape transcription). *2nd International Week of Video* (Geneva: St. Gervais, 1987).

"Primarily Speaking." *Video Communications,* No. 48 (Paris: 1988).

Paragraph and photograph in "Reordering the Hierarchy," by Willard Wood, *Reflex* (May/June 1988).

"And if the Right Hand Did not Know What the Left Hand Is Doing." *Illuminating Video,* eds. Doug Hall and Sally Jo Fifer (New York: Aperture Press in association with the Bay Area Video Coalition, 1990), pp. 91-99.

"BEACON (Two Versions of the Imaginary)," essay from the exhibition catalogue, *ENERGIEEN* (Amsterdam: Stedelijk Museum, 1990). Reprinted in the catalogue, *Bienal de la Imagen en Movimiento '90* (Madrid: Museo Nacional Centro de Arte Reina Sofia, 1990).

"Inasmuch As It Is Always Already Taking Place." *OTHERWORDSANDIMAGES: Video by Gary Hill* (Danish and English). (Copenhagen: Video Gallerie/Ny Carlsberg Glyptotek, 1990), p. 27.

"Site Re:cite" from "Unspeakable Images." *Camera Obscura* No. 24 (San Francisco: 1991).

"Split Time Mystery." *Topographie II: Untergrund, Videoinstallations in the Vienna Subway System* (Vienna: Wiener Festwochen, 1991).

"LEAVES." *Gary Hill—I Believe It Is an Image* (Tokyo: Watari Museum of Contemporary Art, 1992).

Other Projects

Public 7 (Sacred Technologies), ed. Christine Davis (Toronto: Public Access Press, 1993). (project for journal; drawings by Anastasia Hill)

"Gary Hill: Day Seminar," performance by Gary Hill, George Quasha and Charles Stein, November 7, 1993, University of Oxford, Oxford, England.

Monographs

Arranged alphabetically.

Devriendt, Christine. *L'Oeuvre Video de Gary Hill* (French and English). (Rennes: Université de Rennes II, 1990-91).

Gilbert, Christophe. *Maurice Blanchot/Gary Hill: d'une Ecriture l'Autre (et Son Double).* (Paris: DEA Université Paris-III, 1992).

Sarrazin, Stephen. *Chimaera Monographe No. 10 (Gary Hill).* (Montbéliard: Centre International de Création Vidéo Montbéliard, Belfort, 1992).

Exhibition Catalogues and Brochures

Arranged alphabetically.

L'Amour de Berlin (Cavallion: Centre Culturel de Cavallion, 1990).

Art at the Armory: Occupied Territory (Chicago: Museum of Contemporary Art, 1992), pp. 88-91.

Artists ½ Inch Videotape Series 1988 (Toronto: Art Metropole, 1988).

Augaitis, Daina. "As Told To: Structures for Conversation," program essay for exhibition of same title at Walter Philips Gallery, Banff, Alberta, Canada, 1988 (Banff: Walter Philips Gallery, 1990). Also published in the book *Sound by Artists* (Toronto: Art Metropole, 1990).

Bellour, Raymond. "Le dernier homme en croix." *2nd Semaine International de Video* (Geneva: Bel Veder, Centre Génevois de Gravure Contemporaine, 1987). Also published in *Illuminating Video,* eds. Doug Hall, Sally Jo Fifer (New York: Aperture Press in association with the Bay Area Video Coalition, 1990), pp. 425-426, and in *OTHERWORDSANDIMAGES: Video by Gary Hill* (Danish and English). (Copenhagen: Video Gallerie/Ny Carlsberg Glyptotek, 1990), pp. 20-26.

Bellour, Raymond, trans. Lynne Kirby. "Eye for I: Video Self-Portraits." *New American Film and Video Series 48* (New York: Whitney Museum of American Art, 1989).

Bellour, Raymond. "La Double Helice." *Passages de l'Image* (French). (Paris: Musée National d'Art Moderne, Centre Georges Pompidou, 1990), pp. 51-55. Also available in English in the exhibition catalogue of the same name (Barcelona: Centre Cultural de la Fundacio Caixa de Pensions, 1991), pp. 68-73).

1987 Biennial Exhibition (New York: Whitney Museum of American Art, 1987), pp. 150, 168, 201-202, 211.

1989 Biennial Exhibition (New York: Whitney Museum of American Art, 1989), pp. 210-211, 252.

1991 Biennial Exhibition (New York: Whitney Museum of American Art, 1991), pp. 102-105, 378.

Biggs, Simon. "The Author and the Machine (The Electronic Artist in Relation to Evolving Conditions of Production and Consumption)." *Machinations Festival* (Geneva: St. Gervais MJC, 1989).

The Body (2) (Chicago: The Renaissance Society at the University of Chicago, 1991).

Christoffersen, Agnete Dorph, Raymond Bellour and Gary Hill. *OTHERWORDSANDIMAGES: Video by Gary Hill* (Danish and English). (Copenhagen: Video Gallerie/Ny Carlsberg Glyptotek, 1990).

Cooke, Lynne, Bice Curiger and Greg Hilty. *DOUBLETAKE: Collective Memory and Current Art* (London: Hayward Gallery, 1992), pp. 31, 156-159, 225-226, and addendum.

Derrida, Jacques. "Videor." *Passages de l'Image* (French). (Paris: Musée National d'Art Moderne, Centre Georges Pompidou, 1990), pp. 158-161. Also available in English in the exhibition catalogue of the same name (Barcelona: Centre Cultural de la Fundacio Caixa de Pensions, 1991), pp. 174-179.

Documenta IX (Stuttgart: Edition Cantz, 1992), Vol. 1, p. 157; Vol. 2, pp. 222-225, 308. English language edition published in association with Harry N. Abrams, New York, 1992.

L'Ere Binaire: Nouvelles Interactions (Brussels: Musée Communal d'Ixelles, 1992), unpaginated.

Fargier, Jean-Paul. "Magie Blanche." *Gary Hill: DISTURBANCE (among the jars).* (French and English). (Villeneuve d'Ascq: Musée d'Art Moderne, 1988), unpaginated.

Gary Hill (French) (Paris: Centre George Pompidou, 1992). Texts by Christine van Assche, Lynne Cooke, Gary Hill, Jacinto Lageira, and Hippolyte Massardier.

Gary Hill (Spanish and English) (Valencia: IVAM Centre del Carme, 1993). Texts by Christine van Assche, Lynne Cook, Gary Hill, Jacinto Lageira, and Hippolyte Massardier.

Gary Hill (English, Dutch and German) (Amsterdam: Stedelijk Museum Amsterdam and Vienna: Kunsthalle Wien). Texts by Lynne Cooke, Gary Hill, Dorine Mignot, George Quasha, and Willem van Weelden.

Gary Hill: In Light of the Other (Oxford: The Museum of Modern Art, Oxford; The Tate Gallery, Liverpool, 1993). Texts by Corinne Diserens, Bruce Ferguson, Stuart Morgan, Lars Nittve, and Robert Mittenthal.

Gary Hill, Video Installations (Eindhoven: Stedelijk Van Abbemuseum, 1992).

Glowen, Ron and Kim Levin. *Glass: Material in the Service of Meaning* (Tacoma: Tacoma Art Museum, 1991).

Goodman, Cynthia. *Digital Visions: Computers and Art* (New York: Harry N. Abrams, 1987). Published in conjunction with the exhibition "Computers and Art" organized by the Everson Museum of Art, Syracuse, New York, 1987.

Hanhardt, John G. "Commentary..." in *The 3rd Fukui International Video Biennale* (Fukui, Japan, 1985).

Hanhardt, John G. "Gary Hill." *The New American Filmmakers Series 12* (New York: Whitney Museum of American Art, 1983).

Hanhardt, John G. "Gary Hill." *The New American Filmmakers Series 30* (New York: Whitney Museum of American Art, 1986).

Huici, Fernando. "Gary Hill: *Beacon.*" *Bienal de la Imagen en Movimento '90* (Madrid: Museo Nacional Centro de Arte Reina Sofia, 1990).

The Image of Fiction: International Videoart Infermental 5 (Rotterdam, Germany: Con Rumore, 1986), p. 41.

Jenkins, Bruce and John Minkowsky. "Gary Hill." *Beau Fleuve* (Buffalo: Media Study, 1979).

Joachimides, Christos M. and Norman Rosenthal, eds. *METROPOLIS* (Berlin: Martin Gropius Bau, 1991), pp. 154-155, 290.

Kain, Jackie. "L'intime du mot: l'oeuvre video de Gary Hill." *2nd Semaine Internationale de Video* (Geneva: Bel Veder, Centre Génevois de Gravure Contemporaine, 1987).

Kolpan, Steven. "Bateson: Through the Looking Glass." 1986 *Saw Gallery International Festival of Video Art* (Ottawa, Ontario: Saw Gallery, 1986).

Lageira, Jacinto. "Sprachen Video." *Between Cinema and a Hard Place* (French). (Paris: OCO Espace d'Art Contemporain, 1991).

Mittenthal, Robert. "Reading the Unknown: Reaching Gary Hill's *And Sat Down Beside Her"* in *Gary Hill* (Paris: Galerie des Archives, 1990).

Parent, Sylvie. *Cent Jours D'Art Contemporain à Montreal* (Montreal: Centre International D'Art Contemporain de Montreal, 1990), pp. 9-11.

Quasha, George. "Disturbing Unnarrative of the Perplexed Parapraxis (A Twin for DISTURBANCE)." *Gary Hill: DISTURBANCE (among the jars)* (French and English). (Villeneuve d'Ascq: Musée d'Art Moderne, 1988), unpaginated.

Quasha, George. "Notes on the Feedback Horizon." *Glass Onion* (Barrytown, N.Y.: Station Hill Press, 1980).

Rankin, Scott. *Video and Language/Video as Language* (Los Angeles: Los Angeles Contemporary Exhibitions, 1986).

Riley, Bob. *Video Currents—Mediated Narratives.* (Boston: Institute of Contemporary Art, 1987).

Sarrazin, Stephen. "Berlin, Metropolis, La Création, Le Désarroi" in *Chimaera Monograph No. 3.* (Montbéliard: Edition du Centre International de Création Vidéo Montbéliard, Belfort, 1991), pp. 56-61.

Sarrazin, Stephen. "Channeled Silence (Quiet, Something 'is' Thinking)" *Gary Hill—I Believe It Is an Image* (Tokyo: Watari Museum of Contemporary Art, 1992).

Sarrazin, Stephen. "In a Crowded House." *Passageworks* (Malmo: Rooseum—Center for Contemporary Art, 1993), pp. 58-69.

The 2nd International Biennale in Nagoya ARTEC '91 (Nagoya, Japan: Nagoya City Art Museum, 1991), pp. 30-31.

Selections from the Permanent Collection: Recent Acquisitions— Video (San Francisco: San Francisco Museum of Modern Art, 1989).

3. VIDEONALE IN BONN (Bonn: Videonale, 1988).

Van Assche, Christine. "Video Story." *Le Temps des Machines* (Valence: CRAC, 1990). Also reprinted in *Galeries Magazine,* No. 38 (August/September 1990), pp. 10-11).

Video by Artists 2 (Toronto: Art Metropole, 1986).

Videocroniques (Marseille: IMEREC, Vielle Charité, 1991).

Video formes '89 (Clermont-Ferrand: Festival de la Création Vidéo, 1989).

Video Transformations (New York: Independent Curators Incorporated, 1986).

Watari, Shizuko and Gary Hill. Interview with Gary Hill, in *Gary Hill—I Believe It Is an Image* (Tokyo: Watari Museum of Contemporary Art, 1992).

Zippay, Lori. "Gary Hill." *Video* (New York: Electronic Arts Intermix, 1991).

Articles and Reviews

Arranged alphabetically.

Ament, Deloris Tarzan. "Artist Uses Videos to Tease Viewers." *Seattle Times* (February 22, 1993).

Barcott, Bruce. "Gary Hill." *New Art Examiner* (May 1993), p. 51.

Barter, Ruth. "DOUBLETAKE." *Art Monthly* (April 1992).

Bassan, Raphael. "Murs d'Images pour un Art Mur." *Liberation,* Paris (July 31, 1990).

Benichou, Anne. "From Exhibition to Event." *Espace Magazine 6,* No. 2 (Winter 1990).

Berland, Jody. "International Video/Images in Translation." *Vanguard* (April/May 1987), pp. 26-27.

Brown, Richard L. "God and Country." *Tacoma News Tribune* (October 12, 1990).

Burnham, Scott. "Currents Review at ICA." *Boston University Daily Free Press* (January 1991).

Chion, Michel. "La bouche et la video." *L'Image Video,* No. 3 (April/May 1990), pp. 20-22.

Cooke, Lynne. "Gary Hill: 'Who am I but a figure of speech?'" *Parkett,* No. 34 (1992), pp. 16-27.

Cornwell, Regina. "Gary Hill—Museum of Modern Art, New York." *Sculpture* (May/June 1991), p. 69.

Croft, Williams Janis. "Caps Video: Wegman, Hill, Koplan, Lucier." *Afterimage 7* (November 1979).

Devriendt, Christine and Paul-Emmanuel Odin. "L'image comme une aiguille qui ecrit au bout des mots *Site Recite (a prologue)* une video de Gary Hill." *Kanal,* No. 6 (May 1990), pp. 54-56.

Durland, Steven. "CRUX." *High Performance,* No. 37 (1987), pp. 97-98.

Fargier, Jean-Paul. "Z. Rybczinski et G. Hill: La Ligne, Le Point, Le Pli." *Cahiers du Cinema,* No. 415 (January 1989), pp. 60-63.

Fargier, Jean-Paul. "Defense de Doubler." *Art Press,* No. 147 (May 1990).

Furlong, Lucinda. "A Manner of Speaking: An Interview with Gary Hill." *Afterimage* 10 (March 1983), pp. 9-16.

Galloway, David. "Cologne Exhibit is Milestone for Video Sculpture." *International Herald Tribune* (April 2, 1989).

Gay, Jean-Jacques. "Deux temps trois mouvements." *Genlock,* No. 15 (December 1989).

Gay, Jean-Jacques. "Surf, drogue et video." *Museart,* No. 26 (December/January 1992/1993), pp. 122-124.

Glowen, Ron. "Camera of the Mind." *Artweek* (February 22, 1990).

Goggin, Kathleen. "Review of the *Gary Hill* exhibition catalogue published by the Editions du Centre Georges Pompidou." *Parachute,* No. 70 (April/May/June 1993), p. 49.

Gragg, Randy. "The Waning of Modernism." *Seattle Weekly* (November 21, 1990).

Grout, Catherine. "Gary Hill—La condition humaine de la pensée." *Arte Factum,* No. 48 (June/July/August 1993), pp. 8-12.

Grundberg, Andy. "Gary Hill at the Museum of Modern Art." *New York Times* (December 21, 1990).

Gudis, Catherine. "Interview with Gary Hill at MOCA." *The Contemporary 4,* No. 1 (Winter 1987).

Hackett, Regina. "Gary Hill and Gary Reel at And/Or Art Center." *Seattle Post-Intelligencer* (January 21, 1981).

Hackett, Regina. "Gary Hill's Stark Videos Lack Charm but Pack Power." *Seattle Post-Intelligencer* (November 14, 1985).

Hackett, Regina. "20th-Century Art Takes a New Turn at Donald Young." *Seattle Post-Intelligencer* (January 24, 1992).

Hackett, Regina. "Video Sculpture Compels Viewer to Stay Tuned." *Seattle Post-Intelligencer* (February 19, 1993).

Hagan, Charles. "Gary Hill, 'Primarily Speaking' at the Whitney Museum of American Art." *Artforum* (February 1984).

Hagen, Charles. "Tube Art (Take Out)." *The Village Voice* (May 14, 1985).

Hall, Charles. "DOUBLETAKE." *Arts Review* (April 1992).

Horn, Lawrence. "On Video and its Viewer." *Millonnium Film Journal,* No. 14/15 (Fall/Winter 1984/1985).

Huntington, Richard. "'Zone' Animates Common Objects." *Buffalo Courier-Express* (May 15, 1980).

Jarque, Fietta. "La Ier Bienal de la Imagen en Moveimiento ofrecera video y cine interdisciplinar." *El Pais,* Madrid December 8, 1990).

Kolpan, Steven. "Bateson Through the Looking Glass." *Video and the Arts* (Winter 1986), pp. 20, 22, 35, 56.

Lageira, Jacinto. "Gary Hill: The Imager of Disaster." *Galeries Magazine* (December 1990/ January 1991), pp. 74-77, 140, 141.

Lageira, Jacinto. "Une Verbalisation du Regard." *Parachute,* No. 62 (April/May/June 1991), pp. 4-11.

Larson, Kay. "Art Through a Screen Dimly." *New York* (September 12, 1983), pp. 86-87.

Libbenga, Jan. "Videokunst Verlengt Het Bewustzijn." *NRC, Donderdug* (September 15, 1988).

Lord, Catherine. "It's The Thought That Counts." *Afterimage* (October 1983), pp. 9-11.

McManus, Michael. "Video and the Literary Imagination." *Artweek* (March 1987).

Meuris, Jacques. "Art et science ou science et art?" *Art et Culture,* Brussels (September 1992).

Mittenthal, Robert. "Overpowering Ideas." *Reflex* (March/ April 1992).

Morgan, Stuart. "Thanks for the Memories." *frieze* (April/ May 1992).

Morrison, Wolf. "Wizard In Videoland." *The Daily Yomiuri,* Tokyo (April 8, 1985).

Movin, Lars. "Video er Skrift." *Information Onsdag,* Copenhagen (April 18, 1990).

Nash, Michael. "AFI Video Festival." *Artscribe International* (Summer 1989).

Nash, Michael. "Poetic Oversights and Critical Misgivings." *High Performance,* No. 39 (1987).

Nash, Michael. "Video Poetics: A Context for Content." *High Performance,* No. 37 (1987), pp. 67, 70.

Neimann, Susanne and Agnete Dorph Christoffersen. "Blinde i Billedstorm." *Information Onsdag,* Copenhagen (September 27, 1989).

Pencenat, Corinne. "L'Expérience Limite de Gary Hill." *Beaux Arts* (October 1991), p. 113.

Perron, Joel. "Video Show Reflects on Technology's Role." *Japan Times,* Tokyo (March 18, 1990).

Phillips, Christopher. "Between Pictures." *Art in America* (November 1991), pp. 104-114, 173.

Pincus, Robert L. "Watching Machines Ignore Us." *San Diego Union* (May 28, 1987).

Preisner, Brenda. "Sound, Images Conflict in Video 'War Zone'." *Buffalo Evening News* (May 15, 1980).

"Primera Bienal De La Imagen En Movimiento." *RTV Magazine di los Mercados Audiovisuales,* No. 20 (January 1991).

Renouf, Renee. "Video." *Artweek* (July 3, 1982).

Sarrazin, Stephen. "Gary Hill at Galerie des Archives." *Art Press,* No. 147 (May 1990).

Sarrazin, Stephen. "La parole aux objets." *Art Press,* No. 165 (January 1992).

Slemmons, Rod. "Gary Hill—Under New Skins." *Reflex* (May/June 1993), p. 13.

Smallwood, Lyn. "The World as They Know It." *Seattle Weekly* (March 18, 1992).

Sterritt, David. "Multichannel Show *(Primarily Speaking).*" *The Christian Science Monitor* (December 8, 1983).

Sturken, Marita. "Electronic Visions." *Afterimage* (November 1983).

Taubin, Amy. "The Whitney Biennial: Video." *Millennium Film Journal,* No. 13 (Fall/Winter 1983/1984).

Van Assche, Christine. "Interview with Gary Hill." *Galeries Magazine* (December 1990/January 1991), pp. 77, 140-141.

Van Assche, Christine. "Restless Images." *Galeries Magazine* (April/ May 1990).

Van Assche, Christine. "Tendances Multiples." *Tendances Multiples, Videos des Années 80, Petit Journal,* No. 22 (March/May 1990).

Von Graevenitz, Antje. "Living Funeral Art—Video Installations by Bill Viola and Gary Hill." *Archis* 7 (1993), pp. 45-53.

Wooster, Ann-Sargent. "The Heart of Darkness—Film and Video at the Whitney Biennial." *Arts Magazine* (October 1991), pp. 66-71.

Yamamori, Eiji. "Gary Hill." *Aera Magazine* 5, No. 27, Tokyo (July 1992), pp. 72-73.

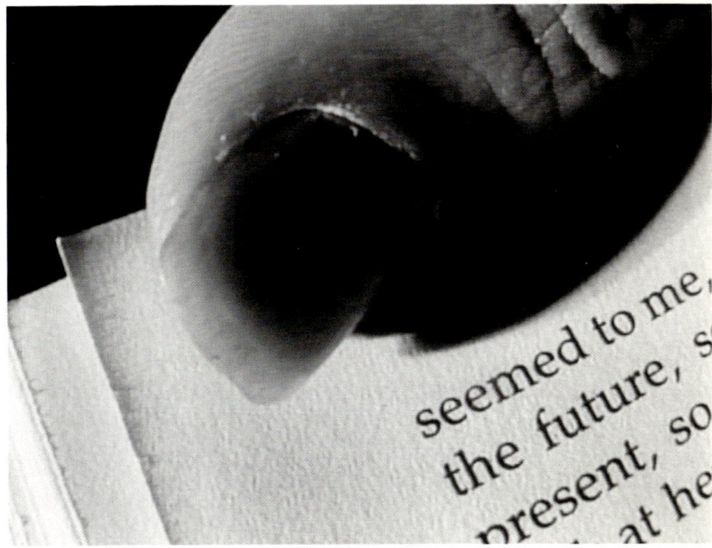

Henry Gallery Association Board of Trustees 1993/94

Ex-Officio Members

Henry Art Gallery Staff

Richard Andrews, Director
Claudia Bach, Public Information Director
Chris Bruce, Senior Curator
Paul Cabarga, Bookstore Manager
Joan Caine, Assistant Director
Fifi Caner, Association Director
Jayson Curry, Assistant to the Director
Laura Downing, Receptionist
Katya Garrow, Development Associate
Anne Gendreau, Loans Registrar
Karla Glanzman, Special Events Coordinator
Dan Gurney, Preparator
Clara Kawanishi, Assistant to the Association Director
Tamara Moats, Curator of Education
Jennifer Reidel, Editorial Assistant
Jim Rittimann, Head Preparator
Kevin Rochat, Facilities/Security Manager
Judy Sourakli, Curator of Collections
Susan Zukov, Finance Manager

Photo credits:

Allison Rossiter: cover, p. 84; Jean-Marc Meunier: p. 8, 10-12, 13; Gary Hill: p. 14, 16, 32, 46-48, 52, 53, 62-64, 78, 79, 82, 83, 90, 91; Mark B. McLoughlin: p. 15, 17, 18, 21-23, 28-31, 33-35, 40, 42-45, 51, 55-57, 62, 66-81, 100-107,; Vicki Demetre: p. 19, 36-39, 98; Carl de Keyzer, courtesy of the Stedelijk Museum, Amsterdam: p. 26-27; Ulam Curjel: p. 41, 50; Philippe Migeat: p. 49, 86; Eduardo Calderon: p. 58, 59; Dirk Bleiker: p. 60; Kathy Bourbonaise: p. 65; Jean-Paul Judon, courtesy Le Creux de L'Enfer, Theirs: p. 76-77; IVAM Centre del Carme: p. 86; Thomas Pederson and Poul Pederson, Aarhus Kunst, Denmark: p. 89; Al Daniels p. 94-95; Marine Hugonnier: p. 97.